EUROPEAN CITIZENSHIP THROUGH THE LENS
OF EU VALUES

European Union Law Series

This series brings together major works in the field of European Union Law. It features a diverse range of publications, including comprehensive handbooks designed to teach European Union Law, treaties for legal practitioners and academics, monographs on specialised topics and some of the best doctoral dissertations from across Europe. Additionally, it includes publications detailing conference proceedings on topical issues, as well as commentaries on major judgments and decisions handed down by the Court of Justice of the European Union.

EUROPEAN CITIZENSHIP THROUGH THE LENS OF EU VALUES

Edited by

Gaëlle Marti

INTERSENTIA

Intersentia
Lefebvre Sarrut Belgium SA
Rue Haute, 139/6
1000 Bruxelles
Belgium
Email: contact@larcier-intersentia.com

Distribution for the UK, Ireland and
Rest of the World (excl. France, Belgium and Luxembourg)
Ingram Publisher Services UK
1 Deltic Avenue, Rooksley
Milton Keynes MK13 8LD
United Kingdom
Tel: +44 1752 202 301 | Fax: +44 1752 202 331
Email: orders@nbninternational.com

Distribution for France and Other Countries (excl. Ireland and the UK)
Interforum Editis
92 avenue de France
75013 Paris
France

Distribution for Belgium and Luxembourg (excl. France, Ireland and the UK)
Larcier-Intersentia
Rue Haute, 139/6
1000 Bruxelles
Belgium

ISBN 978-1-83970-439-0
D/2025/06040/0158
NUR 820

British Library Cataloguing in Publication Data. A catalogue record for this book is available from the British Library

CONTENTS

LIST OF AUTHORS

Andrew Fagan
Senior Lecturer, University of Essex, England

Ninon Forster
Professor of Public Law, Polytechnic University of Hauts-de-France, France

Anastasia Iliopoulou-Penot
Professor of European Law, Paris-Panthéon-Assas University, Centre for European Law, France

Irene Marchioro
Post-Doctoral Fellow, University of Trieste, Italy

Gaëlle Marti
Professor of Public Law, Jean Monnet Chair, Lyon 3 University, Director of the Centre of European Studies, France

Michele Messina
Professor of European Union Law, University of Messina, Italy

Félicie Remlinger
PhD Student at Paris-Panthéon-Assas University (Centre of European Law), France

Quitterie Roccaserra
PhD Student in Public and European law, University Paris-Est Créteil, France

Julie Rondu
Associate Professor, University of Strasbourg, France

Mathieu Rouy
PhD in EU Law, Research Fellow at EDIEC, Jean Moulin Lyon 3 University, France

INTRODUCTION EUROPEAN CITIZENSHIP THROUGH THE LENS OF EU VALUES

Gaëlle MARTI*

What does it mean to be a citizen of the European Union (EU)? What is the relationship between European citizenship and the common values on which the EU is based? Against the backdrop of the 2024 European elections, these questions are all the more crucial as citizenship can only serve as a basis for democratic legitimacy if citizens identify with a set of shared values. From the outset, however, EU citizenship has been the subject of conflicting opinions. Some argue that the market logic that led to the creation of the EU is still very much alive, undermining the concrete and effective implementation of the values enshrined in Article 2 of the Treaty on European Union (also known as the Maastricht Treaty).[1]

And whether these values are indeed shared is also now being questioned, with some Member States advocating for an illiberal conception of democracy. If these European values are not shared, can they be the basis of European citizenship? Conversely, are these values too universal to contribute to the emergence of a specifically European identity? Moreover, should these values be reserved for EU citizens to the exclusion of third-country nationals? And are these values, granted to citizens by Member States, likely to promote civic practices? Is it not time to replace a top-down approach with a bottom-up approach that allows European citizens themselves to define the fundamental values of the social contract and to respond to the major social challenges facing the EU? This volume, the result of a conference held on 17 November 2023 at the Université Jean Moulin Lyon 3, seeks to examine these questions in a critical way.

---

* Professor of Public Law, Jean Monnet Chair, Jean Moulin Lyon 3 University, Director of the Centre of European Studies.

1 Consolidated Version of the Treaty on European Union [2016] OJ C202/13.

The 2024 election year for the European Parliament offers a key moment to take stock of European citizenship: its achievements, the expectations it has raised, but also the challenges it faces. European citizenship, introduced by the Maastricht Treaty, came into force in 1993. For 30 years, Europeans have experienced what it means to belong to a supranational entity superposed on the national community to which they belong. For 30 years, they have been able to vote as European citizens to elect direct representatives to the European Parliament. For 30 years, they have had the right to move, work, trade and reside freely throughout the EU – in principle at least, under the same conditions as nationals of the host Member States – and the Court of Justice of the European Union (CJEU) has been particularly active in guaranteeing the effective rights attached to this status. While 30 is generally considered as the age of maturity, EU citizenship is often criticised for being hollow, devoid of any substance and incapable of creating, on its own, the conditions necessary for the establishment of a genuine democracy at European level. The reasons for this are well-known: the fact that the acquisition and loss of citizenship is mediated by the Member States, which makes it more complex to develop citizens' loyalty to the EU and its institutions; the absence of a public space at European level; the insufficient social dimension of this citizenship; and the weakness of the European Constitution, which some believe could have provided a stronger foundation for the European political project.

Yet the EU is based on a foundation of common values, which would seem conducive to reaffirming the political project of Europe and thus strengthening the basis of European citizenship. Indeed, if citizenship is 'a key mechanism for inclusion and exclusion',[2] values should play a role in drawing the line that separates the beneficiaries of citizenship from the outsiders who are excluded, since these values form the basis of the social contract and define the purpose of the political project. The aim of this volume is to examine European citizenship in the light of the values of the EU after its 30 years of existence.

It does so in a specific and challenging context for the EU. Global structural changes – climate change, the energy crisis, big data, artificial intelligence (AI) – are testing the resilience of societies. On top of the disruption of the Covid-19 pandemic, these are revealing the limits of the current model of economic growth. Externally, there is an unstable geopolitical context, marked by the war in Ukraine, conflicts in the Middle East, the rise of China, and uncertainties surrounding American foreign policy and the continuation of transatlantic alliances. These external factors will have a major impact on a

---

2 P. Mindus, 'Dimensions of Citizenship' (2014) 15(5) *German Law Journal* 735.

number of common EU policies: migration, foreign affairs, defence, energy, as well as enlargement, with pending candidate status for Ukraine, Georgia and Moldova. Internally, the challenges are no less daunting, with the rise of populism, constitutional backsliding by the so-called 'illiberal democracies', increasing attacks on the rule of law and the questioning of the primacy of EU law by constitutional courts (including the Polish Constitutional Tribunal, the German Federal Constitutional Court, the French Conseil d'État and the Belgian Constitutional Court).

All these challenges are acting as a 'stress test' for European values. Sometimes European values are attacked head on (as in the case of the invasion of Ukraine by Russia) or are put under pressure by challenges from Member States (such as Poland and Hungary claiming that they have the right to define their own rule of law and fundamental rights according to their national understanding of these values).[3]

The Court of Justice of the European Union has made its stance on European values clear in a number of recent judgments:

> Article 2 TEU is not merely a statement of policy guidelines or intentions, but contains values which are an integral part of the very identity of the European Union as a common legal order, values which are given concrete expression in principles containing legally binding obligations for the Member States. [...] It follows, inter alia, from the foregoing that compliance by a Member State with the values contained in Article 2 TEU is a condition for the enjoyment of all the rights deriving from the application of the Treaties to that Member State. Compliance with those values cannot be reduced to an obligation which a candidate State is required to comply with in order to accede to the European Union and which it may disregard after its accession [...].[4]

Nonetheless, the pressure on the rule of law, led by illiberal democracies, is not abating. It seems clear that constant vigilance is required to preserve the

---

3 This was the thrust of the arguments put forward by Poland and Hungary in cases opposing these two Member States to the European Parliament and the Council about budgetary conditions. Hungary submitted, in essence, 'that the concept of "the rule of law" does not lend itself to a precise definition and cannot be given a uniform interpretation, because of the obligation to respect the national identity of each of the Member States', see Case C-156/21, *Hungary v. European Parliament and Council of the European Union*, ECLI:EU:C:2022:97, para. 222.
See also Case C-157/21, *Republic of Poland v. European Parliament and Council of the European Union*, ECLI:EU:C:2022:98, para. 312. According to Poland, 'the concept of "the rule of law", as it is defined in Article 2(a) of the contested regulation [...] cannot, as a matter of principle, be given a universal definition since it contains a non-exhaustive number of principles whose meaning may differ from one State to another, depending on the constitutional features or legal traditions specific to the State in question'.

4 Case C-204/21, *European Commission v. Republic of Poland*, ECLI:EU:C:2023:442, paras. 67–68.

rule of law that lies both at the heart of democracies and at the foundation of the European Union. As the CJEU stated:

> [O]nce a candidate State becomes a Member State, it joins a legal structure that is based on the fundamental premiss that each Member State shares with all the other Member States, and recognises that they share with it, the common values contained in Article 2 TEU, on which the European Union is founded. That premiss is based on the specific and essential characteristics of EU law, which stem from the very nature of EU law and the autonomy it enjoys in relation to the laws of the Member States and to international law. That premiss implies and justifies the existence of mutual trust between the Member States that those values will be recognised and, therefore, that the EU law that implements them will be respected [...].[5]

Sometimes values are put under pressure in a less frontal manner, as in the case of solidarity, which is being tested by concerns about migration, energy or Ukrainian grain imports. And EU values face even more pernicious challenges, such as 'fake news', cyberattacks and new disinformation techniques being used as part of a hybrid war led by Russia, with the danger that these will have an impact on European democracy.

All these threats to EU values make it all the more important to think about how these values relate to European citizenship, how they affect citizens' practices at EU level, and how citizenship can, or could be, a means of making them more effective. These values are not only the cornerstone of mutual trust between Member States; they foster the confidence of EU citizens in the European project and, more generally, strengthen their sense of belonging to the European Union.

If values are at the heart of the social contract, underpinning its existence by giving a purpose and boundary to the political power it institutes, they are all the more important for the EU, which cannot be built on the basis of a national identity defined in ethnocultural terms. The whole point of theories of constitutional patriotism, defended by authors such as Jurgen Habermas[6] and Jan-Werner Müller,[7] is to rethink collective identification and civic community beyond the nation, on the basis of commonly shared norms and values. This allows people to remain attached to a unique culture, potentially to their individual countries, but still share a common patriotic identity with other Europeans.

---

5 *Hungary v. European Parliament and Council of the European Union*, above n. 3, para. 125.

6 J. Habermas, *Après l'Etat-nation:Une nouvelle constellation politique* (trans. R. Rochlitz), Paris, Fayard, 2000. See also J. Habermas, *L'intégration républicaine: Essais de théorie politique* (trans. R. Rochlitz), Paris, Fayard, 1998.

7 J.-W. Müller, *Constitutional Patriotism*, Princeton University Press, Princeton (NJ), 2007.

Of course, the possibility of grounding democracy in shared values is seriously contested. One of the most common criticisms is that democracy can only be achieved within the framework of the nation-state, because national identity is the main frame of reference for individuals.[8] But by accepting this criticism, it is impossible to conceive of democracy on a European scale. The only solution would be to transform the EU into a nation-state, sharing the same history, the same culture, the same religion, etc. Given that this assumption is highly unlikely, one would have to conclude that a pluralist democracy is not possible. Yet when citizens are asked what the priorities of the EU should be – for instance, during the Conference on the Future of Europe that took place from April 2021 to May 2022 – they state the protection of values, rights and the rule of law, proving that attachment to universal values is possible.

In any event, these sceptical and even critical readings of the possibility of shared EU values must be addressed. The first concerns EU citizenship itself, which is sometimes seen as the symbol of the politicisation of the EU, and sometimes criticised for granting narrow rights only to wealthy, mobile and economically active citizens.[9] Both views of European citizenship see it as an empty shell, driven solely by an economic logic. Economically inactive citizens are largely deprived of the benefits of this 'market citizenship', as shown by the political rhetoric stigmatising welfare tourism.[10] This is backed up by the recent case law of the CJEU, which shows a noticeable shift towards stricter interpretations of the scope of social solidarity for mobile EU citizens.[11]

Another criticism is that the values in Article 2 are too vague and imprecise to be effectively implemented for the benefit of all EU citizens. More specifically, failure to take account of the inequality that exists in society (resulting from gender, physical condition, race, income, etc.) would make the values of the EU, coupled with the status of citizen, which is impervious to differences, vectors for the perpetuation of inequality.

Other critiques are more ambivalent, claiming either that European values are too universal to be grounds for identity or, on the contrary, that they are too contested, even within the EU, to form the common basis of a political project.

---

8 See P. Manent, *La Raison des nations: Réflexions sur la démocratie en Europe*, Paris, Gallimard, 2006. See also B. Yack, 'The Myth of the Civic Nation' (1996) 10(2) *Critical Review* 193; T. Mertens, 'Cosmopolitan and Citizenship: Kant Against Habermas' (1996) 4(3) *European Journal of Philosophy* 328.

9 See E. Spaventa, 'Earned Citizenship – Understanding Union Citizenship through Its Scope' in D. Kochenov (ed.), *EU Citizenship and Federalism: The Role of Rights*, Cambridge, Cambridge University Press, 2017, pp. 204–25.

10 S. Mantu and P. Minderhoud, 'Exploring the limits of social solidarity: welfare tourism and EU citizenship' (2016) 2(2) *EU Law Journal* 4.

11 Case C-333-13, *Dano*, ECLI:EU:C:2014:2358. See also Case C-67/14, *Alimanovic*, ECLI:EU:C:2015:597.

This volume approaches these questions from two angles. The first part aims to test EU values in the light of EU citizenship: to assess whether these values are citizenship-proof. As it would be impossible to examine all EU values, this citizenship test is applied only to selected values. Human dignity is the first one, as it is the first common value mentioned among those on which the Union is based. Julie Rondu will examine the complex and sometimes ambivalent relationship between human dignity and European citizenship. Then the volume will focus on equality, since this value, which is essential for citizenship, could be said to be endangered by the conditions under which the rights attached to the status of citizen are exercised. The cases of economically inactive citizens (Michele Messina), female citizens (Quitterie Roccaserra) and 'rainbow families' (Irene Marchioro) are put to the test. All these studies come to the same conclusion: namely that European citizenship challenges the value of equality.

The second part of the volume takes a more forward-looking approach to attempt to grasp the potential for the development of EU values through European citizenship. The underlying question is whether citizenship can be a vehicle for European values. One focus is on the way in which the jurisprudence of the CJEU is – or is not – influenced by EU values in determining the scope of EU citizenship (Mathieu Rouy). But the CJEU is not the only architect of the construction of values. The role of citizens' practices is also examined: firstly, the way in which they help to concretely express the value of democracy (Félicie Remlinger), but also the 'litigious path', which can represent a new form of appropriation of EU values by its citizens (Ninon Forster). 'Digital citizenship' will also be explored, understood as the rights granted to individuals in digital society and guaranteed by the CJEU, and its implications for the constitutionalisation of the EU (Anastasia Iliopoulou-Penot). Andrew Fagan will conclude the volume with a critical overview of the human rights-based European citizenship (as stated by the Charter of Fundamental Rights of the EU)[12] showing the shortcomings in the human rights protection within the European order. More precisely, he will show how human rights protection is blind to certain types of identities such as social class identity, and why it should take into account the distinct constituency of vulnerable people being part of the 'precariat' in order to reinforce human rights protection in the European order, and thus ground the European social contract on a rigorous conception of citizenship.

[12] Charter of Fundamental Rights of the European Union [2016] OJ C202/389.

CHAPTER 1
THE AMBIVALENT ROLE OF HUMAN DIGNITY IN EU CITIZENSHIP

Julie Rondu*

Abstract

As a core value of the European Union, human dignity plays a crucial role in defining its identity. This chapter aims to explore the complex relationship between defending human dignity and protecting the rights of EU citizens. Firstly, a connection is emerging between the concept of integration in a host Member State and respect for human dignity. Consequently, EU citizenship rights can be limited if an individual violates the principle of human dignity. In other words, emphasising European identity rooted in human dignity could paradoxically have adverse consequences for citizens. Yet human dignity could also be used to strengthen the rights of EU citizens, for example, through social benefits, although the European Court of Justice has not consistently used human dignity in this way. This analysis also examines how focusing on human dignity, a universal value, might weaken the distinctiveness of EU citizenship.

SECTION I
INTRODUCTION

As Fulvia Ristuccia has highlighted:

> We are witnessing the development of an institutional narrative that defines European legal identity as founded in the values under Article 2 TEU, which are not merely aspirational but have a legally binding nature.[1]

* Associate Professor, University of Strasbourg.

[1] F. Ristuccia, 'European identity through free movement law? The interactions between Union citizenship, free movement of persons, and EU values' (2024) 1 *Quaderni AISDUE*, 1–2.

In that sense, understanding the relationship between European citizenship and these common values is crucial to define the identity of the European Union (EU). Respect for human dignity is the first common value mentioned among those on which the Union is based.[2] Its centrality to the EU legal order is also visible in the EU Charter of Fundamental Rights (CFR), of which Article 1 enshrines human dignity as inviolable.[3] Human dignity thus has an undeniable constitutional dimension in the European legal order. Moreover, it has played an important role in the relationship between EU law and national law. As illustrated by cases such as *Omega*,[4] human dignity can play a 'defensive role'[5] in national constitutional courts. Indeed, the paradigm underpinning freedom of movement within the EU may conflict with national conceptions of common values.

On a national level, human dignity and citizenship are clearly and intimately connected. 'While human dignity is the moral ground on the basis of which all human rights can be derived,[6] the right to citizenship, as the "right to have rights",[7] works as their legal foundation.'[8] For that reason, an individual deprived of citizenship could be regarded as deprived of their human dignity.[9]

However, European citizenship, with its inter-state nature, is less deeply linked with human dignity. Because it is *additional* to nationality of a Member State,[10] EU citizenship is not seen as the very source of fundamental rights. For example, in European Court of Justice (ECJ) case law involving the acquisition or loss of EU citizenship, human dignity is not mentioned. Fundamental rights, notably respect for private and family life[11] and the rights of the child,[12] are expressly referred to as a part of the proportionality test, but not human

---

2 Article 2 of the Treaty on European Union (TEU): Consolidated Version of the Treaty on European Union [2016] OJ C202/13.

3 Charter of Fundamental Rights of the European Union [2016] OJ C202/389. Chapter I in the EU Charter of Fundamental Rights is entitled 'Dignity'.

4 Case C-36/02, *Omega*, ECLI:EU:C:2004:614.

5 M. Avbelj, 'Human Dignity and EU legal pluralism' in G. Davies and M. Avbelj (eds.), *Research Handbook on Legal Pluralism and EU Law*, Cheltenham, Edward Elgar Publishing, 2018, pp. 95–110, p. 100. In another example, the Polish declaration on the EU Charter of Fundamental Rights expressly refers to human dignity.

6 This view is also reflected in Article 1 of the German Basic Law (*Grundgesetz*).

7 According to Hannah Arendt's famous formula: H. Arendt, *The Origins of Totalitarianism*, New York, Harcourt, Brace & Co, 1951.

8 M. Dicosola, 'The right to citizenship and human dignity' in D. Bedford, C. Dupré, G. Halmai and P. Kapotas (eds.), *Human Dignity and Democracy in Europe*, Cheltenham, Edward Elgar Publishing, 2022, pp. 137–54, p. 153.

9 Ibid.

10 Article 20 of the Treaty on the Functioning of the European Union (TFEU): Consolidated Version of the Treaty on the Functioning of the European Union [2016] OJ C202/47. See Case C-673/20, *EP v. Préfet du Gers and Institut national de la statistique et des études économiques (INSEE)*, ECLI:EU:C:2022:449.

11 Article 7 of the EU Charter of Fundamental Rights.

12 Ibid., Article 24.

dignity. Even in the *Rottmann*[13] and *JY*[14] cases, statelessness was not seen as a dignity issue, although it deprives the individual of numerous rights. In *JY*, the Austrian legislation that imposes the prior renunciation of nationality of origin was not considered, in itself, a violation of Article 20 of the Treaty on the Functioning of the European Union (TFEU). In that sense, the added value of human dignity for EU citizens seems to be rather weak: human dignity is not necessarily seen as the essential core of the status of EU citizenship. In the same vein, the notion of 'genuine enjoyment of the substance of the rights attaching to the status [of citizenship]' originating from the *Ruiz Zambrano* judgment[15] is not expressly connected to the value of human dignity. Some authors contend that it could be deduced from this judgment that 'the future exercise of fundamental freedoms rather than the current enjoyment of fundamental rights would be considered at the heart of EU citizenship'.[16]

Nevertheless, it has been argued that the substance of EU citizenship rights should include:

> a core of social entitlements, enabling an individual to lead a life in conditions of dignity, as this would be consistent with the basic tenets of social justice sitting at the core of the constitutional identity of the Union.[17]

As a basis for the project of European integration, the human dignity of EU citizens should be protected in any circumstances. However, a breach to human dignity is not sufficient in itself to make EU law applicable, even if it concerns a mobile EU citizen. Advocate General Jacobs's wish that EU law should give European citizens the assurance that they 'will be treated in accordance with a common code of fundamental values'[18] has not been fully realised. The applicability of fundamental rights requires the previous applicability of a substantial norm of EU law.[19] Thus, a European citizen cannot yet 'invoke that status in order to oppose any violation of his fundamental rights'.[20] In other words, a violation of human dignity does not automatically

13 Case C-135/08, *Rottmann*, ECLI:EU:C:2010:104.

14 Case C-118/20, *JY v. Wiener Landesregierung*, ECLI:EU:C:2022:34.

15 Case C-34/09, *Ruiz Zambrano*, ECLI:EU:C:2011:124.

16 C. Raucea, 'Fundamental Rights: The Missing Pieces of European Citizenship?' (2013) 14(10) *German Law Journal* 2021.

17 A. Bouveresse and A. Iliopoulou-Penot, 'Introductory remarks: Defending the added value of European citizenship in the face of persisting criticism' in A. Bouveresse, A. Iliopoulou-Penot and J. Rondu (eds.), *La citoyenneté européenne, quelle valeur ajoutée? European Citizenship: what added value?*, Brussels, Bruylant, 2023, pp. 11–36, p. 31; D. Sarmiento, 'La justice sociale dans la jurisprudence de la Cour de justice de l'Union européenne' in L. Burgorgue-Larsen (ed.), *La justice sociale saisie par les juges en Europe*, Paris, Pedone, 2013, p. 33.

18 Opinion of AG Jacobs, Case C-168/91, *Konstantinides*, ECLI:EU:C:1992:504, para. 46.

19 Case C-617/10, *Åkerberg Fransson*, ECLI:EU:C:2013:105.

20 Opinion of AG Jacobs, *Konstantinides*, above n. 18, para. 46.

constitute a violation of citizenship rights. In that sense, can it be imagined that in the territory of the EU, as a protective space, being an EU citizen ensures the protection of that person's dignity? This would be essential to truly place human dignity at the heart of European identity. Furthermore, as a fundamental value of the EU, should respect for human dignity be considered an obligation, not only for Member States, but also for EU citizens themselves? In this case, European identity could assert itself against EU citizens.

This chapter aims to answer these questions, highlighting the ambivalence of human dignity in relation to the status of EU citizenship. Section II explores the respect for human dignity as a condition to enjoy EU citizenship rights. Section III looks at the role of human dignity in interpreting citizenship rights. And Section IV examines how a focus on human dignity could potentially dilute EU citizenship.

SECTION II
RESPECT FOR HUMAN DIGNITY AS A CONDITION FOR EU CITIZENSHIP RIGHTS?

As Gaëlle Marti notes in the introduction to this volume:

> [V]alues should play a role in drawing the line that separates the beneficiaries of citizenship [status] from the outsiders who are excluded, since [they] form the basis of the social contract and define the purpose of the political project.[21]

In that sense, violations of human dignity would be likely to justify limitations to citizenship rights. This is particularly noticeable in the context of a paradigm shift in ECJ case law, which has become much more focused on citizens' obligations than on citizens' rights.

For example, the value of human dignity can be encompassed in derogations based on public policy. As in the *Omega* case, in which the ECJ accepted a derogation from the fundamental freedom to provide services, a strand of recent case law more implicitly includes values in public policy derogations from the freedom of movement of EU citizens.

While the integration of an EU citizen in a host Member State is based mainly on the duration of their residence, it also depends on qualitative factors.[22] Consequently, the respect of national fundamental values may be taken into account to define this integration. As Advocate General Bot noted

---

[21] G. Marti, 'Introduction', in this volume.

[22] Case C-325/09, *Dias*, ECLI:EU:C:2011:498, para. 64.

in the *P.I.* case,[23] which involved the repeated rape of a child within a family context, the offender's conduct:

> which constitutes a serious disturbance of public policy, shows a total lack of desire to integrate into the society in which he finds himself and some of whose fundamental values he so conscientiously disregarded for years.[24]

Although human dignity is not expressly referred to, '[a]n offence of that nature',[25] which is regarded by the Court as sexual exploitation of children,[26] violates human dignity. As a 'eurocrime'[27] subject to minimal harmonisation measures concerning the definition of criminal offences and sanctions,[28] it affects common conscience. Therefore, although the applicant had completed an uninterrupted period of ten years of residence, he did not have the right to the enhanced protection provided by this, as set out in Article 28(2) and (3) of Directive 2004/38/EC,[29] as 'his conduct [had] remained hidden owing to the physical and moral violence horribly exercised on the victim for years'.[30] To recognise the right to the applicant's enhanced protection would, according to Advocate General Bot, 'conflict with the values on which citizenship of the Union is based'.[31] Moreover, in this case the Court gave 'a wide definition'[32] to imperative grounds of public security.

In the same vein, in the *Onuekwere* case,[33] the Court considered that:

> The imposition of a prison sentence by the national court is such as to show the non-compliance by the person concerned with the values expressed by the society of the host Member State in its criminal law [...].[34]

---

23 Case C-348/09, *P.I.*, ECLI:EU:C:2012:300.

24 Opinion of AG Bot, Case C-348/09, *P.I.*, ECLI:EU:C:2012:123, para. 60.

25 Ibid., para. 61.

26 Ibid., paras. 25–28.

27 A 'particularly serious crime with a cross-border dimension resulting from the nature or impact of such offences or from a special need to combat them on a common basis': Article 83(1) of the TFEU.

28 Article 83 of the TFEU.

29 Council Directive 2004/38/EC of 29 April 2004 on the right of citizens of the Union and their family members to move and reside freely within the territory of the Member States [2004] OJ L158/77.

30 Opinion of AG Bot, *P.I.*, above n. 24, para. 60.

31 Ibid., para. 62.

32 L. Azoulai and S. Coutts, 'Restricting Union citizens' residence on grounds of public security: where Union citizenship and the AFSJ meet' (2013) 50(2) *Common Market Law Review* 553, 554.

33 Case C-378/12, *Onuekwere*, ECLI:EU:C:2014:13.

34 Ibid., para. 26.

The result is that 'integration in these judgements includes adherence to the values of the host society, which are expressed in the criminal law'.[35] This shows how the value of human dignity is closely linked with the notion of integration, which is essential when ruling on conflicts between the interests of the state and the rights of EU citizens. Charlotte O'Brien calls this a 'restrictive or punitive sense of integration'.[36]

In another example, in the *K* case,[37] an EU citizen made an application for the withdrawal of an entry ban imposed on him by the Netherlands. This demand was rejected, as there were serious reasons for considering that he had participated in war crimes and crimes against humanity two decades before[38] as a member of a Bosnian army unit. The Grand Chamber emphasised that crimes of that nature:

> seriously undermine both fundamental values such as respect for human dignity and human rights, on which, as stated in Article 2 TEU, the European Union is founded, and the peace which it is the Union's aim to promote, under Article 3 TEU.[39]

This legitimated the restriction imposed by the Netherlands on the freedom of movement and residence of an EU citizen. The Court stated that:

> however improbable it may appear that such crimes or acts may recur outside their specific historical and social context, conduct of the individual concerned that shows the persistence in him of a disposition hostile to the fundamental values enshrined in Articles 2 and 3 TEU, such as human dignity and human rights, as revealed by those crimes or those acts, is, for its part, capable of constituting a genuine, present and sufficiently serious threat affecting one of the fundamental interests of society [...].[40]

Consequently, while there is found to be no serious risk of the individual repeating his crimes in the Member State, 'rather it is the morally problematic nature of these historic offences, contrary to the values of the Union, which justify the restriction of the Union citizenship rights'.[41] In this way, the

---

35 S. Coutts, 'The Citizen as Offender and Forfeiture of (EU) Rights' in A. Bouveresse, A. Iliopoulou-Penot and J. Rondu (eds.), above n. 17, pp. 189–209, p. 196.

36 C. O'Brien, *Unity in Adversity: EU Citizenship, Social Justice and the Cautionary Tale of the UK*, Oxford, Hart Publishing, 2017, p. 253.

37 Joined Cases C-331/16 and C-366/16, *K v. Staatssecretaris van Veiligheid en Justitie and HF v. Belgische Staat*, ECLI:EU:C:2018:296.

38 Within the meaning of Article 1(F)(a) of the Convention relating to the Status of Refugees (1951) 189 *UNTS* 137 (Geneva Convention).

39 *K*, above n. 37, para. 46.

40 Ibid., para. 60.

41 S. Coutts, above n. 35, p. 194.

European values enshrined in Article 2 of the TEU, particularly human dignity, are invoked to justify what Stephen Coutts has called a 'moralistic turn in the definition of public policy and public security'.[42]

This definition of public security is more focused on Member States' interests than on EU citizens' rights,[43] but in a subtle manner. While:

> EU law does not impose a uniform scale of values and acknowledges that the requirements of public policy and public security may vary from one country to another and from one era to another[44]

the Court focuses on common values, considering that these crimes are of concern to the Union as a whole. The *K* judgment confirms that:

> there can be no society which does not feel the need of upholding and reaffirming at regular intervals the collective sentiments and the collective ideas which makes its unity and its personality.[45]

In that sense, the connection between expulsion grounds and European values may be seen as 'a step towards a closer link between the citizen and the supranational polity'.[46] However, Luke Dimitrios Spieker has pointed out the risk of a 'tyranny of EU values'.[47] In his view, 'the indeterminacy of these values might provide a gateway for the Luxembourg judges' political, moral, or ideological convictions'.[48] This risk can be particularly significant if EU values are interpreted as limitations to EU citizenship rights.

It is thus possible to deduce in this case law a duty, inherent in the status of EU citizen, to respect common values.[49] Criminal law is a breeding ground for this, as it reflects the values of a society. While EU citizenship has been described as 'citizenship without duties',[50] the role of human dignity in these cases seems to mitigate this conclusion.

---

42 Ibid.

43 See S. Coutts, 'Union Citizenship, Social Integration and Crimes: Duties Through Crime' in L. Azoulai, S. Barbou des Places and E. Pataut (eds.), *Constructing the Person in EU Law: Rights, Roles, Identities*, Oxford, Hart Publishing, 2016, pp. 225–40, p. 227.

44 Opinion of AG Saugmandsgaard Øe, Case C-331/16, *K*, ECLI:EU:C:2017:973, para. 60.

45 E. Durkheim, *The Elementary Forms of the Religious Life*, New York, Free Press, 1965, p. 475, quoted by L. Azoulai, 'Editorial Comments: EU law between common values and collective feelings' (2018) 55(5) *Common Market Law Review* 1329, 1339.

46 F. Ristuccia, above n. 1, 9.

47 L.D. Spieker, *EU Values before the Court of Justice: Foundations, Potential, Risks*, Oxford, Oxford University Press, 2023, p. 243.

48 Ibid.

49 On this relating to a host Member State's values, see L. Azoulai and S. Coutts, above n. 32, 569.

50 D. Kochenov, 'EU Citizenship without Duties' (2014) 20(4) *European Law Journal* 482.

This duty to respect common values is also apparent in nationality-related cases. In *JY*, the person concerned had committed administrative offences and not criminal offences. Nevertheless, the host Member State required a 'positive attitude'[51] from the applicant to acquire naturalisation, and the ECJ accepted the legitimacy of such a requirement, ruling that the Austrian authority's decision lacked only proportionality. The definition of nationality given by the Court – a 'special relationship of solidarity and good faith between it and its nationals'[52] – has a moral dimension. In a case involving criminal offences breaching human dignity, the revocation of the requirement to naturalise on grounds of public policy or public security could be considered by the Court to be legitimate. The judgment in *JY* was limited to a test of proportionality and did not condemn statelessness in itself. As Milena Tripkovic has pointed out:

> [criminal] punishment (in its classical form such as imprisonment) applies to those whose allegiance to the community is indisputable regardless of their infractions; however, those whose citizenship affiliation is taken as a mistaken indication of their loyalty are exposed to more unforgiving sanctions.[53]

In short, human dignity as a fundamental value is not necessarily seen by the ECJ as a right for the individual but can be used as a means to defend European societies against the behaviour of certain individuals. This leads to cases in which the role of human dignity is inherently ambiguous, oscillating between the primacy of Member States' interests and affirmation of a common conscience that is part of the European identity.

SECTION III
HUMAN DIGNITY: EXPANDING RIGHTS FOR EU CITIZENS?

Daniel Sarmiento points out that a future challenge lies in how to turn the constitutional core of the EU, based on the values of Article 2 of the TEU, into rights for individuals, particularly EU citizens.[54] A current in which the value of human dignity has been used to enrich the substance of rights of EU citizens can be seen across two areas of law: firstly, the access to social benefits; and secondly, the protection against torture and inhuman or degrading treatment

---

51 *JY v. Wiener Landesregierung*, above n. 14, para. 57.

52 Ibid., para. 52.

53 M. Tripkovic, 'Transcending the Boundaries of Punishment: On the Nature of Citizenship Deprivation' (2021) 61(4) *British Journal of Criminology* 1044, 1055.

54 D. Sarmiento, 'EU Citizenship as an Autonomous Legal Concept of EU Law' in A. Bouveresse, A. Iliopoulou-Penot and J. Rondu (eds.), above n. 17, pp. 39–60, p. 53.

or punishment. Furthermore, LGBTQ+ rights cases increasingly reflect considerations of human dignity as a basis for legal advancements.

§ 1. ACCESS TO SOCIAL BENEFITS

In the line of cases starting with *Dano*,[55] the ECJ has reacted to the societal fear of so-called 'benefit tourism' by limiting the social dimension of EU citizenship. The result is a 'curious oscillation between common values and collective feelings'.[56]

For example, in the *Alimanovic* case,[57] even the fact that the applicant and her daughter had worker status in the host Member State was not sufficient to allow their access to social benefits. The Court did not adopt the distinction, made by Advocate General Wathelet in his Opinion, between citizens coming to the host Member State for the first time to seek employment and those who have already lived and worked in that state,[58] treating these two categories in the same way. Regarding this case, Charlotte O'Brien has pointed out that whereas the predominant function of a benefit is 'to cover the minimum subsistence costs necessary to lead a life in keeping with human dignity' and not to facilitate access to the labour market, the Court treats it as social assistance, and deprives jobseekers from it.[59] It seems that ensuring a life in conformity with human dignity is the role of the Member State of nationality, and not that of the host Member State, even for a formerly economically active citizen with social integration links in the host state.

In neither *Dano* nor *Alimanovic* are fundamental rights mentioned. In *Dano*, the inapplicability of Directive 2004/38/EC implicitly results in the inapplicability of the CFR, whereas in *Alimanovic*, the ECJ admits that the applicant and her daughter could benefit from the right to residence as jobseekers,[60] which should make the CFR applicable. There is a gap between the statement that the status of EU citizen is '*destined* to be a fundamental status'[61] and this line of cases that do not consider human dignity as an integral part of this status. On the contrary, 'human vulnerability and the needs of EU citizens to "lead a life in keeping with human dignity"' are neglected, and

55 Case C-333/13, *Dano*, ECLI:EU:C:2014:2358.
56 L. Azoulai, above n. 45, 1329.
57 Case C-67/14, *Alimanovic*, ECLI:EU:C:2015:597.
58 Opinion of AG Wathelet, Case C-67/14, *Alimanovic*, ECLI:EU:C:2015:210, para. 94.
59 C. O'Brien, above n. 36, p. 53. See also the conclusions of AG Wathelet, *Alimanovic*, ibid., para. 72, and the *Alimanovic* judgment, above n. 57, para. 45.
60 *Alimanovic*, above n. 57, para. 57. See Directive 2004/38/EC, Article 14(4)(b).
61 Case C-184/99, *Grzelczyk*, ECLI:EU:C:2001:458, para. 31 (emphasis added).

the free movement of poor citizens is discouraged.[62] As Gareth Davies has emphasised, '[w]hat does Union citizenship mean for a penniless and almost uneducated single mother from the Union's poorest state?'[63]

Nevertheless, references to human dignity are not absent from secondary law. Directive 2004/38/EC refers to human dignity, combined with respect of family life, in order to allow family members to retain their right of residence in host Member States 'in the event of the death of the Union citizen, divorce, annulment of marriage or termination of a registered partnership'.[64] However, this value is not mentioned as an interpretative tool of the principle of equal treatment.[65] On the contrary, Regulation (EU) 492/2011[66] establishes a close correlation between dignity and equal treatment: according to recital 6:

> The right of freedom of movement, in order that it may be exercised, by objective standards, in freedom and dignity, requires that equality of treatment be ensured in fact and in law in respect of all matters relating to the actual pursuit of activities as employed persons and to eligibility for housing [...].

Yet this secondary law establishes this correlation only for workers, not for EU citizens, as if the guarantee to live in circumstances in which their human dignity is preserved is limited to economically active or wealthy citizens, i.e. to 'market citizens'.[67]

A departure from this can be seen in the 2021 *CG v. The Department for Communities in Northern Ireland* judgment,[68] in which human dignity was given as the foundation of a protective solution for a citizen in a situation of extreme vulnerability, allowing her access to social benefits. The Court ruled that:

> it is for the host Member State, in accordance with Article 1 of the Charter, to ensure that a Union citizen who has made use of his or her freedom to move and

62 D. Thym and D. Kostakopoulou, 'Conclusion: The Non-Simultaneous Evolution of Citizens' Rights' in D. Thym (ed.), *Questioning EU Citizenship: Judges and the Limits of Free Movement and Solidarity in the EU*, Oxford, Hart Publishing, 2017, p. 317.

63 G. Davies, 'Has the Court changed, or have the cases? The deservingness of litigants as an element in Court of Justice citizenship adjudication' (2018) 25(10) *Journal of European Public Policy* 1442.

64 Directive 2004/38/EC, recital 15.

65 Ibid., Article 24.

66 Council Regulation (EU) 492/2011 of 5 April 2011 on freedom of movement for workers within the Union [2011] OJ L141/1.

67 See M. Everson, 'The legacy of the market citizen' in J. Shaw and G. More (eds.), *New Legal Dynamics of European Union*, Oxford, Clarendon Press, 1995, pp. 73–89; T. Downes, 'Market citizenship: functionalism and fig-leaves' in R. Bellamy and A. Warleigh (eds.), *Citizenship and Governance in the European Union*, London, Continuum, 2001, p. 93; N.N. Shuibhne, 'The Resilience of EU Market Citizenship' (2010) 47(6) *Common Market Law Review* 1597.

68 Case C-709/20, *CG v. The Department for Communities in Northern Ireland*, ECLI:EU:C:2021:602.

> to reside within the territory of the Member States, who has a right of residence on the basis of national law, and who is in a vulnerable situation, may nevertheless live in dignified conditions.[69]

Here, the Court considered that the dignity of the EU citizen, a value enshrined in Article 2 of the TEU, 'can justify the provision of legal protection under free movement rules',[70] departing from the literal interpretation of the Directive 2004/38/EC.

It may be deduced from the reference to vulnerability that the protective solution is limited to exceptional situations, thus protecting only a minority of EU citizens. In this case, the Court notes that the applicant:

> is a mother of two young children, with no resources to provide for her own and her children's needs, who is isolated on account of having fled a violent partner. *In such a situation*, the competent national authorities may refuse an application for social assistance, [...] only after ascertaining that that refusal does not expose the citizen concerned and the children for which he or she is responsible to an actual and current risk of violation of their fundamental rights, as enshrined in Articles 1, 7 and 24 of the Charter.[71]

Consequently, it seems premature to infer from this case the integration of values in the substance of EU citizens' rights. Arguably, 'rather than using the Charter as an interpretative prism for an established and general principle of Union law, the Court relegates fundamental rights to a rather weak, sweeping-up function.'[72] All the same, the *CG v. The Department for Communities in Northern Ireland* case could be interpreted to mean that a vulnerable citizen who is the subject of a deportation order would be protected by fundamental rights. This would be of particular interest for an indigent citizen deported from a host Member State due to their lack of right of residence. The implicit recognition of material destitution as a possible violation of human dignity is welcome. In a similar vein, the European Court of Human Rights has recognised, in the case of national measures affecting persons in a situation of extreme material deprivation and particular vulnerability, an infringement of human dignity.[73] However, in previous ECJ case law, the indigent person was protected on the

---

69 Ibid., para. 89.

70 D. Sarmiento, 'EU Citizenship as an Autonomous Legal Concept of EU Law' in A. Bouveresse, A. Iliopoulou-Penot and J. Rondu (eds.), above n. 17, pp. 39–60, p. 53.

71 *CG v. The Department for Communities in Northern Ireland*, above n. 68, para. 92 (emphasis added).

72 C. O'Brien, 'The great EU citizenship illusion exposed: equal treatment rights evaporate for the vulnerable' (2021) 46(6) *European Law Review* 801.

73 *Moldovan v. Romania*, nos. 41138/98 and 64320/01, §§ 103 and 110, ECtHR, 12 July 2005; *Lăcătuş v. Switzerland*, no. 14065/15, ECtHR, 19 January 2021, concerning the prohibition on begging.

basis of equal treatment, and therefore by virtue of their status as a citizen, without the need to invoke human dignity.[74]

To determine if there is a violation of the core of EU citizens' rights – in the *Ruiz Zambrano* sense – human dignity should play an essential role, like the protection of family life or the superior interest of the child does in judgments such as *Chavez-Vilchez*.[75] This would strengthen the constitutional dimension of the status of EU citizens. Similarly, human dignity should be a fundamental consideration in assessing whether a denial of social benefits has led to a violation of freedom of movement under Article 21 of the TFEU. This would not entail requiring Member States to systematically grant social benefits to EU citizens who have exercised their freedom of movement without fulfilling the conditions to rely on a right of residence, but rather to determine, in individual cases, whether such a refusal would result in a violation of human dignity. The value of solidarity, also enshrined in Article 2, could reinforce this interpretation.

§ 2. PROTECTION FROM TORTURE AND INHUMAN OR DEGRADING TREATMENT OR PUNISHMENT

For obvious reasons, human dignity is at the core of numerous cases about judicial cooperation in criminal matters. The Court has indicated in rulings that Article 4 of the CFR, which prohibits inhuman or degrading treatment or punishment, 'is closely linked to respect for human dignity'.[76] Self-evidently, this absolute prohibition is not conditional on EU citizenship. To find specific protection of EU citizens on this matter, it is necessary to refer to extradition cases, in which the protection of an EU citizen against extradition to a third country relies on the combination of freedom of movement, equal treatment and human dignity.[77] In *Pisciotti*:[78]

> The Union citizen is protected against such physical removal from the territory of the EU by virtue of Union Citizenship law, autonomously and independently of incorporated constitutional law of the Member State of residence. This protection

[74] Case C-85/96, *Martínez Sala*, ECLI:EU:C:1998:217.

[75] Case C-133/15, *Chavez-Vilchez*, ECLI:EU:C:2017:354. In order to assess whether there would be a deprivation of the effective enjoyment of the substance of the rights of a minor citizen in the event of a refusal of residence for his or her parent, it is necessary to examine whether there is an effective relationship of dependency with the parent. In this context, the right to respect for private and family life and the best interests of the child must be taken into account.

[76] Case C-182/15, *Petruhhin*, ECLI:EU:C:2016:630, para. 56.

[77] See, in particular, *Petruhhin*, ibid., or Case C-398/19, *BY*, ECLI:EU:C:2020:1032.

[78] Case C-191/16, *Pisciotti*, ECLI:EU:C:2018:222.

solely depends on the citizen having exercised his or her right to freedom of free movement.[79]

The priority given to European instruments of cooperation, particularly the European arrest warrant,[80] is linked with what Niamh Nic Shuibhne has called the 'protective narrative'.[81] In other words, 'Member States should use tools at their disposal to allow the citizen to live in the EU where their rights are protected and public authorities are ultimately committed to the same shared values'.[82] Nevertheless, there is no absolute protection against extradition for EU citizens, except if there is a risk of violation of Article 19 of the CFR.

In another example, the increased concern about social rehabilitation after criminal sentences enhances EU citizen offenders' rights. Advocate General Bot considered in his Opinion in *Raugevicius* that the Member State's treatment of an extradition request made by a third country must take into consideration 'the rehabilitation function of the sentence, which is closely linked to the concept of "human dignity" enshrined in Article 1 of the Charter of Fundamental Rights'.[83] In that case, because the applicant had lived in a Member State for a considerable length of time and had children with the nationality of this Member State, the conviction handed down in a third country should be enforced in the Member State territory, in order to promote his social rehabilitation.[84] This objective establishes a correlation between individual rights and the interest of the EU as a whole. Human dignity can thus work to strengthen individual rights while simultaneously reinforcing the identity of the Union.

§ 3. LGBTQ+ RIGHTS

In cases involving rainbow families, human dignity is not explicitly mentioned in Court rulings, although in Advocate General Wathelet's Opinion in *Coman*,[85] he highlighted that 'the definition of the concept of "spouse" to be given will necessarily affect'[86] the dignity of the men and women concerned.

[79] V. Roeb, P. Minnerop, P. Telles and J. Snell, 'Revisiting Union citizenship from a fundamental rights perspective in the time of Brexit' (2018) 5 *European Human Rights Law Review* 450.

[80] Council Framework Decision 2002/584/JHA of 13 June 2002 on the European arrest warrant and the surrender procedures between Member States [2002] OJ L190/1.

[81] N.N. Shuibhne, 'The "Territory of the Union" in EU Citizenship Law: Charting a Route from Parallel to Integrated Narratives' (2019) 38 *Yearbook of European Law* 267, 270.

[82] F. Ristuccia, above n. 1, 5.

[83] Opinion of AG Bot, Case C-247/17, *Raugevicius*, ECLI:EU:C:2018:616, para. 61.

[84] Ibid., para. 60.

[85] Case C-673/16, *Coman*, ECLI:EU:C:2018:385.

[86] Opinion of AG Wathelet, Case C-673/16, *Coman*, ECLI:EU:C:2018:2, para. 2.

Some authors regret a finding based mainly on citizenship rights, rather than on fundamental rights.[87] Nevertheless, in *Coman* and *V.M.A.*,[88] the ECJ considered that a national measure hindering the exercise of a citizen's free movement can only be justified if it is in accordance with fundamental rights, establishing a close correlation between fundamental rights and freedom of movement.[89] This could prefigure a closer link between human dignity, when it is at stake, and EU citizens' rights.

In the *Mirin* case, a Romanian court has asked the Court of Justice for a preliminary ruling on the compatibility with citizenship rights of the refusal to recognise the change of gender on the civil status of a transgender person who has exercised their freedom of movement.[90] This could have represented an opportunity for the ECJ to give an interpretation of the substance of EU citizenship rights in full accordance with human dignity, and to contribute to the definition of EU identity. As Myriam Benlolo Carabot has highlighted, the Court 'promotes human rights not primarily as universal values, but as EU foundations and part of EU identity'.[91] In this context, it was of great interest to see if the Court would choose to elude or to rely on human dignity to interpret citizens' rights in a case involving a societal issue. However, despite the reference to dignity in the question referred by the national court, the ECJ makes no mention of that value. The ECJ recalls that any restriction on the right to freedom of movement had to respect fundamental rights,[92] but an interpretation of Article 21 TFEU in the light of the right to respect for private life referred to in Article 7 of the Charter is sufficient to conclude that the national legislation is incompatible with Union law,[93] without there being any need to refer to Article 1 of the Charter.

---

[87] A. Ward and J. MacLennan, 'Citizenship and incremental convergence with Fundamental Rights?' (2019) 78(2) *Cambridge Law Journal* 283.

[88] Case C-490/20, *V.M.A.*, ECLI:EU:C:2021:1008.

[89] *Coman*, above n. 85, para. 32: 'The rights which nationals of Member States enjoy under that provision include the right to lead a normal family life, together with their family members, both in the host Member State and in the Member State of which they are nationals when they return to that Member State'. Also, *V.M.A.*, above n. 88, para. 47.

[90] Case C-4/23, *Mirin*, ECLI:EU:C:2024:845.

[91] M. Benlolo Carabot, 'Citizenship, Integration, and the Public Policy Exception: *B and Vomero* and *K. and H.F.*' (2019) 56(3) *Common Market Law Review* 771, 794.

[92] Case C-4/23, *Mirin*, ECLI:EU:C:2024:845, para. 62.

[93] Case C-4/23, *Mirin*, ECLI:EU:C:2024:845, para. 68.

SECTION IV
CONCLUDING REMARKS: THE TENSION BETWEEN HUMAN DIGNITY AND THE DISTINCTIVENESS OF EU CITIZENSHIP

Because it is a universal fundamental right, human dignity might mitigate the distinctiveness of the status of EU citizenship, levelling the protection offered to EU citizens with that of third-country nationals. This can explain why some authors advocate for refocusing EU citizenship on freedom of movement, which guarantees its added value.[94] Conversely, for Daniel Thym:

> The time may have come [...] to move the debate about Union citizenship beyond cross-border mobility, also considering that the legislation and case law on transnational rights has lost momentum.[95]

In any event, ECJ case law shows points of convergence between the legal framework for mobile EU citizens and that of third-country nationals when human dignity is at stake.

For example, the right of access to the material reception conditions for asylum seekers laid down in Directive 2013/33/EU is not absolute,[96] but according to recital 35, the Directive seeks to ensure full respect for human dignity and to promote the application of Article 1 of the CFR. Consequently, human dignity has been used by the Court to justify a strict interpretation of the possibilities of withdrawing these reception conditions, insofar as they allow asylum seekers to meet their most basic needs.[97] In that regard, respect for human dignity:

> requires the person concerned not finding himself or herself in a situation of extreme material poverty that does not allow that person to meet his or her most basic needs such as a place to live, food, clothing and personal hygiene, and that undermines his or her physical or mental health or puts that person in a state of degradation incompatible with human dignity [...].[98]

---

94 F. De Witte, 'Freedom of Movement Needs to Be Defended as the Core of EU Citizenship' in R. Bauböck (ed.), *Debating European Citizenship*, Cham, Springer, 2019, pp. 93–99.

95 D. Thym, 'Union Citizenship and Third Country Nationals: Overlap, Parallelism, or Distinction?' in A. Bouveresse, A. Iliopoulou-Penot and J. Rondu (eds.), above n. 17, pp. 160–88, p. 186.

96 Article 2(f) and (g) and Article 20 of Council Directive 2013/33/EU of 26 June 2013 laying down standards for the reception of applicants for international protection [2013] OJ L180/96.

97 Case C-233/18, *Haqbin*, ECLI:EU:C:2019:956, para. 46.

98 Ibid. In that sense, see also Case C-163/17, *Jawo*, ECLI:EU:C:2019:218, para. 92.

Daniel Thym argues that 'the case law remains ambiguous, but we cannot exclude that it turns into a fully-fledged guarantee of minimum protection in the future'.[99] Yet while the value of human dignity could enhance the rights of third-country nationals, its role is more ambivalent for EU citizens if it is interpreted in order to mitigate the restrictive interpretation of the scope of application of the principle of equal treatment, as in the judgment in *CG v. The Department for Communities in Northern Ireland.*

In the case *Ordre des barreaux francophones et germanophone*,[100] concerning pre-removal detention, which Belgium had extended to a maximum period of eight months for EU citizens and third-country nationals alike, the Court showed reluctance to criticise the convergence of the legal framework for EU citizens with that of third-country nationals. It stated that these two categories enjoy 'status and rights [that are] entirely different',[101] and that this general lack of comparability justifies EU citizens not necessarily benefitting from a more protective regime.[102] Moreover, detention is not in itself seen as an infringement of the rights and dignity of EU citizens.

Ultimately, while it is desirable that the value of human dignity strengthens individual rights within the EU legal order, this carries the risk of convergence between the status of EU citizens and third-country nationals. Another pitfall is that human dignity is invoked only when a vulnerable person is involved. These tensions mean that the relationship between human dignity and European citizenship is ambivalent. On the one hand, it holds the promise of reinforcing the rights associated with the status of EU citizenship. On the other, asserting a common European identity may come at the expense of certain individuals despite their 'fundamental status' as EU citizens.

---

99 D. Thym, 'Union Citizenship and Third Country Nationals: Overlap, Parallelism, or Distinction' in A. Bouveresse, A. Iliopoulou-Penot and J. Rondu (eds.), above n. 17, pp. 160–88, p. 183. See also D. Thym, *European Migration Law*, Oxford, Oxford University Press, 2023, pp. 351–53 and 412–14.

100 Case C-718/19, *Ordre des barreaux francophones et germanophone*, ECLI:EU:C:2021:505.

101 Ibid., para. 53.

102 Ibid., para. 57.

CHAPTER 2

THE VALUE OF EQUALITY AND ACCESS TO SOCIAL BENEFITS BY 'INACTIVE' EUROPEAN CITIZENS

Michele MESSINA*

Abstract

The question of the access of European citizens to their social rights, in order to guarantee the full enjoyment of EU citizenship, has been the subject of numerous rulings by the EU Court of Justice. It has also been the subject of many doctrinal reflections that concern, more specifically, the access to these rights by all European citizens, economically active or inactive, regardless of their nationality. This chapter analyses recent EU case law to examine the issue of the different treatment reserved to social assistance compared to social security benefits, and to economically inactive European citizens in other Member States depending on the duration of their stay and/or type of residence.

SECTION I
INTRODUCTION

The question of the access of European citizens to their rights – in particular those relating to so-called 'welfare' – in order to guarantee the full benefit of EU citizenship (including social citizenship) has been the subject of numerous rulings by the EU Court of Justice in the last two decades.[1] It has also been

* Professor of European Union Law at the University of Messina.

[1] See *ex multis*, Case C-85/96, *Martínez Sala*, ECLI:EU:C:1998:217; Case C-184/99, *Rudy Grzelczyk*, ECLI:EU:C:2001:458; Case C-224/98, *D'Hoop*, ECLI:EU:C:2002:432; Case C-413/99, *Baumbast and R.*, ECLI:EU:C:2002:493; Case C-138/02, *Brian Francis Collins*, ECLI:EU:C:2004:172; Case C-456/02, *Michel Trojani*, ECLI:EU:C:2004:488; Case C-209/03, *Bidar*, ECLI:EU:C:2005:169; Case C-158/07, *Förster*, ECLI:EU:C:2008:630; Joined Cases C-22/08 and C-23/08, *Vatsouras and Koupatantze*, ECLI:EU:C:2009:344; Case C-140/12, *Brey*, ECLI:EU:C:2013:565; Case C-333/13, *Dano*, ECLI:EU:C:2014:2358; Case C-67/14,

the subject of many doctrinal reflections that concern, more specifically, the access to these rights by all European citizens, economically active or inactive, regardless of their nationality.[2] It is not a coincidence that the Court of Justice,

Alimanovic, ECLI:EU:C:2015:597; Case C-299/14, *García-Nieto*, ECLI:EU:C:2016:114; Case C-308/14, *Commission v. United Kingdom*, ECLI:EU:C:2016:436; Case C-181/19, *Jobcenter Krefeld*, ECLI:EU:C:2020:794; Case C-709/20, *CG v. The Department for Communities in Northern Ireland*, ECLI:EU:C:2021:602; Case C-411/20, *Familienkasse Niedersachsen-Bremen*, ECLI:EU:C:2022:602; and to some extent, Case C-488/21, *GV*, ECLI:EU:C:2023:1013.

2 See *ex multis*, A. Albors-Llorens, 'A Broader Construction of the EC Treaty Provisions on Citizenship?' (1998) 57(3) *Cambridge Law Journal* 461; S. Fries and J. Shaw, 'Citizenship of the Union: First Steps in the European Court of Justice' (1998) 4 *European Public Law* 533; S. O'Leary, 'Putting Flesh on the Bones of European Union Citizenship' (1999) 24(1) *European Law Review* 68; A.J. Menéndez, 'La ciudadanía europea tras *Martínez Sala* y *Baumbast*: la consecución de un derecho europeo más humano pero menos social?' (2010) 89 *Revista Española de Derecho Constitucional* 289; C. Tomuschat, 'Annotation of Case C-85/96, *María Martínez Sala*' (2000) *Common Market Law Review* 449; A. Alemanno, 'La jurisprudence de la Cour de justice et du Tribunal de première instance, Chronique des arrêts, Arrêt "*Rudy Grzelczyk*"' (2001) 4 *Revue du Droit de l'Union Européenne* 1008; F. David, 'La citoyenneté de l'Union, statut fondamental des ressortissant des États membres' (2003) 39(3) *Revue trimestrielle de droit européen* 553; B. Kotschy, 'Droit au minimex en vertu de la citoyenneté? – Arrêt "*Trojani*"' (2004) 2 *Revue du Droit de l'Union Européenne* 327; E. Muir, 'Citoyenneté: Affaire "*Bidar*"' (2005) 1 *Revue du Droit de l'Union Européenne* 193; C. Barnard, 'Of Students and Babies' (2005) 64(3) *Cambridge Law Journal* 560; A.P. Van der Mei, 'Union Citizenship and the "De-Nationalisation" of the Territorial Welfare State: Comments on Case C-456/02 *Trojani* and Case C-209/03 *Bidar*' (2005) 7 *European Journal of Migration and Law* 207; C. Barnard, 'EU Citizenship and the principle of solidarity' in M. Dougan and E. Spaventa (eds.), *Social Welfare and EU Law*, Oxford, Hart Publishing, 2005, p. 157; M. Dougan and E. Spaventa, '"Wish you weren't here...": new models of social solidarity in the European Union' in M. Dougan and E. Spaventa (eds.), *Social Welfare and EU Law*, Oxford, Hart Publishing, 2005, p. 181; S. Giubboni, 'Free movement of persons and European solidarity' (2007) 13(3) *European Law Journal* 360; E. Fahey, 'Interpretative legitimacy and the distinction between "social assistance" and "work-seekers' allowance": Comment on cases C-22/08 and C-23/08 *Vatsouras and Koupatantze*' (2009) 34(6) *European Law Review* 933; S. De La Rosa, 'La citoyenneté européenne à la mesure des intérêts nationaux. A propos de l'arrêt *Förster* (aff. C-158/07 du 18 novembre 2008)' (2009) 2 *Cahiers de droit européen* 549; N.N. Shuibhne, 'The resilience of EU market citizenship' (2010) 47(6) *Common Market Law Review* 1597; D. Kochenov, 'The essence of European citizenship emerging from the last ten years of academic debate: Beyond the cherry blossoms and the moon?' (2013) 62(1) *International and Comparative Law Quarterly* 97; J. Cavallini, 'Citoyen européen économiquement inactif et accès aux prestations d'assistance sociale' (2013) 44–45 *La Semaine Juridique – Social* 39; H. Verschueren, 'Free Movement or Benefit Tourism: The Unreasonable Burden of *Brey*' (2014) 16(2) *European Journal of Migration and Law* 147; J.-Y. Carlier, 'La libre circulation des personnes dans l'Union européenne' (2014) 208 *Journal de droit européen* 167; J. Tomkin, 'Reconciling Integrationist Aspirations with Budgetary Realities. Citizenship and Solidarity in the Union Legal Order' in A. Silveira, M. Canotilho and P. Madeira Froufe (eds.), *Citizenship and Solidarity in the European Union: From the Charter of Fundamental Rights to the Crisis, the State of the Art*, Berlin, Peter Lang, 2014, p. 45; A.V. Garcia Sanchez and W. Kowalczyk, '*Dano*: a Right to Freedom of Movement or Protection against an Unreasonable Burden Imposed upon Member State's Social Security Systems?' (2014) *European Law Reporter* 248; N.N. Shuibhne, '"What I tell you three times is true": Lawful Residence and Equal Treatment after *Dano*' (2016) 23(6) *Maastricht Journal*

in the well-known 2001 *Grzelczyk* ruling, stated, using a formula that has been described as 'quasi-theological',[3] that the status of European citizen was intended to constitute the fundamental status of citizens of Member States, allowing them to obtain, in equal situations and regardless of nationality, the same legal treatment, without prejudice to the expressly provided exceptions.[4] Such a statement had been previously expressed by the Court of Justice, in particular by Advocate General La Pergola, who defined European citizenship as the basic legal status guaranteed by the EU legal system to the citizen of any Member State in his Opinion in the 1997 *Martínez Sala* case.[5]

The affirmation of this fundamental status, together with the extension of the material application of the prohibition of discrimination on grounds of nationality in Article 18 of the Treaty on the Functioning of the European Union (TFEU),[6] has contributed to legitimising the expansion of the beneficiaries of social rights in host Member States. This has brought about a convergence in the status of so-called 'mobile' citizens that does not distinguish between those who are economically active or inactive. This seemed to be the intention of the Citizens' Rights Directive (Directive 2004/38/EC) itself, whose third recital called for the abandonment of the separation of different categories of European citizens, precisely to simplify and strengthen the right

of European and Comparative Law 908; D. Thym, 'When Union citizens turn into illegal migrants: the *Dano* Case' (2015) 40(2) *European Law Review* 249; P. Rodière, 'Quel droit de circulation en Europe pour les personnes inactives et démunies?' (2015) 218 *Journal de droit européen* 146; D. Thym, 'The elusive limits of solidarity: residence rights of and social benefits for economically inactive Union citizens' (2015) 52(1) *Common Market Law Review* 17; A. Iliopoulou-Penot, 'Deconstructing the former edifice of Union citizenship? The *Alimanovic* judgment' (2016) 53(4) *Common Market Law Review* 1007; S. Mantu and P. Minderhoud, 'EU citizenship and social solidarity' (2017) 24(5) *Maastricht Journal of European and Comparative Law* 703; H. Verschueren, 'Economically inactive migrant union citizens: only entitled to social benefits if they enjoy a right to reside in the host state' (2017) 19(1) *European Journal of Social Security* 71; C. O'Brien, 'The ECJ sacrifices EU citizenship in vain: *Commission v. United Kingdom*' (2017) 54(1) *Common Market Law Review* 209; N.N. Shuibhne, 'The Social Market Economy and Restriction of Free Movement Rights: Plus C'est La Même Chose?' (2019) 57(1) *Journal of Common Market Studies* 111; N. Cambien, D. Kochenov and E. Muir (eds.), *European Citizenship under Stress*, Brill Nijhoff, Leiden 2020; H. Verschueren, 'The Right to Social Assistance for Migrating Union Citizens: A Step Forward in the Case Law of the Court of Justice This Time' (2021) 2 *European Journal of Migration and Law* 202; H. Verschueren, 'The Right to Social Assistance for Economically Inactive Migrating Union Citizens: The Court Disregards the Principle of Proportionality and Lets the Charter Appease the Consequences' (2022) 29(4) *Maastricht Journal of European and Comparative Law* 483.

3 A. Iliopoulou-Penot, 'Citoyenneté de l'Union et accès des inactifs aux prestations sociales dans l'État d'accueil' in L. Clément-Wilz (ed.), *Le rôle politique de la Cour de justice de l'Union européenne*, Brussels, Bruylant, 2018, pp. 315, 325.

4 *Rudy Grzelczyk*, above n. 1, para. 31.

5 See Opinion of AG La Pergola, Case C-85/96, *Martínez Sala*, ECLI:EU:C:1997:335, para. 18.

6 Consolidated Version of the Treaty on the Functioning of the European Union [2016] OJ C202/47.

of all EU citizens without distinction to move and reside freely throughout the entire Union.[7] Furthermore, Article 24(1) of the Directive – providing equal treatment for a European citizen resident in a host Member State compared to a national citizen of the state – is considered a specific variation of the principle of non-discrimination on grounds of nationality referred to in Article 18 of the TFEU.[8] However, this equal treatment remains subject, as will be seen, to the limitations provided for in Article 24(2) of Directive 2004/38.[9]

The application of the principle of equal treatment for European citizens of different nationalities becomes rather complicated concerning access to social benefits by economically inactive European citizens residing in a host Member State. There has been copious jurisprudence by the Union on the matter, but this has not led to a coherent, uniform interpretation in the sense of undisputed access to social benefits by European citizens regardless of their Member State of origin. A fundamental role has been played by the EU legislation, which has not always delivered an easy-to-interpret rule to the EU Court. An emblematic case of this is the different treatment reserved to social assistance benefits compared to social security benefits and their different availability to inactive European citizens in other Member States depending on the duration and/or type of residence of the person in question.

This chapter intends to examine these issues, following the ruling of the Grand Chamber of the EU Court of Justice in the 2022 *Familienkasse Niedersachsen-Bremen* case.[10] This ruling presents elements that are absolutely consistent with the well-known 2016 judgment in the *Commission v. United Kingdom* case,[11] thus completing the interpretative framework regarding access to social security benefits pursuant to Regulation 883/2004,[12] in consideration of its complex relationship with Directive 2004/38. At the same time, there are also some interesting aspects to highlight for the future development

---

7 See Council Directive 2004/38/EC of 29 April 2004 on the right of citizens of the Union and their family members to move and reside freely within the territory of the Member States [2004] OJ L158/77. In particular, the third recital of the preamble, where the EU law affirms that: 'Union citizenship should be the fundamental status of nationals of the Member States when they exercise their right of free movement and residence. It is therefore necessary to codify and review the existing Community instruments dealing separately with workers, self-employed persons, as well as students and other inactive persons in order to simplify and strengthen the right of free movement and residence of all Union citizens'.

8 E. Guild, S. Peers and J. Tomkin (eds.), *The EU Citizenship Directive: A Commentary*, 1st ed., Oxford, Oxford University Press, 2014, p. 234.

9 This refers, in particular, to the provision according to which the host Member State is not required to recognise the right to social assistance benefits of European citizens that are nationals of another Member State during the first three months of their stay or during a period longer than the first three months but less than five years.

10 *Familienkasse Niedersachsen-Bremen*, above n. 1.

11 *Commission v. United Kingdom*, above n. 1.

12 Council Regulation (EC) 883/2004 of 29 April 2004 on the coordination of social security systems [2004] OJ L166/1.

of the matter, such as the restrictive interpretation of the derogation from the prohibition of discrimination on grounds of nationality provided in Article 24(2) of Directive 2004/38. Section II will look at the EU founding value of equality, referred to in Article 2 of the Treaty on European Union (TEU),[13] with a specific emphasis on some of its more concrete expressions in EU primary law, such as the general principle of non-discrimination on grounds of nationality enshrined in Article 18 of the TFEU and in Article 21(2) of the Charter of Fundamental Rights of the EU.[14] Rights are further expressed in EU secondary law, in particular, in Article 24 of Directive 2004/38.

SECTION II EQUAL TREATMENT IN THE EU: A GENERAL PRINCIPLE WITH THE STATUS OF A FOUNDING VALUE

Equality is one of the values on which the Union is founded, pursuant to Article 2 of the TEU. This is the solemn legal standing acknowledged by EU Member States following the Reform Treaty signed in Lisbon in 2007 to the EU's previously existing general principle of equal treatment (the Treaty of Lisbon).[15] Article 2 of the TEU enshrines many general principles that may be qualified as having a constitutional nature, with a 'value' alongside a legal foundation, thus constituting the essential core of the EU constituent process. In this sense, equality experienced a change in its legal status – from 'principle' to 'value' – in order to increase its political as well as its moral stance.[16] This was a result of the process of constitutionalisation of the principle of equal treatment whereby this was accorded a higher legal status, more deeply rooting it in the legal system so that it would be less vulnerable to possible change or repeal. If conflicts between legal norms arise, constitutionalised norms will prevail as having a greater weight,[17] and also give the judge a point of

---

13 Consolidated Version of the Treaty on European Union [2016] OJ C202/13.

14 Charter of Fundamental Rights of the European Union [2016] OJ C202/389.

15 See M. Klamert and D. Kochenov, 'Article 2 TEU' in M. Kellerbauer, M. Klamert and J. Tomkin (eds.), *The EU Treaties and the Charter of Fundamental Rights: A Commentary*, 1st ed., Oxford, Oxford University Press, 2019, pp. 22, 25. These authors affirm that 'some of the values appearing under Article 2 TEU are well-known general principles of Union law that are laid out more fully elsewhere in the Treaties'.

16 L. Fumagalli, 'Articolo 2 TUE' in A. Tizzano (ed.), *Trattati dell'Unione europea*, 2nd ed., Milan, Giuffrè, 2014, pp. 11, 13.

17 M. Bell, 'The principle of equal treatment: widening and deepening' in P. Craig and G. de Búrca (eds.), *The Evolution of EU Law*, 2nd ed., Oxford, Oxford University Press, 2011, pp. 611, 625.

reference when considering how to exercise discretion in interpreting anti-discrimination legislation.[18]

The process of constitutionalisation of the principle of equal treatment has also been reinforced by the inclusion of the founding value of equality in the Charter of Fundamental Rights of the EU, in particular in Articles 20 to 26. The value of equality is further expressed in treaties in the form of the general prohibition of discrimination on grounds of nationality provided in Article 18 of the TFEU. The first paragraph of Article 18 of the TFEU prohibits any discrimination on grounds of nationality within the scope of application of the Treaties and without prejudice to any special provision contained therein.[19] As a consequence, every EU citizen has the right not to be discriminated against on the basis of nationality within the substantive scope of EU law.

The principle of equal treatment has contributed extensively to the creation of a 'Europe of citizens'. Alongside the objective of complete integration of the economic market, the EU aimed to guarantee citizens the protection of their rights beyond those related to the exercise of their economic activity. Over the years, the Treaties have gradually been adjusted to uncouple the link between equal treatment and the construction of the internal market. Such a shift has seemed clear since the evolution of the application of the principle of non-discrimination on grounds of nationality to apply it beyond the economic freedoms of all EU citizens independent of their nationality (so long as it fell within the scope of application of the Treaties), making it definitive in determining the relationship between the EU citizen and the host Member State.[20] As a consequence, equality and non-discrimination have become expressions of a principle contributing to the qualification of the EU as a 'union based on the rule of law'.

A national of a Member State, being a citizen of the Union, can rely on Article 18 of the TFEU as well as Article 21 of the TFEU if he or she lawfully resides in another Member State, exercising the right enjoyed by citizens of the Union to move and reside within the territory of the Member States. However, Article 21 of the TFEU also stipulates that these rights are 'subject to the limitations and conditions laid down in the treaties and by the measures

---

18 Ibid., p. 627.

19 See K. Lenaerts and P. Van Nuffel (eds.), *EU Constitutional Law*, Oxford, Oxford University Press, 2022, p. 117; A.P. Van der Mei, 'The Outer Limits of the Prohibition of Discrimination on Grounds of Nationality: A Look through the Lens of Union Citizenship' (2011) 18(1–2) *Maastricht Journal of European and Comparative Law* 62.

20 K. Lenaerts, 'L'égalité de traitement en droit communautaire: Un principe unique aux apparences multiples' (1991) *Cahiers de droit européen* 3, 25. This author affirmed as early as 1991 that the principle of non-discrimination on grounds of nationality went factually beyond the protection of economic freedoms, protecting the EU citizen as such; as a consequence, any discrimination on the grounds of nationality against EU citizens was prohibited in absolute terms. See 28–29.

adopted to give them effect'. The primary rules thus continue to remain subject to the limitations in the rules of secondary law, such as those that stipulate the conditions of possession of adequate health insurance or sufficient resources so as not to constitute a burden on the finances of the host Member State (as expressly prescribed by Directive 2004/38). The attempts of the EU Court of Justice to emancipate the right to free movement and residence of European citizens from an almost exclusively economic profile, through the valorisation of a more social dimension of these rights (combining the rules on free movement and residence and the principle of non-discrimination on grounds of nationality), have often had to contend with a more conservative approach towards the right of residence, in particular with regard to economically inactive European citizens. The EU Court has often shown uncertainty in combining the objective of complete equal treatment of European citizens compared to national citizens, which would guarantee generalised, non-discriminatory access to the social dimension of European citizenship.[21]

In its first rulings on the matter, the EU Court of Justice adopted an approach to the free movement of European citizens that was more sensitive to non-discrimination on grounds of nationality. This was the case of the 1998 *Martínez Sala* ruling,[22] in which the EU Court laid the foundations of the jurisprudence that links European citizenship to non-discrimination on grounds of nationality in the exercise of free movement. In the subsequent 2002 *Baumbast* ruling,[23] the EU Court of Justice affirmed for the first time the direct effect of Article 21 of the TFEU, with regard to the recognition of the right of residence, albeit subject to some limitations. In the 2002 *D'Hoop* ruling,[24] however, the EU Court of Justice understood the mobility of European citizens as an interest to be protected by jurisprudence through the necessary financial solidarity between Member States. In that case, a European citizen had been discriminated against simply for having exercised her freedom of movement. In these rulings it is possible to detect, by analysing the facts, a previous link between the applicants in the main proceedings and the labour market of the host Member State, an aspect that was much more evident in the first two rulings. This suggests a not entirely independent application of the rules on European citizenship, which were invoked rather to perpetuate a pre-existing situation based on the rules on the free movement of workers.[25]

21 See S. Amadeo, 'Il principio di eguaglianza e la cittadinanza dell'Unione: il trattamento del cittadino europeo "inattivo"' (2011) 1 *Il Diritto dell'Unione europea* 59, 61–62.

22 *Martínez Sala*, above n. 1.

23 *Baumbast and R.*, above n. 1.

24 *D'Hoop*, above n. 1.

25 See M. Messina, 'I cittadini europei inattivi e le condizioni per l'accesso alle prestazioni di assistenza sociale in uno Stato membro ospitante: quale lezione dall'ordinamento USA?' (2018) 3 *Freedom, Security & Justice: European Legal Studies* 44, 49.

SECTION III
ACCESS TO SOCIAL BENEFITS BY INACTIVE EU CITIZENS IN A HOST MEMBER STATE

As early as 2001, financial solidarity was the subject of the ruling in the *Grzelczyk* case, to the extent that the Court of Justice seemed to allow this, at least in part. This ruling clarified that students' right of residence could be enjoyed as long as they did not become an 'excessive' burden (not simply a generic burden) for the public finances of the host Member State. It added, however, that the difficulties faced by a beneficiary of the right of residence must be of a temporary nature.[26] In the subsequent *Trojani* ruling in 2004, the EU Court affirmed for the first time the principle of non-discrimination exclusively on the basis of European citizenship without taking into account whether or not the applicant submitting a request for social benefits in a host Member State was economically productive or financially independent. The task of the Court of Justice was made simpler in that case by the fact that the applicant was legally resident in the host Member State in accordance with the applicable national law, and thus did not have to satisfy other conditions for lawful residence established by EU law.[27] In the 2004 *Collins* ruling,[28] the EU Court extended access to social advantages to European citizens seeking a first job in a host Member State, ensuring that these citizens, although inactive, did not have to satisfy the condition of sufficient resources.[29] Yet the Court of Justice limited the scope of this by specifying that access to an allowance for jobseekers could still be made subject to the residence requirement, establishing a link between the person seeking employment and the labour market in question.

Directive 2004/38, adopted by the EU legislature following the aforementioned EU Court rulings, continued to provide such differentiations between the different categories of European citizens with regard to their eligibility to access social benefits in a host Member State. It added to the condition of the possible exercise of an economic activity based on the duration of residence in that Member State, while also providing for three main categories of European citizens. The first is EU citizens who stay in another Member State for a period not exceeding three months (Article 6 of Directive 2004/38), for whom no particular formalities are foreseen for their stay except possession of a valid identity document. Yet the combined provisions of Article 14(1) and Article 24(2) of Directive 2004/38 show how the

---

26 *Rudy Grzelczyk*, above n. 1, para. 44.

27 *Michel Trojani*, above n. 1.

28 *Brian Francis Collins*, above n. 1.

29 M. Dougan, 'Free Movement: The Workseeker as Citizen' (2001) 4 *Cambridge Yearbook of European Legal Studies* 93, 119.

right of residence, even when short and unconditional, can only be enjoyed as long as the EU citizens in question 'do not become an unreasonable burden on the social assistance system of the host Member State',[30] taking into account that 'the host Member State shall not be obliged to confer entitlement to social assistance during the first three months of residence'.[31] This is clear discrimination against migrant Union citizens staying for short periods, without distinguishing between economically active or inactive EU citizens. The second category is European citizens who stay in a Member State for a period exceeding three months (Article 7 of Directive 2004/38). Under this provision, economically inactive EU citizens can exercise their right to reside in another host Member State for a period exceeding three months, provided they have: 'sufficient resources [...] not to become a burden on the social assistance system of the host Member State during their period of residence and have comprehensive sickness insurance cover in the host Member State'.[32] The status of economically inactive EU citizens is then further clarified by Article 14(2) of Directive 2004/38, which subordinates their right of residence to the conditions set out in Article 7, stating that EU citizens who are neither active nor self-sufficient cannot derive from EU law any right of residence in another Member State.[33] The third category provides for the acquisition of the right of permanent residence in the host Member State for the EU citizen who has resided legally and continuously there for five years (Article 16 of Directive 2004/38). In this case, the enjoyment of the right of permanent residence is not subordinate to the need to have sufficient resources.

The regulatory framework outlined by Directive 2004/38 with regard to the application of the principle of non-discrimination on grounds of nationality in the enjoyment of social rights by European citizens who have exercised their right to free movement is thus strongly linked to the requirement of lawful residence, without neglecting the duration thereof, in a host Member State. Following the entry into force of Directive 2004/38, an economically inactive EU citizen who requests access to certain forms of social assistance if he/she does not have sufficient resources will maintain the right of residence, pursuant to the same Directive, until this right is revoked due to the fact that he/she has become an excessive burden on the social assistance system of the host Member State, as can be deduced from the combined provisions of Articles 14 and 24 of Directive 2004/38, and of recital 16 thereof.[34]

In light of the current regulatory framework and the related rulings of the EU Court of Justice, European citizens thus do not enjoy unconditional access

30 Directive 2004/38, Article 14(1).

31 Ibid., Article 24(2).

32 Ibid., Article 7(1)(b).

33 M. Messina, above n. 25, 54.

34 S. Mantu and P. Minderhoud, above n. 2, 709.

to social benefits in the host Member State, given that the fundamental and essential condition for such access is the residence of the citizen in the host Member State. The Court of Justice has added further conditions to this, such as a genuine link with the labour market of the Member State involved,[35] or the degree of integration into the host country's society.[36] The 2008 ruling in *Förster* was absolutely consistent with this, legitimising that a state should grant aid to cover the maintenance costs of students from other Member States only to those who have demonstrated a certain degree of integration into the society of that state. According to the EU Court, the condition of uninterrupted residence for five years ensured that the applicant for a study grant was integrated into the host Member State.[37] To further support this, the Court then referred to Article 24(2) of Directive 2004/38, which does not provide any obligation for Member States to grant maintenance subsidies to students who have not yet achieved the right of permanent residence, referred to in Article 16, regardless of the fact that this legislation could not apply timewise to the facts of that case. This ruling placed economically inactive migrant European citizens in a position of absolute inequality not only in relation to national citizens of the host Member State, but also in relation to migrant EU workers with access to certain social benefits. Such a distinction between those who carry out an economic activity and those who do not, and why the latter category can be excluded from access to certain benefits for at least five years, is not entirely convincing for some commentators.[38]

The possibility of economically inactive EU citizens accessing social benefits, and therefore the recognition of forms of social and financial solidarity between Member States and European citizens, has also been the object of more recent jurisprudence by the Court of Justice. Over the last few years, there has been a change in the interpretation of the provisions on European citizenship towards a more restrictive stance.[39] This is a clear step backwards from the original position on European citizenship, to the advantage of an interpretation that reaffirms the centrality of the link of nationality, with the responsibility towards the most vulnerable individuals falling exclusively on the

35 *Brian Francis Collins*, above n. 1, paras. 67–69.

36 *Bidar*, above n. 1, para. 57.

37 *Förster*, above n. 1, para. 52.

38 See, for example, A.P. Van der Mei, 'Union citizenship and the legality of durational residence requirements for entitlement to student financial aid' (2009) 16(4) *Maastricht Journal of European and Comparative Law* 477, 488. Other authors have taken a less radical position in this regard, hoping that the lack of maturation of the right of permanent residence did not automatically mean that a migrant EU citizen could be excluded a priori from access to certain categories of social benefits. See E. Guild, S. Peers and J. Tomkin (eds.), above n. 8, p. 227.

39 See A. Nato, *La cittadinanza sociale europea al tempo della crisi economica*, Cacucci, Bari 2020, p. 57; and M. Messina, above n. 25, 61.

Member State of origin.[40] This distances European citizenship from the idea of a 'status' that goes beyond traditional connections related to nationality in the country of origin.

In the *Brey* case ruling in 2013, despite presenting a certain degree of transnational solidarity,[41] the EU Court moved backwards towards a return to a narrow functional interpretation of the rules on European citizenship. It stated that nothing prevented, in principle, making the granting of social benefits to economically inactive EU citizens conditional on the fulfilment of the conditions of the right of residence in the host Member State.[42] This close link between access to social benefits and the right of residence in the host Member State was further developed in the subsequent 2014 *Dano* ruling,[43] which consolidated the reversal of EU jurisprudence to reduce the possibility of access to social benefits by economically inactive European citizens. This reversed the dynamic promoted by the *Martínez Sala* ruling to give EU citizens access to the welfare systems of host countries on equal terms with respect to national citizens. It is worth highlighting how, in these rulings, the main object of the cases concerned the right or not to social benefits in the host Member State and not the question of the right of residence.[44]

In the *Dano* ruling, the reversal occurred when the EU Court stated that the right to legally reside in the host Member State, an essential condition for benefitting from equal treatment with national citizens in accessing social benefits, was subject exclusively to the conditions set out in Article 7(1)(b) of Directive 2004/38, i.e. the provision of sufficient economic resources by the economically inactive European citizen.[45] The recognition of the right of access to benefits by those who cannot exercise a right of residence pursuant to Directive 2004/38 would have been in conflict with one of the objectives of the Directive itself, which is to prevent citizens of other Member States from becoming an excessive burden on the social assistance system of the host Member State.[46] In doing so, any unequal treatment in the access to social

40 E. Spaventa, 'Earned Citizenship – Understanding EU citizenship through its scope' in D. Kochenov (ed.), *EU Citizenship and Federalism: The Role of Rights*, Cambridge, Cambridge University Press, 2017, pp. 204, 208. See also S. Mantu and P. Minderhoud, above n. 2, 710.

41 The Court of Justice, on this occasion, demonstrated a certain degree of transnational solidarity by stating that 'the mere fact that a national of a Member State receives social assistance is not sufficient to show that he constitutes an unreasonable burden on the social assistance system of the host Member State'. See *Brey*, above n. 1, para. 75.

42 *Brey*, above n. 1, para. 44.

43 *Dano*, above n. 1.

44 A. Nato, above n. 39, p. 59.

45 *Dano*, above n. 1, para. 73.

46 The Court, on this occasion, reversed the objective of Directive 2004/38, which had previously been identified as facilitating the exercise of the primary and individual right for EU citizens to move and reside freely. See D. Thym, 'The elusive limits of solidarity: residence rights of and social benefits for economically inactive Union citizens', above n. 2, 25.

benefits between EU citizens would derive from Directive 2004/38 itself, based on the relationship between the need to have sufficient economic resources as a condition for legal residence, and the need not to create a burden on the social assistance system of the host Member State. The EU Court, in the *Dano* ruling, attributed greater importance to the requirement of sufficient economic resources, which would allow a citizen to benefit from the right of residence, than to the assessment of whether the social benefit requested constituted an excessive burden, which was also a condition foreseen by Directive 2004/38. This interpretation has made the requirement of sufficient economic resources an insurmountable limitation, given that the law of a Member State can be considered satisfied, for the purposes of refusing access to certain social benefits by an EU citizen of another Member State, by the mere insufficiency of available economic resources, without even evaluating whether the provision of the requested service constitutes an excessive burden on its national budget. Consequently, the *Dano* ruling inaugurated the trend of jurisprudence tending to hinder the construction of social European citizenship based on the creation of an authentic space of supranational solidarity.[47] Instead, the *Dano* ruling produced a paradoxical situation in which a European citizen would have free access to social assistance in another Member State only if he/she had sufficient resources (which would presuppose that the individual in question did not need any form of social assistance). This ruling by the Court is absolutely consistent with the provisions of Directive 2004/38, the only instrument to which an excessively 'economic' interpretation of the notion of European citizenship can be attributed.[48] It is regrettable that the EU Court has opted for an excessively literal interpretation of the provisions in question, including Articles 7 and 24 of Directive 2004/38.

The jurisprudence initiated with the *Dano* ruling was confirmed in the subsequent *Alimanovic* case in 2015, in which the EU Court found that only European citizens with a right of residence, pursuant to Article 7 of Directive 2004/38, enjoy equal treatment with the nationals of the host Member State. In the latter case, the applicant, in contrast to the *Dano* case, maintained a right to lawful residence in the host Member State as a former employed worker for a period exceeding six months, a condition expressly regulated by Article 7(3)(c) of Directive 2004/38. After that period, Ms Alimanovic would have enjoyed a right of residence, pursuant to Article 14(4)(b) of Directive 2004/38, i.e. as an EU citizen who goes to another Member State for the first time as a jobseeker.

---

47 See M. Messina, 'La Corte di giustizia UE si pronuncia, positivamente, nei confronti della normativa nazionale di uno Stato membro UE che esclude i cittadini economicamente inattivi di un altro Stato membro, che soggiornano nel proprio territorio, dall'accesso a talune prestazioni sociali a parità di trattamento rispetto ai cittadini nazionali dello Stato membro ospitante' (2014) 5 *Ordine internazionale e diritti umani* 1130, 1132.

48 Ibid., 1134.

The latter case is one of those regulated by Article 24(2) of Directive 2004/38, in which the host Member State is left with the possibility of denying access to social assistance benefits.[49] Consequently, the Court of Justice concluded that EU law did not preclude national legislation from excluding citizens of other Member States who had gone to another Member State for the first time as a jobseeker from certain social assistance benefits, pursuant to Article 14(4)(b) of Directive 2004/38.[50]

In the subsequent ruling in the 2016 *García-Nieto* case,[51] the EU Court reiterated that a European citizen can invoke the principle of non-discrimination on grounds of nationality, pursuant to Article 24(1) of Directive 2004/38, only if his/her stay in the host Member State is in compliance with the conditions established by the Directive, with a clear reference to Article 7, but also to Article 6, given the specific circumstances of the case. The case at stake concerned the stay of a European citizen in the host Member State for a period of less than three months. For that reason, the denial of access to social assistance benefits by the partner of the European citizen in question was entirely compliant with EU legislation, given the derogation from the application of the principle of non-discrimination provided for in Article 24(2) of Directive 2004/38, which expressly provides for such a hypothesis.

Within this line of jurisprudence, the 2016 *Commission v. United Kingdom* case is of particular interest, although concerning only indirectly the application of Directive 2004/38, as it is more focused on Regulation 883/2004 on the coordination of national social security systems.[52] In this ruling, the Court of Justice, once again, confirmed the close link between the right of access to social benefits and the satisfaction of the criterion of the right of residence in the host Member State, pursuant to Directive 2004/38. This effectively provided an additional condition for the access to benefits governed by Regulation 883/2004, which, on the contrary, did not contain any reference to the residence requirement referred to in Directive 2004/38 for the access to social security benefits in the Regulation itself.[53] The EU Court, in this ruling, confirmed with particular emphasis the *Brey* and *Dano* rulings regarding the granting of social benefits to economically inactive European citizens, making

49 *Alimanovic*, above n. 1, para. 58.

50 Ibid., para. 63.

51 *García-Nieto*, above n. 1.

52 Council Regulation (EC) 883/2004 of 29 April 2004 on the coordination of social security systems [2004] OJ L166/1.

53 M. Messina, above n. 25, 66. In this regard, it is worth highlighting how the Commission, which initiated the infringement procedure and the subsequent action for failure to fulfil obligations against the United Kingdom, considered sufficient, for the access to the benefits referred to in the case, the habitual residence of the European citizen in question and not the possession of a right of residence pursuant to Article 7 of Directive 2004/38.

this subject to the right of residence in the host Member State.[54] The right of residence, according to the Court, would become a substantial condition that economically inactive citizens must satisfy.[55] The Court found that EU law did not preclude the national legal systems of the Member States from requiring economically inactive European citizens to provide proof of their right to lawful residence in order to access social benefits, deducing this from Article 7(1)(b) of Directive 2004/38. This ruling allows host Member States to make the recognition of the right of residence in their territory of citizens of other Member States conditional on the fact that they do not become an excessive burden on the social assistance system of the host Member State.[56]

In the *Commission v. United Kingdom* ruling, the Court of Justice seemed to achieve the maximum consolidation of jurisprudence tending to restrict the rights of European citizenship by inactive EU citizens intending to access social benefits in a host Member State. The right of residence, pursuant to Article 7 of Directive 2004/38, has now become a formal and irrefutable requirement, as well as an insurmountable obstacle for economically inactive European citizens. It creates paradoxical situations in which the formal requirement of the right of residence in the host Member State is required to access social benefits, while one of the conditions for obtaining this right is precisely the availability of sufficient economic resources so as not to constitute an excessive burden on the social assistance system of the Member State. It follows that the mere request for access to social benefits is considered evidence of a lack of sufficient resources, suitable for denying the right of residence necessary to access the social benefits.[57]

---

54 Many have highlighted, in doctrine, the excessive importance given to the condition of the right of residence. In this case, compared to the *Brey* ruling (above n. 1), the EU Court did not make any reference to the fact that the legitimacy of this condition must be consistent with and respectful of EU law. In fact, unlike the *Brey* ruling, in the *Commission v. United Kingdom* (above n. 1) ruling, the Court did not state that the imposition of the right of residence should never lead to the automatic exclusion of economically inactive citizens from access to social benefits without an adequate assessment of their individual situation. See C. O'Brien, above n. 2, 232.

55 *Commission v. United Kingdom*, above n. 1, para. 72.

56 It has been argued that the part of the ruling in which the EU Court distanced itself most from social and financial solidarity was considering discrimination on grounds of nationality to be indirect, thus opening up the possibility of its justification. This is in fact what happened when the Court deemed the UK's defence legitimate, justifying the difference in treatment between EU citizens, and therefore the possibility of checking the lawfulness of residence before granting social benefits to inactive people from other Member States. This justification was given as the need to protect the finances of the host Member State, considering such verification to be proportionate because it would not have a systematic nature, excluded by the second paragraph of Article 14(2) of Directive 2004/38. See *Commission v. United Kingdom*, above n. 1, para. 84 as well as M. Messina, above n. 25, 67.

57 This vicious circle was highlighted as early as the *Dano* case (above n. 1) and was already quite clear from the provisions of Directive 2004/38 itself, which the EU Court interpreted by ignoring the fact that these were exceptions to the free enjoyment of fundamental

The formal requirement of the right of residence, pursuant to Article 7 of Directive 2004/38, has today taken on an absolute character, which deprives EU citizens of the right to be able to demonstrate their integration, or even their desire to integrate into the host Member State. This seems to preclude any control of the proportionality of the specific measures, or any case-by-case evaluation of the personal circumstances concerning the people involved.[58] Any request for sufficient resources ceases once the right of permanent residence has been obtained, pursuant to Article 16 of Directive 2004/38, confirming a system based on increasing protection with increasing duration of residence in the host Member State, making the free enjoyment of social rights in the EU by European citizens subject to satisfying a temporal requirement.

SECTION IV THE DEROGATION FROM EQUAL TREATMENT IN ACCESSING SOCIAL SECURITY BENEFITS IN RECENT CASE LAW

In the summer of 2022, the Grand Chamber of the Court of Justice rendered a judgment in the *Familienkasse Niedersachsen-Bremen* case that was fully compliant with the same line of jurisprudence.[59] The case concerned the right of access of inactive European citizens to family benefits during the first three months of stay in another EU Member State (whether a citizen who returns to a state after having stayed in another Member State in accordance with EU law can access benefits from it on his/her return). In essence, the applicable German legislation, following an amendment by the German legislature made in 2019, differentiates the treatment between a citizen of another EU Member State who establishes domicile or habitual residence in Germany, and a German citizen who establishes domicile or habitual residence in Germany following a stay in another EU Member State in accordance with EU law. As noted by the referring judge, in application of the relevant German legislation, citizens

---

freedoms provided by the Treaties. See M.E. Bartoloni, 'La libera circolazione dei cittadini europei economicamente inattivi tra principio di non discriminazione e tutela dei sistemi nazionali di welfare' (2015) 9 *Diritti umani e diritto internazionale* 476, 480. This author affirms that the national welfare system would thus become accessible only to those who, in principle, do not need social benefits.

58 Such a lack of control on the proportionality of the relevant national measures was later confirmed in two other important judgments rendered by the Court of Justice: see *Jobcenter Krefeld*, above n. 1, and *CG v. The Department for Communities in Northern Ireland*, above n. 1. Also see H. Verschueren, 'The Right to Social Assistance for Economically Inactive Migrating Union Citizens: The Court Disregards the Principle of Proportionality and Lets the Charter Appease the Consequences', above n. 2, 489–93.

59 *Familienkasse Niedersachsen-Bremen*, above n. 1.

of another EU Member State are not entitled to family allowance during the first three months of their stay if they do not demonstrate that they receive an income deriving from a paid working activity in the host Member State, while German citizens are entitled to that benefit even if they do not carry out such an activity.

This discrimination on grounds of nationality introduced by the German legislation was strongly inspired by the restrictive approach adopted by the EU Court concerning social rights of migrant European citizens since the *Dano* ruling. As highlighted by the referring judge, the German legislature considered the difference in treatment between citizens of the Union, introduced by national legislation in 2019, as entirely compliant with EU law, since this made it possible to avoid an influx of citizens of other Member States likely to generate an excessive burden on the German social security system.[60] Such a difference in treatment was based on Article 24(2) of Directive 2004/38, which expressly allows the host Member State not to grant the right to social benefits in the first three months of residence, as access to family allowance by citizens of another Member State who do not carry out paid work would have the same effect of a social benefit. The German legislation, in justifying this difference in treatment by the need to protect the finances of the host Member State, also relied on the ruling in the *Commission v. United Kingdom* case.

What the German national legislation, perhaps a little too simplistically, did not take into due consideration when adopting the 2019 reform was the question of the impact of Article 4 of Regulation 883/2004 on the coordination of the social security systems of the Member States. Indeed, as noted by the referring judge, although Regulation 883/2004 allows a Member State to establish certain requirements for the granting of family benefits to citizens of other Member States who reside in its territory without carrying out paid work, Article 4 of the same Regulation requires equal treatment and does not contain any provision that allows for different treatment based on the nationality of the beneficiary.

These circumstances led the referring judge to suspend the national proceedings and to submit to the Court of Justice a fundamental question necessary for the resolution of the main dispute. The referring judge argued that the resolution depended on the EU Court's answer to the question whether discrimination on grounds of nationality in the national legislation after the

---

60 See Opinion of AG Szpunar, Case C-411/20, *Familienkasse Niedersachsen-Bremen*, ECLI:EU:C:2021:1017, para. 20. In this regard, some commentators have noted that the jurisprudence of the EU Court gave importance to the limitation of the principle of equal treatment referred to in Directive 2004/38 precisely to prevent the onset of abuses of the right of free movement and residence of Union citizens. See S. Poli, 'Le preoccupazioni degli Stati membri per l'abuso delle libertà di circolazione delle persone alla luce della giurisprudenza della Corte di giustizia' (2017) 3 *Il diritto dell'Unione europea* 565.

2019 reform was contrary to Article 4 of Regulation 883/2004, or whether it could be justified by virtue of the derogation from the principle of equal treatment referred to in Article 24(2) of Directive 2004/38. This would result in discrimination against an economically inactive European citizen of another Member State who had established habitual residence in the host Member State in relation to an inactive national citizen in accessing certain family benefits. In essence, the EU Court was called upon to establish whether the derogation from equal treatment referred to in Article 24(2) of Directive 2004/38 applied directly, or by analogy, to family or social security benefits requested by the applicant. In the case it did apply, the Court would have to find a way to reconcile this provision with that of Article 4 of Regulation 883/2004,[61] which does not provide for any derogation from equal treatment in access to social security benefits.[62] In fact, it explicitly expresses, in the context of access to social security benefits, the general principle of non-discrimination on grounds of nationality referred to in Article 18 of the TFEU.

The Court of Justice, in answering the question posed by the referring judge, started from the assumption that every EU citizen can avail him/herself of the prohibition of discrimination on grounds of nationality in the exercise of the freedom of movement and residence within the territory of the Member States, pursuant to the combined provisions of Articles 18 and 21 of the TFEU. At the same time, the EU Court also noted the limitations and conditions provided for by the Treaties and measures adopted in application of the latter, to which Article 21 of the TFEU itself refers. It is at this point that Directive 2004/38 comes into play, as in order to provide for a gradual system of integration of European citizens in other Member States, it establishes specific conditions for lawful residence, not excluding limitations on the application of the principle of non-discrimination on grounds of nationality, such as that

---

61 See A. Iliopoulou-Penot, 'L'arrêt *S/Familienkasse Niedersachsen-Bremen*, nouvelle pierre à l'édifice de la citoyenneté européenne sociale' (2022) 3 *Revue des affaires européenne* 571.

62 At least, in the current version of Article 4 of Regulation 883/2004, given that, in the proposal to reform the Regulation presented by the Commission in December 2016, paragraph 2 of Article 4 introduced the possibility for the host Member State to make access to social security benefits by economically inactive European citizens of other Member States conditional on having right of residence in the first Member State, pursuant to Directive 2004/38, thus limiting the legitimacy of the residence of the inactive European citizen of another Member State in the host Member State only to the conditions in Directive 2004/38. See 'Proposal for a Regulation of the European Parliament and of the Council amending Regulation (EC) No. 883/2004 on the coordination of social security systems, and Regulation (EC) No. 987/2009 laying down the procedure for implementing Regulation (EC) No. 883/2004', COM(2016) 815 final. This proposal, although presented after the Brexit referendum on the withdrawal of the UK from the EU, was undoubtedly inspired by the decision of the heads of state meeting at the European Council in February 2016, which was supposed to reshape the UK's position within the EU. For more on that decision, see N.N. Shuibhne, 'Reconnecting Free Movement of Workers and Equal Treatment in an Unequal Europe' (2018) 43(4) *European Law Review* 477.

provided for in Article 24(2) of Directive 2004/38, with regard to access to social assistance benefits. The EU Court found that the applicant, despite being economically inactive, had a right of residence in the first three months of residence in Germany in compliance with the conditions (or more accurately, absence of conditions) set out in Article 6 of Directive 2004/38. The Court then drew attention to the definition of 'family benefits' pursuant to Regulation 883/2004, a rather decisive issue for the resolution of the dispute, stating, in a not particularly innovative way, that the family allowance provided for by the German legislation fell within this notion of 'family benefits'.[63] For the purposes of granting family benefits, it was therefore necessary to establish whether, in the presence of lawful residence pursuant to Article 6 of Directive 2004/38, an economically inactive EU citizen could rely on the principle of equal treatment with economically inactive citizens of the host Member State on their return after exercising their right to reside in another EU Member State. The Court of Justice proceeded to evaluate whether the family benefits at issue could be considered social assistance within the meaning of Article 24(2) of Directive 2004/38, for the purposes of applying the derogation from the principle of equal treatment. This gave the EU Court a new opportunity to rule on the definition of the notion of social assistance within the meaning of the Directive.[64]

The Court of Justice, after highlighting that the right of residence of migrant European citizens is based on a system of increasing and gradual protections by virtue of the degree of integration in the host Member State, affirmed a restrictive reading of the notion of social assistance and, consequently, of the scope of the derogation from equal treatment during the first three months of residence referred to in Article 24(2) of Directive 2004/38. The EU Court confirmed that the notion of social assistance refers to the set of public schemes that can be used by those who do not have sufficient resources to meet their own and their family's basic needs, thus risking becoming a burden on the public finances of the host Member State.[65] The family allowance referred to,

[63] In particular, the Court of Justice made reference to the provisions in Article 3(1)(j) of Regulation 883/2004, combined with Article 1(z) to consider 'family benefits' those 'benefits that are granted automatically to families meeting certain objective criteria relating in particular to their size, income and capital resources [...], without any individual and discretionary assessment of personal needs, and [that] are intended to meet family expenses' (*Familienkasse Niedersachsen-Bremen*, above n. 1, para. 34). The EU Court confirmed the notion affirmed in *Commission v. United Kingdom*, above n. 1, para. 60 and *Martínez Sala*, above n. 1, para. 22.

[64] This notion, interpreted broadly or narrowly, is decisive for the scope of the right of short-term residence and the principle of equal treatment of inactive citizens in the host Member State. See A. Iliopoulou-Penot, above n. 61, 574.

[65] *Familienkasse Niedersachsen-Bremen*, above n.1, para. 46. In this case, the EU Court took up what was stated in the *Brey* (above n. 1) and *Dano* (above n. 1) cases, respectively at paras. 61 and 63 of the judgments.

according to the EU Court, is granted regardless of the state of need of the beneficiary, therefore not aiming to guarantee the latter's means of subsistence, but only to compensate for some family burdens. For this reason, the allowance at issue did not fall within the notion of social assistance provision referred to in Article 24(2) of Directive 2004/38.[66] The Court then had to evaluate whether the derogation from equal treatment contained in the provision also applied to the granting of benefits other than social assistance, provided that the applicant is a citizen of the Union in a situation of lawful residence in the host Member State, pursuant to Article 6 of Directive 2004/38, read in conjunction with Article 14(1): that is, in the first three months of stay.[67]

In answering this question, the EU Court opted to respect the literal wording of the provision of Article 24(2) of Directive 2004/38, stating that it cannot be interpreted as if EU law has intended to allow the host Member State to derogate from the principle of equal treatment from which European citizens who legally reside in its territory must benefit. With regard to benefits other than social assistance, the same provision allows the host Member State not to grant the right only to social assistance during the first three months of stay or during a longer period if looking for a job. The Court said that this interpretation was confirmed by the legal context of Article 24(2) of Directive 2004/38 and Article 14(1), dealing with the right of residence for a period not exceeding three months, which provides that social assistance can be maintained until the EU citizen and his/her family members do not become an excessive burden for the social assistance system of the host Member State. This interpretation confirms that the derogation from the principle of equal treatment referred to in Article 24(2) of Directive 2004/38 is limited to social assistance benefits and cannot be extended to social security benefits.[68] All this is in accordance with the objective of the provision in question, which aims, according to recital 10 of the Directive, to preserve the financial balance of the social assistance system of a Member State, not of its social security system. Although the Court's jurisprudence on the rights of European citizens has not been entirely uniform over the years, the derogation from the application of the principle of equal treatment provided for in Article 24(2) of Directive 2004/38 can only be interpreted restrictively, as a derogation from the principle in the

---

66 Ibid., para. 48.

67 This was the position taken by the German government that emerged from the written observations submitted in the case, in which it was argued that the exclusion of economically inactive citizens of other Member States from access to family allowance during the first three months would discourage such citizens from settling in Germany, thus protecting national public finances. The German government's position is well described in the Opinion of AG Szpunar, *Familienkasse Niedersachsen-Bremen*, above n. 60, paras. 83–86.

68 *Familienkasse Niedersachsen-Bremen*, above n. 1, para. 53.

first paragraph of Article 18 of the TFEU, of which Article 24(1) of Directive 2004/38 is only a specific expression.[69]

Starting from the impossibility of extending the application of the derogation from the principle of equal treatment to access to social security benefits, the EU Court then examined the case, basing its assessment exclusively on the application of Article 4 of Regulation 883/2004, which conflicted with the measure adopted by the German legislature, resulting in direct discrimination. Article 4 concretises the principle of equal treatment in favour of EU citizens, and Regulation 883/2004 does not contain any provision that allows a host Member State to differentiate treatment between economically inactive citizens of another Member State and its own citizens regarding the conditions for granting family benefits.

In light of this, the Court of Justice concluded that the German legislation in force did not comply with Regulation 883/2004, to the extent that it operated direct discrimination on grounds of nationality in access to social security benefits between economically inactive German citizens who have returned to Germany after exercising their right to reside in another Member State, and inactive citizens of other Member States who reside in Germany. At the same time, the Court subordinated the application of the principle of equal treatment concerning obtaining family benefits to the fact that economically inactive citizens who stay in a Member State other than that of which they are a national have established habitual residence in the host Member State, pursuant to Article 6(1) of Directive 2004/38, read in conjunction with Article 14(1).[70]

SECTION V
ACCESS TO SOCIAL ASSISTANCE AND SOCIAL SECURITY BENEFITS: IS THERE ANY DIFFERENCE?

Based on this last aspect, highlighted by the Court of Justice in the *Familienkasse* ruling, it is possible to evaluate its real meaning for the purposes of guaranteeing equal treatment in access to social benefits by economically inactive EU citizens compared to national citizens of the host Member State.

First, as underlined by authoritative doctrine,[71] the judgment in question has certainly placed another keystone in the construction of European social citizenship. There is little doubt that the restrictive interpretation of the notion of 'social assistance', and consequently of the derogation from the principle of equal treatment, has contributed and will continue to contribute

---

69 Ibid., para. 50.

70 Ibid., para. 65.

71 See A. Iliopoulou-Penot, above n. 61.

to guaranteeing almost unconditional access to social security benefits by economically inactive European citizens in host Member States. The states will not be able to impose any exception to this access based on the protection of state finances in general, or of its social assistance system. The relevant legislation is that contained in Regulation 883/2004, which, unlike Directive 2004/38, at least for the moment, does not impose any particular conditions for access to social security benefits. This results in a non-negligible difference in the first three months of stay between access to social security benefits (in principle without particular conditions) and access to social assistance benefits (which, by derogation from the general rule of equal treatment, may be limited by the condition that the economically inactive European citizen does not become an excessive burden on the finances of the host Member State). This is what could seemingly be deduced from the ruling of the Court of Justice in the *Familienkasse* case, at least on a prima facie evaluation. In refusing an application by analogy of the derogation from equal treatment provided for in Article 24(2) of Directive 2004/38 beyond the boundaries of access to social assistance benefits that the provision specifically refers to, the intention of the EU Court was to dispel any residual doubt or stem any strenuous or even potential attempts of a more general application of this provision, as a broader mechanism for protecting the interests of the public finances of the Member States. The Court of Justice, therefore, concluded in favour of the definitive exclusion of any broad interpretation of the scope of derogation from equal treatment referred to in Article 24(2) of Directive 2004/38, which would otherwise cover all social benefits.[72]

Yet against this step forward, analysing the *Familienkasse* ruling more specifically, it is possible to identify the EU Court's desire to seek consistency with its previous jurisprudence on the matter, connecting access to the benefits at issue in the main proceedings (social security) by economically inactive European citizens to residence in the host Member State. In fact, the Court of Justice, referring to previous rulings, confirmed the legitimacy of the national legislation of Member States, which subordinates the granting of benefits referred to in Regulation 883/2004 to the requirement that economically inactive EU citizens fulfil the conditions for right of residence in the host Member State under Directive 2004/38.[73] This requirement, definitely restrictive in other circumstances, did not raise particular problems in the *Familienkasse* case, as the request for access to family benefits by the applicant referred only to the first three months of her stay in the host Member State – a period of stay that, pursuant to Article 6(1) of Directive 2004/38, does

72 Ibid., 576.

73 *Familienkasse Niedersachsen-Bremen*, above n. 1, para. 62. The EU Court made express reference to the previous judgments in the *Brey* (above n. 1), *Dano* (above n. 1) and *Commission v. United Kingdom* (above n. 1) cases.

not impose any conditions or formalities, except the possession of a current identity card or valid passport. This absence of conditions is not even altered by not becoming an 'unreasonable burden', which Article 14(1) provides with reference to the first three months of stay. Its relevance was excluded by the Court of Justice by virtue of the fact that the literal wording of the provision refers to 'an unreasonable burden on the social assistance system of the host Member State' and not to its social security system.

In light of this, the Court of Justice had no particular difficulty stating that an economically inactive EU citizen who resides in a Member State other than that of which he/she is a national, pursuant to Article 6(1) of Directive 2004/38 in conjunction with Article 14(1), can obtain family benefits in the host Member State, pursuant to Regulation 883/2004. The European citizen in question could make use of the principle of equal treatment, provided, as the EU Court pointed out, that he/she had established habitual residence in that territory and is not residing there only temporarily.[74] The EU Court here understands habitual residence as 'effective', i.e. implying that the:

> intention to establish, in actual fact, the habitual centre of his or her interests in that Member State and that he or she shows that his or her presence on the territory of that Member State demonstrates a sufficient degree of stability, which distinguishes it from temporary residence.[75]

In the *Familienkasse* ruling, the Court of Justice returned to deal with the difficult relationship between the notion of the right of residence pursuant to Directive 2004/38, and that of habitual residence pursuant to Regulation 883/2004. The EU Court had already addressed this issue in the *Commission v. United Kingdom* case, in which, rather hastily and somewhat formally, it had stated that the right of residence pursuant to Directive 2004/38 constituted a condition independent of the habitual residence required by Regulation 883/2004 to guarantee access to certain social benefits. On that occasion, the Commission considered that the relevant British legislation provided for the condition of the right of residence pursuant to Directive 2004/38 as a further criterion for determining habitual residence in the Member State in question, compared to those already provided for by Regulation 883/2004.[76] The *Familienkasse* ruling

---

74 Ibid., para. 70.

75 Ibid., paras. 71–72. The Court makes reference to Council Regulation (EC) 987/2009 of 16 September 2009 laying down the procedure for implementing Regulation (EC) No 883/2004 on the coordination of social security systems [2009] OJ L284/1 on the determination of residence (Article 11(2) states the concept of residence within the meaning of Regulation 883/2004) and, by analogy, to the notion of habitual residence of a spouse in case of divorce, making reference to Case C-289/20, *IB*, ECLI:EU:C:2021:955, para. 58.

76 For a critical view on that specific aspect of the judgment, see *ex multis*, C. O'Brien, above n. 2, 220–21.

does not give a broader reflection on this issue, in truth not departing from the previous ruling in *Commission v. United Kingdom*. In fact, the illusion of the sole condition of habitual residence to be able to access family benefits in *Familienkasse* was due to the fact that the applicant had requested access to these benefits only with reference to the first three months of her stay in the host Member State – a period that, pursuant to Article 6 of Directive 2004/38, does not provide for any particular condition for right of residence. Formally, however, in the *Familienkasse* ruling, the Court of Justice once again stated that economically inactive EU citizens in the first three months of stay, in order to access family benefits pursuant to Regulation 883/2004 on equal terms with national citizens, must not only have established habitual residence in the host Member State, but also benefit from right of residence pursuant to Article 6(1) of Directive 2004/38, read in conjunction with Article 14(1). This places the EU Court in absolute consistency with its previous jurisprudence, which subordinated access to social benefits in another Member State to satisfying the condition of lawful residence pursuant to Directive 2004/38. In fact, it is only because the applicant requested family benefits for solely the first three months, and specifically because of the absence of further conditions for lawful residence during this short period, that she was granted the right on equal terms with national citizens of the host Member State. It is quite clear that if the applicant had requested access to the same benefits for the period following the first three months of residence, the Court of Justice would likely have responded in a similar way to its judgment in *Commission v. United Kingdom*. Consequently, access to social benefits for a period exceeding the first three months of residence would have been legitimately rejected due to the fact that the applicant did not satisfy the conditions in Article 7 of Directive 2004/38 for lawful residence in the host Member State. These conditions are linked to the substantial self-sufficiency of a non-national European citizen in a host Member State.

The 2022 ruling of the EU Court in the *Familienkasse* case, if not a step forward, is perhaps at least a setback (albeit partial) to the trend in jurisprudence of the Court of Justice, which for over a decade has put the construction of European citizenship to a severe test by undermining its original meaning. It must be acknowledged, however, that this test originates from Directive 2004/38 itself, which, in the noblest intentions, should have facilitated the exercise of perhaps the most representative freedom of European citizenship, namely that of being able to move or reside within the territory of the entire Union. The difference in treatment between non-national and national European citizens is in fact an inevitable consequence of the provisions of Directive 2004/38. This difference in treatment is based precisely on the subordination of the status of lawful residence in a host Member State to the need to have sufficient economic resources to do so, so as not to create a burden for the social assistance system of the Member State, as established by EU law in Article 7 of the Directive. The condition of lawful residence in the host Member State would not in itself represent a problem; a very different matter is that Directive 2004/38 creates a link between lawful residence and the provision of sufficient economic resources.

It is true that the necessary level of integration that an EU citizen and his/her family must achieve in a host Member State, consisting of a genuine link with the country, can be attained in other ways than those attributable to sufficient economic resources. In this regard, the very notion of habitual residence evoked by the EU Court in the *Familienkasse* ruling could come to the rescue, since this implies the manifestation of the desire to effectively establish the habitual centre of one's interests in a Member State, by demonstrating that one's presence attests to a sufficient degree of stability, differentiating it from a temporary stay. The demonstration of such an intention does not necessarily have to be linked to the availability of sufficient economic resources; as has been argued elsewhere, it could also be shown by the mere registration of one's residence at the relevant municipal offices in which one intends to establish habitual residence, an act in itself expressing the desire to settle there.[77]

Unfortunately, the revision of Directive 2004/38 in this sense appears very remote, due to the continuous push of the Member States towards a change of priority in the pursuit of the objectives of the Directive itself, increasingly favouring an objective that aims to avoid 'an unreasonable burden on the finances of the state' rather than one that facilitates and strengthens the right to free movement and residence of all EU citizens without distinction.[78] As a consequence, it is necessary to rely once again on the EU Court to perhaps reverse its course in the jurisprudence compared to that over the last decade. The *Familienkasse* ruling may represent a first, if rather small and timid, step in this direction.

---

[77] M. Messina, above n. 25, 81–82.

[78] Reference should be made to another recent Grand Chamber judgment in *GV*, above n. 1, in which the EU Court faced yet another attempt from some EU Member States to affirm the justification based on the 'unreasonable burden on the social assistance system of the host Member State' in order to limit access to a special non-contributory cash benefit (a disability allowance in this case), even by a 'dependent direct ascendant' of a mobile EU worker. While the Court rejected the attempt, by applying existing case law on the rights of dependent direct descendants and spouses of active EU citizens or workers, the Opinion of AG Ćapeta in the case is of interest, as in quite a provocative way, she seemed to challenge EU Member States' willingness to consider free movement rights as an abuse, even in a situation when the economically inactive citizen derives his or her right of residence and right to equal treatment from a mobile EU worker who is an economically active citizen in the exercise of a fundamental Treaty-based right, as in this case. See the Opinion of AG Ćapeta, Case C-488/21, *GV*, ECLI:EU:C:2023:115, para. 142.

CHAPTER 3
AN ANALYSIS OF GENDER DISCREPANCIES IN EU CITIZENSHIP

Quitterie ROCCASERRA*

Abstract

This chapter explores the links between EU citizenship and gender within both primary and secondary law, and within European Court of Justice (ECJ) case law. While citizenship in the EU, the 'fundamental' status of Member State nationals, marked a constitutional turning point in the Union's integration process, the enshrinement of this status does not appear to be adapted to the specific characteristics of women. First, its roots, inherited from the internal market, make the enjoyment of these rights conditional on economic conditions that feminist studies have shown to be ill-suited to the reality of women's personal and professional lives. Secondly, as the prohibition of discrimination against men and women is not an integral part of EU citizenship, the status in itself does not offer a response to women's vulnerability. Above all, the Court of Justice, in giving substance to citizenship status, has produced variable results with regard to its holders, but also with regard to female third-country nationals who are family members of European citizens. This view of EU citizenship embeds women in a gendered and stereotyped family pattern, while at the same time increasing their vulnerability in terms of the family unit.

SECTION I
INTRODUCTION

The status of EU citizenship was constitutionalised in primary law by the Treaty of Maastricht in 1992 and is defined in Article 9 of the Treaty on European Union (TEU) and Article 20 of the Treaty on the Functioning of

* PhD student in public and European law, University Paris-Est Créteil, France, Markets, Institutions, Liberties (MIL) research unit (quitterie.roccaserra@u-pec.fr).

the European Union (TFEU),[1] which states that this status – as D. Kochenov calls it, this '*ius tractum*'[2] – guarantees rights to and imposes duties on EU nationals.[3] As EU citizenship is included in the title of Part II of the TFEU ('Non-discrimination and Citizenship of the Union'), it might seem that the equality of men and women would be linked to this status. However, an analysis of the provisions of primary law does not reveal any distinction according to gender in the Treaties. Article 9 of the TEU states that:

> In all its activities, the Union shall observe the principle of the *equality of its citizens*, who shall receive equal attention from its institutions, bodies, offices and agencies. *Every national* of a Member State shall be a citizen of the Union. Citizenship of the Union shall be additional to and not replace national citizenship.[4]

So is the status of citizen, the 'fundamental status' of nationals of Member States as described in the ECJ's ruling in the 2001 *Grzelczyk* case,[5] the fundamental status of all nationals, regardless of gender? If so, can one ask how EU citizenship, an apparently gender-neutral status, negatively affects women? This issue has been little addressed by scholars in France.[6] The shortcomings of a labour-oriented perspective of citizenship as concerns women has been analysed regarding the status of worker, but it is of interest to ask what the broader gender-specific implications of EU citizenship are.

This chapter will focus specifically on the intersectionality between EU citizenship and gender, without considering the full diversity of situations relating to women (for example, intersectionality between race and gender or sexual orientation).[7] The notion of 'gender' will be that defined in the Convention of Istanbul[8] to mean: 'the socially constructed roles, behaviours,

---

1 Article 8A of the Maastricht Treaty. See Consolidated Version of the Treaty on European Union [2016] OJ C202/13 and Consolidated Version of the Treaty on the Functioning of the European Union [2016] OJ C202/47.

2 D. Kochenov, '*Ius Tractum* of Many Faces: European Citizenship and the Difficult Relationship between Status and Rights' (2009) 15(2) *Columbia Journal of European Law* 169.

3 Article 20(2) of the TFEU.

4 Emphasis added.

5 Case C-184/99, *Rudy Grzelczyk v. Centre public d'aide sociale d'Ottignies-Louvain-la-Neuve*, ECLI:EU:C:2001:458.

6 However, see C. Marzo, 'La femme citoyenne européenne' in P. Icard and J. Olivier-Leprince (eds.), *Les femmes dans le droit de l'Union européenne*, Brussels, Bruylant, 2014, pp. 121–55; M. De Walsche and P. Dupont, 'La citoyenne dans la jurisprudence de la Cour de Justice de l'Union européenne' in A. Bouveresse, A. Iliopoulou-Penot and J. Rondu (eds.), *La citoyenneté européenne, quelle valeur ajoutée? European Citizenship: what added value?*, Brussels, Bruylant, 2023, pp. 211–45.

7 Regarding the question of intersectionality and a criticism of rigid categorisation, see I. Solanke, 'Putting Race and Gender Together: A New Approach to Intersectionality' (2009) 72(5) *Modern Law Review* 723.

8 Council of Europe Convention on preventing and combating violence against women and domestic violence, Istanbul, 11 May 2011, CETS No. 210 (hereafter, the Convention of Istanbul).

activities and attributes that a given society considers appropriate for women and men'.[9] The term 'women' is used to refer to females, including 'girls under the age of 18'.[10]

This analysis will seek to demonstrate how EU citizenship has been developed by the Court of Justice to try to guarantee the teleological interpretation of the 'fundamental status of EU nationals', but without taking into account specificities relating to women as highlighted by feminist scholars. Section II discusses how these shortcomings in terms of gender are partly linked to the market-oriented basis of EU citizenship, going back to the very foundations of the EU, which are deeply rooted in the market. Section III looks at how the ECJ's 'gender-blind' approach to citizenship status has had varying results in terms of protecting female applicants. Section IV argues that the status of EU citizen is inadequate with regard to the specificities of the gender of the bearer, and that this status also creates dependence of both EU citizens and third-country nationals on male EU citizens – a situation that tends to reflect the gendered division of roles between men and women.

SECTION II
HOW DOES A CITIZENSHIP ROOTED IN THE MARKET DEAL WITH GENDER?

While the enshrinement of EU citizenship has undeniably been a constitutional step forward in the EU's legal order, the liberal roots of the status make the enjoyment of its rights conditional on being an economically active citizen. This raises issues for female EU citizens, as this status is not correlated with the prohibition of discrimination on the grounds of sex and can thus fail to alleviate the specific difficulties faced by women.

§ 1. THE MARKET-ORIENTED ROOTS OF CITIZENSHIP AND THE ISSUES THIS RAISES FOR WOMEN

I. EU CITIZENSHIP: A MARKET-ORIENTED STATUS

The Treaty of Maastricht made EU citizenship constitutional, but the rights related to this status pre-existed it. It has been argued that the 1968 right of freedom of movement of workers constituted 'an incipient form – still

9 Ibid., Article 3(c).
10 Ibid., Article 3(f).

embryonic and imperfect – of European citizenship'.[11] This ancillary form of EU citizenship existed almost from the beginning of the construction of the European Economic Community as seen through the lens of the status of worker and the internal market.[12] This evolving notion of 'worker' has led some scholars to conceptualise the idea of 'market citizenship' as 'paradoxical' or 'oxymoronic',[13] highlighting the market-oriented roots that shaped the 'fundamental status' of citizen. Essentially, the status of worker has determined the form of EU citizenship.[14] The autonomous notion of citizenship defined by the ECJ[15] has been subject to evolving interpretation in ECJ case law, extending its *ratione personae* scope to individuals in three Directives in the 1990s.

Today, the voluntary dissociation of EU citizenship from the market perspective can be found in the change of vocabulary attached to this status,[16] highlighting 'the transition from an economic to a political community, as expressed by an EU founded under the Treaty of Maastricht'.[17] This 'transnational' citizenship[18] is determined primarily by its horizontal dimension, which derives directly from the evolution of 'market citizenship' embodied in the two main rights laid down in Article 20 of the TFEU: the right to move freely[19] and the right to non-discrimination.[20] As such, EU citizenship offers the possibility of enjoying the same rights as those of the nationals of the host state by expanding their *ratione personae* benefits, making the most important aspect of EU citizenship the conjunction of freedom of movement and non-discrimination regarding nationality. In this way, citizenship has a

11 L. Sandri, 'Free Movement of Workers in European Community' (1968) *Bulletin of the European Communities* 5.

12 Article 2 of the Treaty establishing the European Economic Community (Treaty of Rome). Since the Single European Act in 1986, the EU area has been defined as a 'common internal market': an area without internal frontiers where capital, goods, services and workers can move without obstacle, as provided by Articles 48 to 51 of the Treaty of Rome.

13 N.N. Shuibhne, 'The Resilience of EU Market Citizenship' (2010) 47(6) *Common Market Law Review* 1597. M. Everson, 'The legacy of the market citizen' in J. Shaw and G. More (eds.), *New Legal Dynamics of European Union*, Oxford, Clarendon Press, 1995, p. 73.

14 Articles 48 to 51 of the Treaty of Rome.

15 Case 66/85, *Deborah Lawrie-Blum v. Land Baden-Württemberg*, ECLI:EU:C:1986:284.

16 See, for example: F. Wollenschläger, 'A New Fundamental Freedom beyond Market Integration: Union Citizenship and its Dynamics for Shifting the Economic Paradigm of European Integration' (2011) 17(1) *European Law Journal* 1. While the market is listed as an objective of the EU, in Article 3(3) of the TEU, EU citizenship now falls under the Area of Freedom, Security and Justice (AFSJ), created in Article 3(2) and 'offered' to EU citizens: 'The Union shall offer its citizens an area of freedom, security and justice without internal frontiers, in which the free movement of persons is ensured [...]'.

17 F. Wollenschläger, above n. 16, 30.

18 Y.N. Soysal, *Limits of Citizenship: Migrants and Postnational Membership in Europe*, Chicago (IL), University of Chicago Press, 1994.

19 TFEU, Article 20(2)(c) and Article 21.

20 Ibid., Article 18.

'status of social integration',[21] meaning that it guarantees equal treatment in the Member States where an EU citizen chooses to reside.[22]

Yet if EU citizenship can be considered as 'an equalising tool',[23] as it 'grants every citizen of the Union the opportunity to move and reside freely within the territory of the Member States',[24] these two rights can also create a gender discrepancy. Because while the right of free movement has been enlarged by *ratione personae* to include those who are economically inactive, this 'fundamental' right[25] is still 'subject to the limitations and conditions laid down in the Treaties'.[26] These are set out in the Citizens' Rights Directive (Directive 2004/38/EC),[27] which replaces several pre-existing instruments. This Directive states that a citizen must be economically active (falling under the definition of employed or self-employed)[28] or self-sufficient in order not to become an unreasonable burden on the social assistance system of the host Member State,[29] as laid down in Article 7 of the Directive.[30]

It is true that freedom of movement for workers is broader today than that in the European Community (EC) before the adoption of EU citizenship, but there remains a distinction between the economically active and inactive and between those who have sufficient resources and who are considered a 'burden' on the host society,[31] reflecting the economic roots of the status of citizenship.

---

21 L. Azoulai, 'La citoyenneté européenne: un statut d'intégration sociale' in J.-C. Piris, O. De Schutter, L. Azoulai and A. Barav (eds.), *Chemin d'Europe: Mélanges en l'honneur de Jean-Paul Jacqué*, Paris, Dalloz, 2010, pp. 1–28.

22 D. Kochenov, see above n. 2, 194.

23 C. Juverdeanu, 'The different gears of EU Citizenship' (2021) 47(7) *Journal of Ethnic and Migration Studies* 1596, 1597.

24 D. Kochenov, see above n. 2.

25 Case C-413/99, *Baumbast and R v. Secretary of State for the Home Department*, ECLI:EU:C:2002:493.

26 Article 21(1) of the TFEU.

27 Council Directive 2004/38/EC of 29 April 2004 on the rights of citizens of the Union and their family members to move and reside freely within the territory of the Member States [2004] OJ L158/77.

28 Ibid., Article 7(1)(a).

29 See ibid., recital 16. Article 7 of the Citizens' Rights Directive states that the right of residence to stay more than three months in another Member State is conditional on citizens providing that they have self-sufficient resources and comprehensive medical insurance so as not to become an unreasonable burden on the welfare system of the host state. These conditions were laid down in the free movement Directives (Council Directive 90/364/EEC of 28 June 1990 on the right of residence [1990] OJ L180/26, Council Directive 90/365/EEC of 28 June 1990 on the right of residence for employees and self-employed persons who have ceased their occupational activity [1990] OJ L180/28, and Council Directive 93/96/EEC of 29 October 1993 on the right of residence for students [1993] OJ L317/59).

30 For an analysis, see A. Iliopoulou-Penot, 'Article 7' in A. Iliopoulou-Penot (ed.), *Directive 2004/38 relative au droit de séjour des citoyens de l'Union européenne et des membres de leur famille*, Brussels, Bruylant, 2020, pp. 159–87.

31 A. Iliopoulou-Penot, 'Les catégories des travailleurs et des citoyens' in B. Bertrand (ed.), *Les catégories juridiques du droit de l'Union européenne*, Brussels, Bruylant, 2016, p. 245.

II. EU CITIZENSHIP: A STATUS DISCONNECTED FROM GENDER EQUALITY

How does this market-oriented conception of citizenship correlate to gender equality? From the outset of the European Economic Community (EEC), the Treaty of Rome contained Title III on 'social policy' and gender equality, which were developed within the framework of the internal market. The issue of gender equality was initially linked to equal pay, as is still found in Article 157 of the TFEU (the 'equal pay for equal work provision').[32] The establishment of a common social policy was not a key concern of the Treaties, but was seen more as a means of guaranteeing undistorted competition.[33] Nevertheless, in the 1976 *Defrenne II* case, the ECJ stated that, regarding Article 157:

> this provision forms part of the social objectives of the Community, which is not merely an economic union, but is at the same time intended, by common action, to ensure social progress [...].[34]

This recognition of the social dimension of the 'equal pay principle' has been argued to:

> assist in reorienting its centre of gravity away from the economic needs of employers to the situation of women workers and is important in establishing that hard and formal legal norms have to be considered according to a more substantive objective of equal pay.[35]

Currently, gender equality is one of the EU's cardinal values provided in Article 2 of the TEU,[36] correlated with Article 3(3) of the TEU,[37] which

---

32 Ex-Article 141 of the Treaty establishing the European Community (TEC).

33 The ECJ clearly stated in *Defrenne II*: '[...] in the light of the different stages of the development of social legislation in the various Member States, the aim of Article 119 [now 141] is to avoid a situation in which undertakings established in States which have actually implemented the principle of equal pay suffer a competitive disadvantage in intra-Community competition as compared with undertakings established in States which have not yet eliminated discrimination against women workers as regards pay' (Case 43/75, *Gabrielle Defrenne v. Société anonyme belge de navigation aérienne Sabena* (*Defrenne II*), ECLI:EU:C:1976:56, para. 9).

34 Ibid., para. 10.

35 S. Millns, 'Gender Equality, Citizenship, and the EU's Constitutional Future' (2007) 13(2) *European Law Journal* 218, 232.

36 Article 2 of the TEU: 'The Union is founded on the values of respect for human dignity, freedom, democracy, equality, the rule of law and respect for human rights, including the rights of persons belonging to minorities. These values are common to the Member States in a society in which pluralism, non-discrimination, tolerance, justice, solidarity and *equality between women and men* prevail' (emphasis added).

37 Article 3(3) of the TEU: 'It shall combat social exclusion and discrimination, and shall promote social justice and protection, equality between women and men, solidarity between generations and protection of the rights of the child'.

guarantees the right to equality between women and men. Gender equality is also enshrined in the horizontal clauses of Article 8 of the TEU, which enshrines equal treatment for men and women as a mission of the Union,[38] and Article 10 of the same Treaty. Moreover, Articles 153 and 157 of the TFEU respectively concern women in the labour market and treatment at work, and gender equality in terms of wages and, more generally, positive discrimination. In 1978, in *Defrenne III*,[39] the ECJ declared that the elimination of discrimination on the grounds of sex was one of the fundamental rights it was responsible for ensuring were respected.[40] In today's Charter of Fundamental Rights (CFR), Articles 21 and 23 guarantee gender equality:[41] both the Union and the Member States are bound to respect this fundamental right as a general principle of law when this falls within the scope of EU law.[42]

With regard to secondary legislation, since 1975 there have been a number of specific texts to guarantee equal treatment, mostly based on Article 157 of the TFEU.[43] The EU has stated that it wants to address gender equality as an objective.[44] However, the legal provisions that exist are not included in Title II of the TFEU on citizenship, suggesting that they are not attached to this status.

---

38 Ex-Article 3(2) of the TEC.

39 Case 149/77, *Gabrielle Defrenne v. Société anonyme belge de navigation aérienne Sabena (Defrenne III)*, ECLI:EU:C:1978:130.

40 See Joined Cases 60/84 and 61/84, *Cinéthèque SA v. Fédération nationale des cinémas français*, ECLI:EU:C:1985:329.

41 Charter of Fundamental Rights of the European Union [2016] OJ C202/389 (CFR). Article 21(1) of the CFR (on non-discrimination): 'Any discrimination based on any ground such as sex, race, colour, ethnic or social origin, genetic features, language, religion or belief, political or any other opinion, membership of a national minority, property, birth, disability, age or sexual orientation shall be prohibited'. Article 23 of the CFR (on equality between women and men): 'Equality between women and men must be ensured in all areas, including employment, work and pay. The principle of equality shall not prevent the maintenance or adoption of measures providing for specific advantages in favour of the under-represented sex'.

42 Article 51(1) of the CFR.

43 See, notably, Council Directive 75/117/EEC of 10 February 1975 on the approximation of the laws of the Member States relating to the application of the principle of equal pay for men and women [1975] OJ L45/19. In addition, Council Directive 2004/113/EC of 13 December 2004 implementing the principle of equal treatment between men and women in the access to and supply of goods and services [2004] OJ L373/37 was the first to implement the principle of equal treatment between women and men beyond the sphere of the workplace (see E. Caracciolo di Torella, 'The Goods and Services Directive: Limitations and Opportunities' (2005) 13(3) *Feminist Legal Studies* 337). Two recent Directives have also been adopted in the legislation: Council Directive (EU) 2022/2381 of 23 November 2022 on improving the gender balance among directors of listed companies and related measures [2022] OJ L315/44 and Council Directive (EU) 2023/970 of 10 May 2023 to strengthen the application of the principle of equal pay for equal work or work of equal value between men and women through pay transparency and enforcement mechanisms [2023] OJ L132/21.

44 See, for example, the Gender Equality Strategy 2020–2025, which sets out policy objectives and actions in this area ('Communication from the Commission to the European Parliament, the Council, the European Economic and Social Committee and the Committee of the Regions: A Union of Equality: Gender Equality Strategy 2020–2025', COM(2020) 152 final).

The non-discrimination clause of Article 19 of the TFEU (ex-Article 13 of the TEC),[45] which stipulates that the EU may take appropriate action to fight against discrimination based on sex, racial or ethnic origin, religion or belief, disability, age or sexual orientation, does appear prima facie to be capable of including the legal basis of EU citizens. Yet although the Article is located in Title II of the TFEU entitled 'Non-discrimination and Citizenship of the Union', citizenship is not attached to this principle, so it does not constitute a right directly attached to this status. Moreover, although equal treatment was correlated with citizenship in ECJ case law in the 1998 *Martínez Sala* ruling,[46] which the constituent power subsequently enshrined by amending the title of Title II,[47] this right was related to non-discrimination on grounds of nationality and not to gender equality. Thus, C. Marzo stresses the 'misleading' nature of Title II, in that 'when citizenship is mentioned, it does not cover equality, and vice versa'.[48] While EU citizens benefit from a set of rights,[49] an analysis of the rights attached to the status of citizen, as listed inter alia in Article 20(2) of the TFEU,[50] shows the absence of any reference to equality, and more specifically to equality between men and women.

It can be concluded that EU citizenship does not offer a guarantee of gender equality: the liberal roots of the status are not counterbalanced by the gender equality provisions.

---

45 E. Dubout, *L'article 13 du traité CE: la clause communautaire de lutte contre les discriminations*, Brussels, Bruylant, 2006.

46 Case C-85/96, *Martínez Sala v. Freistaat Bayern*, ECLI:EU:C:1998:217.

47 Until the Treaty of Lisbon, it was entitled 'Citizenship of the Union' with no mention of discrimination.

48 C. Marzo, above n. 6, p. 130.

49 See Articles 21 to 25 of the TFEU.

50 Article 20 of the TFEU enshrines the following rights: '(a) the right to move and reside freely within the territory of the Member States; (b) the right to vote and to stand as candidates in elections to the European Parliament and in municipal elections in their Member State of residence, under the same conditions as nationals of that State; (c) the right to enjoy, in the territory of a third country in which the Member State of which they are nationals is not represented, the protection of the diplomatic and consular authorities of any Member State on the same conditions as the nationals of that State; (d) the right to petition the European Parliament, to apply to the European Ombudsman, and to address the institutions and advisory bodies of the Union in any of the Treaty languages and to obtain a reply in the same language'.

§2. INCOMPATIBILITY REGARDING EU CITIZENSHIP, GENDER AND THE MARKET THROUGH THE PRISM OF GENDER STUDIES

Two main issues can be raised regarding the roots of EU citizenship and gender: the first is that there are certain gender specificities regarding work activities that citizenship does not take into account, implying that this status is 'gendered'; the second issue is that citizenship is based on a gendered understanding of family relationships.

I. THE CONSEQUENCES OF THE LIBERAL ROOTS OF CITIZENSHIP: A GENDERED STATUS INADEQUATE TO WOMEN'S SOCIAL AND ECONOMIC REALITIES

Although the enjoyment of the rights attached to the status of citizen is no longer reserved for the economically active alone, the broader scope of application does not create de facto compatibility with the specific circumstances faced by women. Indeed, it is harder for women to respect the conditions laid down in Article 7 of the Citizens' Rights Directive in order to benefit from these rights.[51] As highlighted by feminist scholars who have criticised the market approach linked to the enjoyment of EU citizenship rights, a market-oriented view does not take into account the specificities of women regarding work,[52] including the fact that they are often employed part-time,[53] in lower-qualified jobs,[54] and on lower remuneration compared to men.[55] Women frequently face direct and indirect gender-based pay discrimination, which can lead to the

---

51 S. Mantu, 'Women as EU Citizens: Caught between Work, (Sufficient) Resources, and the Market' in T. de Lange, W. Maas and A. Schrauwen (eds.), *Money Matters in Migration: Policy, Participation, and Citizenship*, Cambridge, Cambridge University Press, 2021, pp. 188–204.

52 L. Ackers, 'Citizenship, gender and dependence in the European Union: Women and internal migration' (1996) 3 *Social Politics* 316.

53 See Eurostat, 'Women more likely to have worked part-time in Q3 2023', *ec.europa.eu* (7 March 2024) <https://ec.europa.eu/eurostat/web/products-eurostat-news/w/ddn-20240307-2>.

54 See, for example, the 'Report of the European Parliament on women's poverty in Europe', 2021/2170(INI).

55 In 2022, women's gross hourly earnings were on average 12.7% below those of men in the EU, 'with significant variations across Member States, and this has decreased only minimally over the last ten years' ('Gender pay gap: Parliament adopts new rules on binding pay-transparency measures', *European Parliament* (30 March 2023) <https://www.europarl.europa.eu/news/en/press-room/20230327IPR78545/gender-pay-gap-parliament-adopts-new-rules-on-binding-pay-transparency-measures>). See Eurostat, 'Gender pay gap statistics', *ec.europa.eu* (8 March 2025) <https://ec.europa.eu/eurostat/statistics-explained/index.php?title=Gender_pay_gap_statistics>.

feminisation of poverty.[56] In that regard, the Covid-19 pandemic provided a clear demonstration of the intersectional specificities of work and gender,[57] involving falling participation of women in the labour market, a decrease in working hours, and a rise in work–life conflicts,[58] demonstrating the vulnerability of women in the workplace.

There is no question that the EU is taking steps to ensure that women's work and status are better adapted, particularly in terms of equal pay for men and women,[59] in an attempt to free women through the market.[60] But while this may be a way of integrating women through the ability to work, there is still a notion of 'contributing economically' to the society of a host Member State as a condition of enjoying the rights attached to EU citizenship.[61] The socio-economic reality women face makes it more difficult for them to achieve these conditions.

Another factor, highlighted by feminist literature, is that this notion does not take into account the personal dimension of women's lives, as this does not interact directly with the market. For example, the household division of labour and informal activities of care, which are mainly carried out by women,[62] affect the ability to have the same career as those who do not have to carry out these activities. Gender studies have shown how the market impacts women, notably regarding unpaid care,[63] an area acknowledged by the EU in the recent 'Communication on the European care strategy'.[64] Although women

---

56 See the survey of the European Institute for Gender Equality, available at European Institute for Gender Equality, 'Women with low skills have fewer opportunities in the EU labour market', *eige.europa.eu* (10 May 2017) <https://eige.europa.eu/newsroom/news/women-low-skills-have-fewer-opportunities-eu-labour-market>.

57 See Directive (EU) 2023/970 and recital 13 of Directive (EU) 2023/970. See also Eurofound, *Women and labour market equality: Has COVID-19 rolled back recent gains?*, Publications Office of the European Union, Luxembourg 2020.

58 Eurofound, *Women and labour market equality: Has COVID-19 rolled back recent gains?*, Publications Office of the European Union, Luxembourg 2020.

59 See, for example, Council Directive 2006/54/EC of 5 July 2006 on the implementation of the principle of equal opportunities and equal treatment of men and women in matters of employment and occupation (recast) [2006] OJ L204/23.

60 See, for example, L. Ackers, *Shifting Spaces: Women, Citizenship and Migration within the European Union*, Bristol, Policy Press, 1998.

61 H. Askola, 'Tale of Two Citizenships? Citizenship, Migration and Care in the European Union' (2012) 21(3) *Social & Legal Studies* 341, 350.

62 The Commission has acknowledged this great discrepancy between women and men: unpaid care responsibilities concern around 7.7 million women in Europe and only 450,000 men: 'Communication from the Commission to the European Parliament, the Council, the European Economic and Social Committee and the Committee of the Regions on the European care strategy', COM(2022) 440 final.

63 For an analysis of this intersectionality see, for example, A.A. Marphatia and R. Moussié, 'A question of gender justice: Exploring the linkages between women's unpaid care work, education, and gender equality' (2013) 33(6) *International Journal of Educational Development* 585.

64 COM(2022) 440 final, above n. 62.

are increasingly economically independent and have entered the paid labour market, they still carry out most domestic work and care, to an extent that these can be qualified as 'gendered responsibilities'. As H. Askola highlights, 'it can be argued that EU law's lingeringly market-oriented citizenship fails to recognise gendered divisions in caring roles, which also result in divisions in the labour market'.[65] As the EU Commission itself notes, care:

> leads to women taking long absences for family leave, reducing working time and withdrawing early from the labour market. For many women, it results in fewer career opportunities and lower wages and pensions than those enjoyed by their male peers.[66]

Some doctrinal studies argue that the family dimension should be seen as a motor for the ECJ to extend *ratione personae* to economically inactive individuals to adapt the scope and protect women.[67]

Another argument seems to refute the analysis of not taking care activities into account as this falls outside the scope of the market.[68] While traditional welfare states 'have evolved around the relationship between paid work and welfare',[69] unpaid care work in fact has a public dimension: a few studies have shown the impact of unpaid care on the welfare state.[70] As S. Millns highlights:

> Feminist research has shown [...] that such a relationship between work and welfare has been mediated by another far more 'subterranean' relationship, one that links men's waged labour to women's unpaid domestic work.[71]

As the rules around free movement and citizenship do not take these factors into account, some feminist scholars have defined this status as 'gendered'.[72]

65 H. Askola, see above n. 61, 345.

66 COM(2022) 440 final, above n. 62.

67 See, for example, K. Scheiwe, 'EC Law's Unequal Treatment of the Family: The Case Law of the European Court of Justice on Rules Prohibiting Discrimination on Grounds of Sex and Nationality' (1994) 3(2) *Social and Legal Studies* 243. The *Dano* case law (Case C-333/13, *Elisabeta Dano and Florin Dano v. Jobcenter Leipzig*, ECLI:EU:C:2014:2358) shows the importance of justifying willingness to work.

68 Indirectly related to the market, the idea of the 'global care chain' shows the centrality of care activities for the market, as professional care could not exist without the lowest chains of care, which are unpaid (see L. Marla and L. Baldassar, 'Les dynamiques de soin transnationales entre émotions et considérations économiques' (2010) 41(1) *Recherches sociologiques et anthropologiques* 1 <http://journals.openedition.org/rsa/182>).

69 S. Millns, above n. 35, 234.

70 See N. Cambien, 'EU Citizenship and the right to care' in D. Kochenov (ed.), *EU Citizenship and Federalism: The Role of Rights*, Cambridge, Cambridge University Press, 2017, pp. 489–508.

71 S. Millns, above n. 35.

72 L. Ackers, above n. 52; see also L. Ackers, above n. 60.

II. GENDERING THE FAMILY RELATIONSHIP

A second issue, arising from the first, is linked with the implications of the delimitation of the family as regards EU citizenship. If free movement rules are gendered,[73] this could have implications on gender equality regarding citizenship as defined by stereotypical gendered family relationships related to the sponsor, the worker, and today, within Directive 2004/38, the citizen.

This has its roots in deriving the right of residence from family members.[74] Feminist studies point out the problematic 'parasitic' nature of family rights,[75] which results in dependency on the (male) sponsor,[76] as 'family members are seen as being dependent on and subordinated to the worker'.[77] The ECJ has made clear in its case law regarding family members of workers (and transposed in the case law of EU citizenship):

> any rights conferred on third-country nationals by the Treaty provisions on citizenship of the Union are not autonomous rights of those nationals but rights derived from those enjoyed by the Union citizen.[78]

Problematically, EU citizenship and the status of worker were created during a period when the roles of family members were defined in a stereotyped way. In that sense, Regulation 1612/68[79] has been analysed as centring on masculine vocabulary[80] that promotes a traditional concept of the family.[81] It is striking that from the beginning of the EC, the apparently 'neutral' vocabulary employed in secondary legislation took a 'family' approach to determine the beneficiaries of rights deriving from the right of residence, viewing women

---

73 L. Ackers, above n.52.

74 Case 40-76, *Slavica Kermaschek v. Bundesanstalt für Arbeit*, ECLI:EU:C:1976:157.

75 For a critique, see L. Ackers, 'Citizenship, Migration and the Valuation of Care in the European Union' (2004) 30(2) *Journal of Ethnic and Migration Studies* 373, 396.

76 Regarding the question of dependency, see below, (Section IV, § 2, I).

77 I. Moebius and E. Szyszczak, 'Of raising pigs and children' (1998) 18(1) *Yearbook of European Law* 125, 144.

78 Case C-165/14, *Alfredo Rendón Marín v. Administración del Estado*, ECLI:EU:C:2016:675, para. 73.

79 Council Regulation (EEC) 1612/68 of 15 October 1968 on freedom of movement for workers within the Community [1968] OJ L257/2.

80 Such male-oriented vocabulary is seen, for example, in Article 10(1) stating of family members: '(a) *his* spouse and their descendants who are under the age of 21 years or are dependents; (b) dependent relatives in the ascending line of the worker and *his* spouse' (emphasis added). See also G. Milios, 'Defining "Family Members" of EU Citizens and the Circumstances under Which They Can Rely on EU Law' (2020) 39 *Yearbook of European Law* 293, 295–96. See also I. Moebius and E. Szyszczak, above n. 77.

81 It defined the term 'spouse' as legally married partners, excluding partnership and homosexual couples (Joined Cases C-122/99P and C-125/99P, *D. and Sweden v. Council*, ECLI:EU:C:2001:304).

in a stereotypical way.[82] The 'adult worker' model implicitly perceived the man as the breadwinning sponsor, with the woman mainly dependent on the husband's right of residence, as women who were not working or seeking employment fell outside the scope of the EC. This understanding of the family unit, considering the wife's place as dependent on her working husband's right of residence, led L. Ackers to argue that freedom of movement is a gendered freedom.[83]

The wording of the current Directive 2004/38 contains more neutral vocabulary and admits a family model more in tune with social trends,[84] but does this neutrality create equality between men and women? Admittedly, the preamble provides that the Directive should be implemented without any discrimination between beneficiaries on grounds of:

> sex, race, colour, ethnic or social origin, genetic characteristics, language, religion or beliefs, political or other opinion, membership of an ethnic minority, property, birth, disability, age or sexual orientation.[85]

Yet aside from this statement, the Directive does not contain any gender-specific provisions; as feminist scholars have argued, gender-neutral vocabulary does not mean equal treatment.[86] Moreover, as S. Mantu highlights, the Directive contains provisions that could specifically affect women,[87] 'yet these provisions do not consider fully the potentially circumscribed status of women affected by family breakdown or bereavement'.[88] Without any adaptation related to women's work and its intersectionality with family life, L. Ackers argues that:

> The invisibility of care and the specificities of women's economic activities in migration theory is echoed in the development of European citizenship, which continues to presuppose a very traditional and normative model of family relations

[82] See, for example, K. Scheiwe, above n. 67.

[83] L. Ackers, above n. 60; see also L. Ackers, above n. 52.

[84] The Court of Justice has also interpreted the family model in a dynamic way, through the recognition of same-sex marriages and same-sex filiation (Case C-673/16, *Relu Adrian Coman v. Inspectoratul General pentru Imigrări et Ministerul Afacerilor Interne*, ECLI:EU:C:2018:385; Case C-490/20, *V.M.A. v. Stolichna obshtina, rayon 'Pancharevo'*, ECLI:EU:C:2021:1008).

[85] Recital 31 of Directive 2004/38.

[86] See K.T. Bartlett, 'Feminist Legal Methods' (1990) 103(4) *Harvard Law Review* 829.

[87] For example, Articles 11, 12 and 13, regarding the autonomous right of residence of family members in the event of death, departure from the host state, divorce, annulment or termination of registered partnership of the EU citizen exercising the right of residence.

[88] S. Mantu, '(En)gendering EU Citizenship' in E. Fornalé (ed.), *Gender Equality in the Mirror: Reflecting on Power, Participation and Global Justice*, Leiden, Brill Nijhoff, 2022, pp. 95–109, p. 98.

and migration behaviour. Citizenship rights, under the free movement of persons, radiate from the 'citizen-worker' positioned at the nucleus of the male breadwinning family.[89]

In short, the formalisation of the liberal vision of EU citizenship leads to problems with regard to the social and economic realities faced mainly by women. Nonetheless, the ECJ has adapted this status in litigation, with varying results for women claimants.

SECTION III
HOW CASE LAW HAS SHAPED EU CITIZENSHIP WITH VARYING EFFECTS ON WOMEN

An analysis of the intersectionality between gender and EU citizenship must involve a review of ECJ case law, as the Court is the main artisan of this status. This section will attempt to draw up a typology of case law rulings regarding the consolidation of 'social citizenship',[90] based on the how the Court of Justice has taken on board the particular situation of women and gender-specific vulnerability. Two main trends in case law can be identified. The first consists of rulings which, although dealing with vulnerability experienced by female citizens, remain silent on this issue, with variable results in terms of the protection of female citizens. The second consists of rulings that try to reconcile the specific characteristics of women to the status of citizen, resulting in a conditional protection of women. These rulings seem to suggest the emergence of a form of citizenship based on 'merit', which is necessarily more difficult for women to enjoy.

§ 1. SILENCING GENDER IN CASE LAW REGARDING EU CITIZENSHIP

The ECJ's creative jurisprudence on EU citizenship seems to silence the status of women, even when the cases brought before the Court deal with specific issues of women's vulnerability. This silence leads to paradoxical results, enshrining a protective status for citizens but taking a restrictive approach on social rights that leads to the greater vulnerability of women.

---

89 L. Ackers, above n. 75.

90 T.H. Marshall, *Citizenship and Social Class and Other Essays*, Cambridge, Cambridge University Press, 1950.

I. SHAPING EU CITIZENSHIP WITH PARADOXICAL EFFECTS ON WOMEN

In what J. Shaw refers to as the first period of constitutionalisation of citizenship status,[91] the ECJ enforced the ethos of 'fundamental status' in a series of cases.[92] A line can be drawn from the 1998 *Martínez Sala* case[93] to the 2002 *Baumbast* case[94] to the 2004 *Zhu and Chen* case,[95] including the seminal 2001 *Grzelczyk* case. The underlying link between these cases is that they all dealt with insufficient resources of economically inactive people. This line of case law – with the exception of *Grzelczyk* – also dealt with family matters related to the specificities of women's situations and was used to consolidate citizenship status.

The landmark *Martínez Sala* case was the first in which the ECJ based its decision on citizenship after the latter's institutionalisation within the Treaty of Maastricht, coupled with the principle of equality in order to protect EU citizens' social rights. Ms Martínez Sala, a Spanish woman, lived in Germany, and was employed from time to time punctuated by periods of unemployment due to pregnancies and childcare. In its *ratio decidendi*, the ECJ found that Martínez Sala enjoyed a right of residence in the host Member State and was protected by the right to non-discrimination, entitling her to social benefits.[96] This landmark case is a clear example of how a social security matter related to a woman's situation consolidated the status of citizen by extending its scope to the economically inactive.

The mother's situation was also at stake in *Baumbast*, directly affecting Article 21 of the TFEU, while the *Zhu and Chen* case also related to the role of a primary carer of a third-country national other than an EU citizen, extending the *ratione materiae* of citizenship. These cases were founded on the premise that citizenship is a 'fundamental status',[97] resulting in the protection of the most vulnerable categories of individuals. By granting the right of residence to mothers of EU citizens as those responsible for their children, these two rulings centralised the Court's reasoning in terms of care.

---

91 J. Shaw, 'Citizenship: Contrasting Dynamics at the Interface of Integration and Constitutionalism' (2010) *University of Edinburgh School of Law Working Paper*, No 2010/14. V. Réveillère, 'Le juge et le travail des concepts juridiques. Le cas de la citoyenneté de l'Union européenne' (2017) *European University Institute PhD Thesis*.

92 Regarding the teleological interpretation of citizenship status, see K. Lenaerts and J.A. Gutierrez-Fons (eds.), *Les méthodes d'interprétation de la Cour de justice de l'Union européenne*, Brussels, Bruylant, 2020.

93 *Martínez Sala v. Freistaat Bayern*, above n. 46.

94 *Baumbast and R v. Secretary of State for the Home Department*, above n. 25.

95 Case C-200/02, *Kunqian Catherine Zhu and Man Lavette Chen v. Secretary of State for the Home Department*, ECLI:EU:C:2004:639.

96 *Martínez Sala v. Freistaat Bayern*, above n. 46, para. 65.

97 This was not yet affirmed by the ECJ in *Martínez Sala* (above n. 46).

All three cases during this period of the constitutionalisation of citizenship can be seen as a clear consolidation of the status. The ECJ extended the protection of citizenship either by protecting individuals without sufficient resources or by giving the right of residence to the carer of an infant EU citizen (in *Zhu and Chen*) – rulings that had a greater impact on women than men.[98] In that regard, C. Marzo has noted that through these rulings, the Court has built a citizenship that 'reflects a certain societal role, a certain acceptance of women'.[99] The *Zhu and Chen* case, for example, can be seen as:

> an important example of what might be called jurisprudential gender mainstreaming – that is, integrating a gender perspective through the European Court of Justice's case law in order to recognise the reality of women's role in the care work associated with family life.[100]

This values care work, notwithstanding the fact that it falls outside the EU's market framework.[101]

However, while these rulings offer a certain appreciation of the value of care, they are also open to criticism. First, the observation can be made that, even though these cases protect women and consolidate their status, gender specificities were not directly considered by the Court, resulting in a certain 'gender blindness' in the resolution.[102] In the *Martínez Sala* case, there is an absence of mentions of gender specificities regarding the activity of care. While the specific situation of the mother seems to be at the centre of the case, the resolution still confirms that unpaid care does not fall under the definition of 'work' in EU law.[103] As such, it has been criticised for its missed attempt to root citizenship 'in the development of social rights as well as market rights'.[104] In this way, while the *Martínez Sala* ruling aims to protect vulnerable people in their individuality, at the same time it overlooks an essential element at the root of female vulnerability: that women are more likely to have to take care of children alone; in the vast majority of cases, a single-parent family is headed by a woman.[105] Because of the 'gender

---

98 Since there are statistically more unemployed women than men (see COM(2022)440 final, above n. 62).

99 C. Marzo, above n. 6, p. 125.

100 S. Millns, above n. 35, 235.

101 Ibid., 235.

102 S. Mantu, above n. 51.

103 H. Askola, above n. 61.

104 J. Shaw, 'The European Union and gender mainstreaming: Constitutionally embedded or comprehensively marginalized?' (2002) 10 *Feminist Legal Studies* 213, 223.

105 For example, in France only 18% of single-parent families are fathers living with their children: see Institut national de la statistique et des études (INSEE), 'Families in France in 2020: 25% single-parent families, 21% large families', *insee.fr* (13 September 2021) <https://www.insee.fr/en/statistiques/5428547>.

blindness' of the Court, citizenship is shaped in a way that creates a 'gendered effect',[106] which:

> reinforces existing gender stereotypes of inter-dependency within the family and of migration behaviour, which permeate the legislative structure and judicial interpretation of the provisions on free movement of workers.[107]

By enshrining EU citizenship as a status that protects the vulnerable, the ECJ's case law protects women, while at the same time ignoring the specific nature of the vulnerability that characterises care.

II. INCREASING THE VULNERABILITY OF FEMALE CITIZENS

If the ruling in *Martínez Sala*, later confirmed in *Trojani*,[108] based equality on the legality of residence, a different line of case law inverses this interpretation of the ECJ regarding the situation of women. This more 'reactionary' line of case law began with the 2014 *Dano* case[109] and was later confirmed in the 2015 *Alimanovic* case[110] and the 2016 *García-Nieto* case.[111]

In the *Dano* case, a Romanian woman from the Roma community claimed a non-contributory benefit for her son. The Court found that Ms Dano failed to meet the conditions set out in Article 7 of Directive 2004/38, since asking for social benefits proved that she did not meet the condition of sufficient resources required for a long period of residence. As such, she could not benefit from equal treatment as outlined in Article 24 of the Directive. The ECJ stated that special non-contributory benefits can be refused for those moving to a Member State for the sole purpose of claiming those benefits, qualifying them as 'social assistance'. This ruling shows a tendency of the Court to try to address the risk of 'welfare tourism'.[112]

In *Dano*, an assessment of the individual is totally silenced: this case marks the abandonment of an analysis *in concreto* of the proportionality test, enacting that the host Member State does not need to provide that a situation creates

---

106 I. Moebius and E. Szyszczak, above n. 77.

107 Ibid., 127.

108 Case C-456/02, *Michel Trojani v. Centre public d'aide sociale de Bruxelles (CPAS)*, ECLI:EU:C:2004:488.

109 *Elisabeta Dano and Florin Dano v. Jobcenter Leipzig*, above n. 67.

110 Case C-67/14, *Jobcenter Berlin Neukölln v. Nazifa Alimanovic*, ECLI:EU:C:2015:597.

111 Case C-299/14, *Vestische Arbeit Jobcenter Kreis Recklinghausen v. Jovanna García-Nieto*, ECLI:EU:2016:114.

112 This non-judicial notion can be defined as an individual moving to another Member State for the sole purpose of benefitting from social assistance.

an unreasonable burden.[113] Consequently, the Court completely silenced the particular specificity of the situation of a single mother (it should be noted that some elements of her personal situation seem to corroborate that she moved for the sole purpose of claiming social benefits,[114] indicating that her situation was taken into account in the ruling of the case). A more individualistic approach underlies the reasoning of the ECJ, as the applicant's individual situation is assessed *in abstracto*, while her general situation – in particular, her family situation – is not taken into account. The subjective consideration of so-called 'welfare tourism' is at the heart of the judgment.

A similar reversal was confirmed in cases regarding jobseekers in *Alimanovic* and *García-Nieto*, showing what one scholar has called the 'lack of traction of EU citizenship'.[115] In none of these cases did the ECJ mention the 'fundamental' dimension of EU citizenship, while considerably reducing the protection of women in situations of vulnerability. In that regard:

> in a system where only the economically active are valued and allowed to take full advantage of the opportunities of EU citizenship, women will be generally disadvantaged as they are less likely to take up paid work or stay in paid work once they have children, even if they migrated as workers.[116]

This opens these rulings up to criticism in terms of their impact on women, marking a 'reactionary' jurisprudence that represents a step backwards in the evolution of social citizenship, and consequently, a step backwards in the protection of women. Although the EU clearly wishes to encourage the full participation of women in the labour market, its policies can generally be seen as reinforcing gendered stereotypes in terms of work and private lives rather than achieving gender equality. Given that the majority of care activities are performed by women, combined with the fact that the majority of single parents are women and that single-parent families have a high risk of poverty, denying the consideration of family situation necessarily has a much greater statistical impact on women.[117] Citizenship thus serves a protective status only for those who meet the economic criteria set out in the Citizens' Rights

113 J. Rondu, 'Le contrôle de proportionnalité in concreto est-il toujours plus protecteur du citoyen de l'Union?' (2023) 665 *Revue de l'Union européenne* 96.

114 Ms Dano was considered not well-integrated in the host country, as she had no job, was not seeking one either in Germany or in Romania and she lived at her sister's with her child.

115 C. O'Brien, 'Civis captialist sum: Class as the new guiding principle of EU free movement rights' (2016) 53(4) *Common Market Law Review* 937.

116 S. Mantu, 'Concepts of Time and European Citizenship', (2013), *European Journal of Migration and Law*, vol. 15, no 4, pp. 447–464, pp. 458-459.

117 In the words of the 'Report of the European Parliament on women's poverty in Europe', 2021/2170(INI), above n. 54: 'whereas single-parent families are at greater risk of poverty and social exclusion and bear a higher probability of transmission of poverty over several

Directive – a paradoxical situation, as the most vulnerable will not benefit from protection, while those who do not need it will.

§ 2. TAKING GENDER INTO ACCOUNT: RECONCILING GENDER AND CITIZENSHIP?

An approach that seems fairer, and can be found in some ECJ case law, would be to address the specificities of gender, firstly in the interpretation of the notion of worker, enabling the definition to be adapted to women's work, and secondly, in analysing these specificities in light of women's vulnerability.

I. FOCUSING ON GENDER SPECIFICITIES REGARDING WORK

The possibility of reconciling the rights attached to the status of citizen and the specificities relating to women can be found within the ECJ interpretation of the notion of worker.[118] The first impact can be seen as indirect: a broader understanding of the notion of 'worker' allowed the Court to include marginal economic activities, often characteristic of women's employment.[119] This was the case in the ECJ's 1982 *Levin* ruling, in which the Court held that the concept of worker should not be restrictively interpreted: that a person was still a 'worker' if they earned below a subsistence salary. The applicant, Ms Levin, was a British national who lived and worked part-time in the Netherlands and whose remuneration fell below the minimum wage in the host country. The Court held that free movement covers those 'who pursue or are desirous of pursuing an economic activity', defined as 'effective and genuine activities, to the exclusion of activities on such a small scale as to be regarded as purely marginal and ancillary'.[120] As such, the Court equated low-remuneration economic activities (which tend to be carried out mostly by women) with the notion of worker.[121] This was incidental to women, in that it did not seek to protect women directly, but aimed to guarantee the integration process by extending workers' freedom of movement to a wider range of people. Women, who account for the majority of the lowest-paid

generations; whereas 85% of single-parent families are headed by women; whereas in 2020, 42.1% of the EU population living in single-adult households with dependent children were at risk of poverty or social exclusion' (Point I).

118 *Deborah Lawrie-Blum v. Land Baden-Württemberg*, above n. 15.

119 See Section II, § 2, I.

120 Case 53/81, *D.M. Levin v. Staatssecretaris van Justitie*, ECLI:EU:C:1982:105, para. 17.

121 See ibid., and Case C-413/01, *Franca Ninni-Orasche v. Bundesminister für Wissenschaft, Verkehr und Kunst.*, ECLI:EU:C:2003:600.

activities and part-time jobs, would consequently benefit from this flexible definition. In this case, 'the way the notion of EU worker has been defined by the Court of Justice plays an important role in shaping women's exercise of free movement rights'.[122]

The second possibility for reconciling citizenship and gender specificities is direct, for example, regarding the protection of EU citizens who leave work under specific circumstances related to pregnancy. In two cases, *Dias*[123] and *Jessy Saint Prix*,[124] the ECJ had to determine if women who were either taking care of their infant or had to take maternity leave would benefit from the right of residence in the host Member State. In *Saint Prix*, the Court interpreted the status of EU worker as including pregnancy, as long as the woman plans to return to the work market within a reasonable period of time.[125] In contrast, in the *Dias* ruling, the Court stated that the year-long gap taken by Ms Dias to take care of her child prevented her from being considered a worker. These different decisions suggest that the Court tries to adapt the notion of worker to the specificities of motherhood and to find an equilibrium between the different interests at stake – a gender-friendly approach regarding the specificities faced by women in maternity and the protection of the status of worker. Yet while the concept of worker is sometimes adapted to fit the specificities of a female worker, the rights linked to EU citizenship are still dependent on economic activity. As S. Mantu argues, this can be seen as the 'magnetic force of the labour market',[126] as 'it points toward the importance of being and remaining an EU *worker* when it comes to fully enjoying EU citizenship rights'[127].

II. FOCUSING ON THE VULNERABILITY OF WOMEN: GENDER-SPECIFIC PROTECTION?

The 2021 *CG* case[128] was the first to introduce the criteria of vulnerability regarding the social rights of EU citizens. In this case, an unemployed mother who was a victim of domestic violence had taken refuge in a shelter with her children and had applied for social benefits. The ECJ's reasoning was initially

[122] S. Mantu, above n. 88, p. 99.
[123] Case C-325/09, *Secretary of State for Work and Pensions v. Maria Dias*, ECLI:EU:C:2011:498.
[124] Case C-507/12, *Jessy Saint Prix v. Secretary of State for Work and Pensions*, ECLI:EU:C:2014:2007.
[125] The Court stated 'that Article 45 TFEU must be interpreted as meaning that a woman who gives up work, or seeking work, because of the physical constraints of the late stages of pregnancy and the aftermath of childbirth retains the status of "worker", within the meaning of that article, provided she returns to work or finds another job within a reasonable period after the birth of her child' (para. 47).
[126] S. Mantu, above n. 51, p. 197.
[127] Ibid., p. 200.
[128] C-709/20, *CG v. The Department for Communities in Northern Ireland*, ECLI:EU:C:2021:602.

based on the *Dano* case,[129] holding that the mother was not entitled to social assistance, as she did not have sufficient resources, and therefore could not invoke equal treatment by virtue of Article 24(1) of the Citizens' Rights Directive.[130] However, the ECJ added a second stage in its reasoning, which was based on the Charter of Fundamental Rights (CFR).[131]

The Court asserted that Member States must take into account the specific vulnerability of a woman and her children in light of their fundamental right to dignity (Article 1 of the CFR) and to private and family life (Article 7 of the CFR), read in conjunction with the obligation to take into consideration the best interests of the child, as recognised in Article 24(2) of the CFR, in order to analyse whether the refusal to grant social assistance violates the fundamental rights of the applicant.[132] Consequently, the refusal to grant aid will only be possible if the applicant's fundamental rights are respected.

The distinction from the *Dano* ruling is articulated through the centrality of the consideration given to the vulnerability of this mother, which is mentioned twice in the ruling.[133] Moreover, this vulnerability regarding the woman's specific family situation is emphasised by the ECJ in para. 92, just before the operative part of the judgment stating that:

> In the present case, it is apparent from the order for reference that CG is a mother of two young children, with no resources to provide for her own and her children's needs, who is isolated on account of having fled a violent partner.[134]

The woman's vulnerability is clearly taken into account in the Court's unorthodox reasoning, becoming an element of applicability of the CFR and directly linking EU citizenship to fundamental rights. This justifies the triggering of extended protection and gives substance to the status of citizen in that it protects the most vulnerable individuals.[135] While this criterion is currently not very precise, if it were to be made permanent it would have a greater impact on women. Indeed, the Court of Justice's reasoning in this case can be argued to have been determined by a conjunction of factors that

---

129 The Court reiterated the *Dano* ruling (above n. 67) nine times between paras. 60 and 79 of the judgment.

130 *CG*, above n. 128, para. 80.

131 Ibid., paras. 84–92.

132 Ibid., paras. 89–90.

133 Ibid., paras. 89 and 91

134 Ibid., para. 92.

135 On the contrary, for a critical analysis of the effects of this case on EU citizenship, see J. Rondu, 'Les droits fondamentaux, enrichisement ou dilution du statut de citoyen?' in A. Bouveresse, A. Iliopoulou-Penot and J. Rondu (eds.), *La citoyenneté européenne, quelle valeur ajoutée? European Citizenship: what added value?*, Brussels, Bruylant, 2023, pp. 293–324.

affect women more broadly: domestic violence, single-parent families and unemployment.

In that sense, one could argue that the instrumentalisation of the specific family situation of vulnerable women – either by silencing this or putting it at the core of the reasoning – offers the possibility for the ECJ to limit or to extend the protection of female EU citizens in need.

§ 3. 'MERIT' IN ECJ CASE LAW AND GENDER DISCREPANCY

Case law on EU citizenship has seen the emergence of what D. Kochenov describes as the citizenship of 'personal circumstances',[136] or as S. Ganty calls it, 'merizenship'.[137] This term derives from 'merit' and 'citizenship', and refers to the fact that citizenship of the EU must be merited. Studies have analysed the emergence of two types of citizen (the 'good' and the 'bad' citizen);[138] one can now see the parallel emergence of the 'meritorious' citizen and the 'demeritorious' citizen. This gives citizenship a moral dimension: one must prove one's willingness to comply with requirements to integrate within a host Member State. However, in ECJ case law, this moral dimension ultimately depends on the Court's judgment to offer protection, or, on the contrary, an absence of protection.

Some of the Court's jurisprudence can certainly be explained in this way: it was Ms Dano's lack of willingness to integrate that justified excluding her from benefits; conversely, it was Ms Saint Prix's merit of continuing work while pregnant and returning to it soon after giving birth that was valued. In the case of *CG*, it was the specific intensity of the woman's vulnerability that gave a moral dimension to her situation and justified the protection of her and her children.[139]

---

136 D. Kochenov, 'The citizenship of personal circumstances in Europe' (2017) *European University Institute Working Paper 2017/7* <https://cadmus.eui.eu/bitstream/handle/1814/46005/LAW_2017_07.pdf>.

137 S. Ganty, *L'intégration des citoyens européens et des ressortissants de pays tiers en droit de l'Union européenne: Critique d'une intégration choisie*, Brussels, Bruylant, 2021.

138 L. Azoulai, 'Transfiguring European Citizenship: From Member State Territory to Union Territory' in D. Kochenov (ed.), *EU Citizenship and Federalism: The Role of Rights*, Cambridge, Cambridge University Press, 2017, pp. 178–203.

139 This moral dimension can be interpreted in the use of the 'language of emotion' in this case. M. De Walsche and P. Dupont, above n. 6, p. 226; see also M. Benlolo-Carabot and A. Iliopoulou-Penot, 'Citoyenneté 2022' in C. Blumann and F. Picod (eds.), *Annuaire de droit de l'Union européenne*, Paris, Éditions Panthéon-Assas, 2022, pp. 405–22.

The assessment of the moral dimension depends on the focus of the Court's analysis, and necessarily affects the applicant – in these cases, women. The choice of focus and its effects on women are even more apparent in the *Alimanovic* ruling. In that case, the ECJ set aside the vulnerability of the applicant (a woman looking after her children on her own while working). With its focus on the individual merit of the woman and not the family situation, the Court did not address the possibility for Ms Alimanovic to benefit from the right of residence based on the right of residence of her children due to their schooling in the Member State under Article 10 of Regulation 492/2011,[140] as stated in the ECJ case law of *Teixeira*,[141] *Ibrahim*,[142] and *Baumbast*. If this had been the case, the mother would have been considered deserving in that she allowed her children to continue to enjoy this right in the host Member State. But instead of focusing on the right of the children as EU citizens, the ECJ focused on the presumption of the burden generated by the woman on the finances of the state, demonstrating the impact on women if the sole focus is their personal situation.[143] However, in a later case, *Jobcenter Krefeld*,[144] the ECJ stated that the silence of the referring court as to the possibility of children benefitting from right of residence on the basis of Regulation 492/2011 led to its own silence on this question.

These examples show to what extent not taking into account the family dimension, whether this is a result of the formulation of the preliminary question by the referring court or a choice on the part of the ECJ, exacerbates women's vulnerability by focusing on an individual, liberal, moral judgment that is a legacy of a market-oriented vision.[145] Women are particularly hard hit when the specific vulnerability linked to their status as single mothers is not considered.

---

140 Council Regulation (EU) 492/2011 of 5 April 2011 on freedom of movement for workers within the Union [2011] OJ L141/1. Opinion of AG Wathelet, Case C-67/14, *Jobcenter Berlin Neukölln v. Nazifa Alimanovic*, ECLI:EU:C:2015:210, paras. 117–22.

141 Case C-480/08, *Maria Teixeira v. London Borough of Lambeth and Secretary of State for the Home Department*, ECLI:EU:C:2010:83.

142 Opinion of AG Mazák, Case C-310/08, *London Borough of Harrow v. Nimco Hassan Ibrahim and Secretary of State for the Home Department*, ECLI:EU:C:2009:641.

143 K. Hyltén-Cavallius, 'Who Cares? Caregivers' Derived Residence Rights from Children in EU Free Movement Law' (2020) 57(2) *Common Market Law Review* 399, 430.

144 Case C-181/19, *Jobcenter Krefeld*, ECLI:EU:C:2020:794.

145 According to G. Davies, it is the factual elements of each case that enable the Court of Justice to rule in a more or less favourable direction. G. Davies, 'Has the Court changed, or have the cases? The deservingness of litigants as an element in Court of Justice citizenship adjudication' (2018) 25(10) *Journal of European Public Policy* 1442.

SECTION IV THIRD-COUNTRY NATIONAL FAMILY MEMBERS: CATALYSING GENDER DISCREPANCIES

There is a particularly protective interpretation of residence rights for family members who are third-country nationals within EU citizenship, which guarantees the effective enjoyment by citizens of the rights attached to their status.[146] In this sense, the fundamental freedom of movement now implies the prerogative to enjoy this right in conditions of dignity, and, as a correlation, to benefit from the right to protection of family life. However, this appraisal, centred on the needs of 'mobile' citizens, can lead to distortions in family relations, by anchoring women in a stereotyped vision of their role within the family unit. The consequences of such an instrumental and stereotyped understanding can result in the particularly problematic dependence of female third-country nationals on their family members.

§ 1. EU CITIZENSHIP AND GENDER STEREOTYPES OF CARE IN CASE LAW

Jurisprudence relating to EU citizenship specifically protects children, guaranteed by the presence of the family. Yet this protection granted by ECJ case law reinforces a gendered assessment of the citizen's intra-family relationships, which tends to make presumptions in favour of the mother, to the detriment of the relationship between the father and his child.

I. A STEREOTYPED UNDERSTANDING OF THE ROLE OF MOTHER

As has been seen, Regulation 1612/68 promoted a stereotyped vision of intra-family relations, placing the male breadwinner at the centre of the family unit and proclaiming the woman as the 'caregiver' of the children. This vision of the family has been renewed in ECJ case law in the interpretation of the notion of 'dependence' between EU citizens and third-country nationals. While Directive 2004/38 breaks with the gendered wording of Regulation 1612/68 and offers a gender-neutral formulation, the Court appears to analyse the place of women

[146] See case law on the right of return to the host Member State, for example, Case C-127/08, *Blaise Baheten Metock and Others v. Minister for Justice, Equality and Law Reform*, ECLI:EU:C:2008:449.

in the family in light of the stereotyped notion of 'dependence'. Despite the fact that Directive 2004/38 does not apply to parents who are third-country nationals caring for EU citizens, the case law of the Court of Justice has come to offer an extensive interpretation through the needs of children to benefit from a family presence in the host Member State in accordance with Article 3 of the Directive, notably in *Baumbast* and *Zhu and Chen*.[147]

Another case that gives a particularly gendered assessment of intra-family relations in light of the question of care is *Carpenter*.[148] The 'stereotypical' role of women in the family can be seen in this ruling. Mrs Carpenter, the wife of a service provider, is presented as instrumental to the family unit, with the Court stating that 'Mrs Carpenter continues to lead a true family life there, in particular by looking after her husband's children from a previous marriage'.[149] The ruling continues:

> It is clear that the separation of Mr and Mrs Carpenter would be detrimental to their family life and, therefore, to the conditions under which Mr Carpenter exercises a fundamental freedom. That freedom could not be fully effective if Mr Carpenter were to be deterred from exercising it by obstacles raised in his country of origin to the entry and residence of his spouse [...].[150]

This wording indicates that the applicant is presented as a caretaker for her husband's children, enabling him to devote himself to his professional activities.

This appraisal highlights the divide between the assessment of mothers who are EU citizens and mothers who are not. The distinction made between mothers who are EU citizens and mothers who are third-country nationals by the ECJ is particularly illuminating: while the former are expected to fulfil their potential by entering the labour market, the latter enable EU citizens – their husbands or children – to fulfil their potential in the labour market. Motherhood is 'over-protected' in the context of a relationship of dependency,[151] supporting the gendered analysis of intra-family relations, with the 'breadwinner father' on the one hand, and the third-country national mother on the other, who is judged by a particularly maternalistic conception.

---

147 *Zhu and Chen*, above n. 95, para. 45.

148 Case C-60/00, *Mary Carpenter v. Secretary of State for the Home Department*, ECLI:EU:C:2002:434.

149 Ibid., para. 44.

150 Ibid., para. 39.

151 M. De Walsche and P. Dupont, above n. 6, p. 229.

II. A DEVALUED CONCEPTION OF THE FATHER'S ROLE

The centrality of the mother's role in the analysis of the bond of dependence entails a correlative sidelining of the father's role in intra-family relations, which is particularly illustrated in the *Ruiz Zambrano* case.[152] Here, the third-country national parents of minor EU citizens are at the centre of the Court's reasoning. The specificity of the role of a mother towards her children will emerge in later case law with the emergence of the notion of 'primary caregivers'.[153] As explained by the ECJ in the subsequent case, *Dereci*,[154] the core role of the parent, regarding situations such as *Ruiz Zambrano*, is materialised in the dependency that affects the citizen by analysing if the departure of the third-country national parent will result in the departure of the child.[155] In such an analysis:

> it is important to determine, in each case at issue in the main proceedings, *which parent is the primary carer* of the child and whether there is in fact a relationship of dependency between the child and the third-country national parent.[156]

As highlighted by L. Lonardo in cases dealing with the custody of a child who is an EU citizen in a separation/divorce, these parents find themselves in competition to determine which family relationship will be in the child's best interests, with the result that 'a parent may have recourse to strategic behaviour (which might entail lying)'.[157] In the *Dereci*, *Chavez-Vilchez* and *K.A.*[158] cases in particular, the ECJ had to determine which parent could benefit from the right of residence derived from that of the child who was a citizen. Although the Court of Justice does not treat cases concerning the infringement of the essential rights of the child as a parental custody dispute, the underlying litigation is related to this issue.[159] So while the ECJ confirmed that a child can have a plurality of caregivers,[160] taking into account the statistics regarding care

---

152 Case C-34/09, *Gerardo Ruiz Zambrano v. Office national de l'emploi (ONEm)*, ECLI:EU:C:2011:124.

153 Case C-133/15, *H.C. Chavez-Vilchez v. Raad van bestuur van de Sociale verzekeringsbank*, ECLI:EU:C:2017:354.

154 Case C-256/11, *Murat Dereci and Others v. Bundesministerium für Inneres*, ECLI:EU:C:2011:734.

155 See, for example, Joined Cases C-356/11 and C-357/11, *O and S v. Maahanmuuttovirasto and Maahanmuuttovirasto v. L*, ECLI:EU:C:2012:776, para. 56.

156 *Chavez-Vilchez*, above n. 153, para. 70 (emphasis added).

157 L. Lonardo, 'The best interests of the child in the case law of the Court of Justice of the European Union' (2022) 29(5) *Maastricht Journal of European and Comparative Law* 596, 612.

158 Case C-82/16, *K.A. and Others v. Belgische Staat*, ECLI:EU:C:2018:308.

159 *Chavez Vilchez*, above n. 153, para. 71.

160 Ibid.

activities,[161] in the vast majority of cases mothers will be presumed to be the primary carers of minors.[162]

This analysis of the relationship of dependence in the *Ruiz Zambrano* situation reveals the introduction of 'affective dependence'[163] in case law, which leads to specific protection of the relationship between mother and child to the detriment of the father's place in the family. This is shown with an emotional turn in the Court's reasoning: 'It is undeniable that this new interpretation of dependence was taken to protect the mother, as the affectionate relationship between a child and its mother is well-known'.[164] Taking into consideration an affective dimension of dependence certainly makes it possible to guarantee a right of residence to the mother even if the father may be responsible for the child's care. This affective dependence gives rise to a maternalistic conception of the family through the link between the citizen and his/her parent. In this sense, it would appear that the child's dependence on the mother, as measured by the criterion of affective dependence, is presumed, whereas dependence on the father must be demonstrated. By deduction, women are then at the centre of protection of the 'substance of rights' of the children – which leads to a 'right to care' attached to the status of the infant[165] – protecting the child against a de facto privation of their citizens' rights,[166] which correlatively leads to a depreciation of the father's role.

Thus, case law on primary caregivers is particularly favourable to women who are third-country nationals, maintaining traditional stereotypical patterns, and implying a certain vulnerability on the part of men. And yet, while this case law is favourable to mothers, the effects of family relationships lead to increased dependence of women on EU citizens.

---

161 See Section II, § 2, I.

162 For an analysis of this notion, see Section IV, § 2, II.

163 *Chavez-Vilchez*, above n. 153, para. 71 ('the extent of his emotional ties both to the Union citizen parent and to the third-country national parent').

164 In French: '*Il est inconstatable que cette nouvelle interprétation de la dépendance ait été prise pour protéger la mère, la relation d'affection d'un enfant et sa mère étant notoire*', C. Dagot, 'La fonction de la citoyenneté européenne dans la détermination d'un modèle familial européen' (2019) 4 *Revue du droit de l'Union Européenne* 109, 123.

165 See N. Cambien, above n. 70.

166 See C. Marzo, above n. 6, pp. 149–50.

§2. EU CITIZENSHIP AS A CATALYST OF VULNERABILITY OF FEMALE THIRD-COUNTRY NATIONALS

Just as citizenship status is shaped by the instrumentalisation of family matters in which gender has a core role, citizenship also shapes family matters,[167] and more specifically, the role of third-country national spouses and mothers of EU citizens, resulting in dependence on the EU national. Such a situation has its roots in the definition of the beneficiaries of the right of residence derived from the sponsor. The Citizens' Rights Directive states that a criterion of dependency[168] should be used to determine if a family member can claim the right of residence derived from a citizen directly benefitting from this right based on the Treaties.[169] While this requires dependency only to be shown, it can be argued that the centrality of this criterion regarding female members of an EU citizen's family in fact causes dependency. Dependency tends to have two side effects regarding women. The first is the induced dependency of EU citizens' spouses, referred to by E. Dubout as '"aggravated" dependency'.[170] And a second effect is emerging: 'reversed dependency', which occurs when a mother cannot benefit from an autonomous right of residence and has to depend on her child's right of residence.[171]

I. AGGRAVATING WOMEN'S DEPENDENCY ON HER SPOUSE

Two cases resulted in a generous interpretation of the beneficiaries of the right of residence derived from an EU national spouse in order to protect family members from the spouse: the first was *Diatta*,[172] whose ruling was transposed in the *Ogieriakhi* case.[173] In both cases, the ECJ allowed the possibility for the partner/spouse of an EU citizen to enjoy the right of residence even if they do not live together, as long as they stay in the same Member State. By interpreting a de jure and not de facto conjugal link, the Court sought to

167 However, the EU does not have jurisdiction regarding family law (see Articles 2 to 5 of the TFEU).

168 For an overview of the notion of dependency, see K. Hyltén-Cavallius, above n. 143.

169 Based either on the right of residence in Articles 20 and 21 of the TFEU, or solely based on Article 20 of the TFEU.

170 E. Dubout, 'The European Form of Family Life: The Case of EU Citizenship' (2020) 5(1) *European Papers* 3, 35. See also Opinion of AG Sharpston, Case C-456/12, *O v. Minister voor Immigratie, Integratie en Asiel*, ECLI:EU:C:2013:837, para. 48.

171 E. Dubout, above n. 170, 37.

172 Case 267/83, *Aissatou Diatta v. Land Berlin*, ECLI:EU:C:1985:67.

173 Case C-244/13, *Ewaen Fred Ogieriakhi v. Minister for Justice and Equality*, ECLI:EU:C:2014:2068.

protect the spouse from a possible threat from the EU citizen. However, this protection was paradoxically limited by the *Kuldip Singh*[174] ruling, in which the ECJ had to interpret Article 13(2)(a) of Directive 2004/38, stipulating the terms for a personal right of residence following divorce or termination of a registered partnership.

In the *Kuldip Singh* case, the ECJ literally interpreted the Article, claiming that the EU citizen's departure from the host Member State meant that the spouse also lost the right of residence, which could not be transformed into an autonomous rather than a derived right, as it must still exist for this to occur.[175] This ruling implies a strict interpretation of the conjugal link as de facto and not de jure, contrary to the *Ogieriakhi* ruling. In fact, the conjugal bond was strictly analysed in terms of whether the derived rights were effective, instrumentalising the family relationship to presume they were not, as the EU citizen sponsor and his spouse were not living in the same Member State. As many women are economically dependent on their spouse,[176] such an interpretation can induce dependency, notwithstanding the fact that this family link is supposed to be exempt from such dependency.[177]

The consequences of such an understanding of the Directive can lead to aggravated dependency, specifically regarding situations of domestic violence that third-country national women may be subject to. The Convention of Istanbul on domestic violence[178] recognises that, while such violence can affect both men and women, statistics show that it affects women far more:[179] in that sense, domestic violence is considered gender-based violence. The first case brought before the ECJ regarding women victims of domestic violence based on the interpretation of the Citizens Rights' Directive was *NA*.[180] The applicant, NA, was a Pakistani national married to a German national, with whom she had children. While in the UK, she was a victim of domestic violence. The referring

174 Case C-218/14, *Kuldip Singh and Others v. Minister for Justice and Equality*, ECLI:EU:C:2015:476.

175 Ibid., paras. 66–67.

176 See previous explanation regarding the specificities of women's economic activities and work situations.

177 Article 2 of Directive 2004/38 does not mention dependency linking a spouse to the sponsor.

178 Article 3(b) of the Convention of Istanbul states that domestic violence 'shall mean all acts of physical, sexual, psychological or economic violence that occur within the family or domestic unit or between former or current spouses or partners, whether or not the perpetrator shares or has shared the same residence with the victim'.

179 Article 3(a) of the Convention of Istanbul states that '"violence against women" is understood as a violation of human rights and a form of discrimination against women and shall mean all acts of gender-based violence that result in, or are likely to result in, physical, sexual, psychological or economic harm or suffering to women, including threats of such acts, coercion or arbitrary deprivation of liberty, whether occurring in public or in private life'.

180 Case C-115/15, *Secretary of State for the Home Department v. NA*, ECLI:EU:C:2016:487.

national court asked the ECJ about the interpretation of Article 13(2)(c):[181] the ECJ literally interpreted the Article, as it had in the *Kuldip Singh* ruling, but offered a diametrically opposed opinion to the Advocate General. The ECJ stated that, as the EU citizen left the country before beginning the divorce procedure, the spouse could not benefit from an autonomous right to stay on the basis of the Article.[182] This literal analysis implies that the special protection allowed in the legislation could only be used in very specific conditions, leading some scholars to ask if the ECJ was 'protecting the perpetrator over the victim' of domestic violence, and that such a ruling could be used by the sponsor to threaten the spouse.[183] This problematic ruling seems to have been partially overruled by the ECJ in the later case of *X v. Belgium*,[184] which offered a more adequate solution to the specificities of domestic violence faced by women.[185]

The most striking aspect of this case is that third-country national victims of domestic violence perpetuated by third-country national spouses would be more protected than those who suffered domestic abuse by an EU citizen.[186] Directive 2003/89/EC does not specify the necessity for a third-country national family member to have sufficient resources and comprehensive health insurance in order to benefit from the right of residence. This shows how the teleological interpretation of EU citizenship can lead to women's even greater dependency on an EU national compared to third-country nationals.

---

181 Article 13(2) states: 'Without prejudice to the second subparagraph, divorce, annulment of marriage or termination of the registered partnership referred to in point 2(b) of Article 2 shall not entail loss of the right of residence of a Union citizen's family members who are not nationals of a Member State where: […] (c) this is warranted by particularly difficult circumstances, such as having been a victim of domestic violence while the marriage or registered partnership was subsisting'.

182 *NA*, above n. 180, para. 48.

183 H. Oosterom-Staples, 'Residence Rights for Caring Parents who are also Victims of Domestic Violence' (2017) 19(4) *European Journal of Migration and Law* 396, 411.

184 Case C-930/19, *X v. Belgium*, ECLI:EU:C:2021:657. For an extended analysis relating to French doctrine, see P. Dumas, 'Le renforcement a minima de la protection du conjoint de citoyen de l'Union victime de violence domestique' (2021) 3 *Revue des affaires européennes* 715. It is noteworthy that this case dealt with a male spouse of Algerian nationality who was the victim of domestic violence from his spouse, a French national with whom he lived in Belgium.

185 The ECJ stated that the 'divorce proceedings may be initiated after the departure of the EU citizen from the host Member State', as long as the proceedings are initiated 'within a reasonable period following such departure' (*X v. Belgium*, above n. 184, para. 43).

186 Article 15(3) of Council Directive 2003/86/EC of 22 September 2003 on the right to family reunification [2003] OJ L251/12.

II. THE REVERSED DEPENDENCY OF MOTHERS ON THEIR CHILDREN

There is a significant line of ECJ case law that instrumentalises the primary caregiver to guarantee the right to education for the children of a former worker,[187] or of a sponsor EU citizen who has fled the country,[188] or the protection of the right to free movement of a child too young to have started school,[189] or to stay within the territory of the Union.[190] The underlying justification of this derived right of residence relies on the protection of the *effet utile* of the rights of the child that could not be enjoyed without the primary caregiver.

This case law leads to a sort of reversed dependency, with the right of residence of the mother deriving from that of her child. The centrality of the mother's dependency is particularly seen in situations such as *Ruiz Zambrano*. This 'reversed dependency'[191] is based on the centrality of the protection of the best interests of the child, found in Article 24(2) of the CFR in conjunction with the protection of family life in Article 7 of the CFR,[192] which emerges in ECJ case law.[193] The ECJ's interpretation of EU primary and secondary law regarding the best interests of the child can lead to deleterious effects on the mother as it reinforces a stereotypical analysis of the family relationship, viewing her role as a caregiver of her children. In that sense, in the *Ibrahim* and *Teixeira* cases, the mother's initial dependence on the spouse is simply transferred to the child. The most representative case showing reversed dependency of the mother on her child is *NA*. In this case, the woman could not benefit from the autonomous right of residence as a victim of domestic violence, reducing her solely to a primary caregiver of her child, silencing the specific vulnerability that she faced as a victim of domestic violence. As A. Weiss asserted:

> This empowering gesture of compromise is a strange solution for people who experience domestic abuse and have lived in a relationship defined by power imbalance between the spouses.[194]

---

187 *Baumbast*, above n. 25.

188 See *Ibrahim* (above n. 142) and *Teixeira* (above n. 141).

189 *Zhu and Chen*, above n. 95.

190 *Gerardo Ruiz Zambrano v. Office national de l'emploi (ONEm)*, above n. 152.

191 E. Dubout, above n. 170.

192 *Alfredo Rendón Marín v. Administración del Estado*, above n. 78.

193 Ibid.

194 A. Weiss, 'Transnational Families in Crisis: An Analysis of the Domestic Violence Rule in E.U. Free Movement Law' (2009) 30(3) *Michigan Journal of International Law* 841, 853.

The paradox of such dependency is that the right of the child is an instrument guaranteeing the mother's right to stay. In this way, the child can be seen as a 'field of protection' for the mother, who cannot benefit from a right of residence on her own. The vulnerability of the mother's situation is that her right of residence is granted only as long as the relationship of dependency continues. This is the apparently paradoxical effect of the right of residence derived by parents: while it is seen as an indirect way of protecting the mothers, it induces dependency on their children. As the duration of this derived right is linked to the *effet utile* of their presence with their children, the right ends when the relationship of dependency disappears.[195] This termination depends on the right of residence of the child, and on the nature of the dependency.

While the *Ruiz Zambrano* case law allows mothers to benefit from an autonomous right of residence on the basis of Directive 2003/109,[196] this is not the case for mothers who benefit from a right of residence on the basis of their children's schooling.[197] Moreover, third-country national mothers have to prove that they have sufficient resources to be allowed to stay, even if they are victims of domestic violence.[198] This shows that the effects of the *Dano* case are applied even in cases of vulnerability, situations that are more typically faced by women. These economic conditions seem detached from the social reality of women who find themselves in particularly vulnerable situations and are unable to find a job due to psychological harm, language barriers, or the fact that they look after their children alone.[199] In that sense, the protection intended to be granted with the possibility of the autonomous right to residence becomes 'less effective as the vulnerability of the individual it is designed to protect increases'.[200]

---

195 See *Ibrahim* (above n. 142) and *Teixeira* (above n. 141).

196 Council Directive 2003/109/EC of 25 November 2003 concerning the status of third-country nationals who are long-term residents [2004] OJ L16/44. Case C-624/20, *E.K. v. Staatssecretaris van Justitie en Veiligheid*, ECLI:EU:C:2022:639.

197 Case C-529/11, *Olaitan Ajoke Alarape and Olukayode Azeez Tijani v. Secretary of State for the Home Department*, ECLI:EU:C:2013:290.

198 *X v. Belgium*, above n. 184.

199 See, for example, Point AH of the 'Report of the European Parliament on women's poverty in Europe', 2021/2170(INI), above n. 54.

200 A. Weiss, above n. 194, 853.

SECTION V
EU CITIZENSHIP: A CATALYST FOR GENDER DISCREPANCY INSIDE THE FAMILY FRAMEWORK?

In 1791, Olympe de Gouges wrote a parallel version of the French 'Declaration of the Rights of Man and of the Citizen' (1789): the 'Declaration of the Rights of Women and the Female Citizen' ('*Déclaration des droits de la femme et de la citoyenne*'). This document demonstrates how the specificities of gender necessitate citizenship to be adapted accordingly. Citizenship of the EU is no exception.

The liberal market-oriented view of EU citizenship can be incompatible with the specific socio-economic conditions experienced by women. Simultaneously, this view can catalyse gender stereotypes of the family unit. To overcome this problematic situation, two solutions seem appropriate. First, linking EU citizenship directly to the non-discrimination clause of Article 19 of the TFEU would counterbalance the shortcomings regarding women's specific vulnerabilities. Secondly, in the case of third-country nationals, the dependency effects of EU citizenship could be mitigated by granting citizenship on the basis of residence, amending Article 9 of the TEU and Article 20 of the TFEU. These women could then enjoy autonomous residence rights on the basis of the existence of their residency in Europe as opposed to their derived right from a spouse or child who is an EU citizen.

As things stand, there is still a long way to go before EU citizenship is a status that guarantees equality between men and women. Much work needs to be done for women to be able to fully benefit from the provision in Article 3(2) of the TEU that '[t]he Union shall offer its citizens an area of freedom, security and justice without internal frontiers'.

CHAPTER 4

FROM *CHEN* TO *PANCHAREVO* AND BEYOND: A BRIEF HISTORY OF ECJ CASE LAW ON THE FREEDOM TO MOVE AND RESIDE OF FAMILY MEMBERS

Irene MARCHIORO*

Abstract

This chapter examines European Court of Justice case law and how it has extended the scope of the freedom to move and reside for EU nationals and their family members through an expansive interpretation of Treaty provisions and of the Citizens' Rights Directive (Directive 2004/38). The analysis explores the practical outcomes of ECJ judgments and the corresponding obligations on Member States, and also looks at their impact on the recognition of new forms of marriage and parenthood, including parenthood resulting from surrogacy.

SECTION I
INTRODUCTION

The influence of European Court of Justice (ECJ) case law on the application of the freedom to move and reside of EU citizens and their relatives is substantial and varied. The latest trend in this vein is seen in a number of decisions through which the ECJ has introduced, for the purpose of granting the right to move and reside, a particular form of recognition of family status,[1] which has been defined

* Post-doctoral fellow at the University of Trieste.

[1] J. CROON-GESTEFELD, 'Der Einfluss der Unionsbürgerschaft auf das Internationale Familienrecht' (2022) 86(1) *Rabels Zeitschrift für Ausländisches und Internationales Privatrecht* 32; L. HÜBNER, 'Die Integration der primärrechtlichen Anerkennungsmethode in das IPR' (2021) 85(1) *Rabels Zeitschrift für Ausländisches und Internationales Privatrecht* 106; P. MANKOWSKI, 'Nun sag, wie hast Du's mit dem Anerkennungsprinzip? – Im EU-Ausland "unrechtmäßig" erlangte Namen als Prüfstein' (2020) 40 *Praxis des Internationalen Privat- und Verfahrensrechts* 323; M. LEHMAN, 'Recognition as a Substitute for Conflict of Laws?' in S. LEIBLE (ed.), *General*

as 'functionally oriented' or 'functionally limited'.[2] The milestones of this new approach of the Court, which represents both an alternative and a shortcut to the traditional recognition method in private international law,[3] are the judgments rendered by the Court in *Coman*[4] and in *Pancharevo*.[5]

Principles of European Private International Law, Alphen aan den Rijn, Wolters Kluwer, 2016, pp. 11–43; B. Cortese, *L'ordinamento dell'Unione Europea, tra autocostituzione, collaborazione e autonomia*, Turin, Giappichelli, 2018, p. 279; D. Coester-Waltjen, 'Das Anerkennungsprinzip im Dornröschenschlaf?' in H.-P. Mansel (ed.), *Festschrift für Erik Jayme*, Munich, Sellier, 2004, pp. 121–30; E. Jayme and C. Kohler, 'Europäisches Kollisionsrecht 2001: Anerkennungsprinzip statt IPR?' (2001) 21 *Praxis des Internationalen Privat- und Verfahrensrechts* 501.

2 J. Meeusen, 'Functional Recognition of Same-sex Parenthood for the Benefit of Mobile Union Citizens – Brief Comments on the CJEU's Pancharevo Judgment', *EAPIL blog* (3 February 2022) <https://eapil.org/2022/02/03/functional-recognition-of-same-sex-parenthood-for-the-benefit-of-mobile-union-citizens-brief-comments-on-the-cjeus-pancharevo-judgment/>; O. Feraci, 'Il riconoscimento "funzionalmente orientato" dello status di un minore nato da due madri nello spazio giudiziario europeo: una lettura internazional privatistica della sentenza Pancharevo' (2022) 105 *Rivista di diritto internazionale* 563, 571; G. Rossolillo, 'Art. 10 della risoluzione dell'Institut de Droit International su Human Rights and Private International Law: la continuità degli status come garanzia del rispetto della vita privata e familiare' (2022) 16(3) *Diritti umani e diritto internazionale* 531, 534; E. di Napoli, G. Biagioni, O. Feraci, R. Calvigioni and P. Pasqualis, 'La circolazione dello status dei minori attraverso le "frontiere" d'Europa: intersezioni tra diritto dell'Unione e diritto internazionale privato alla luce della sentenza Pancharevo' (2023) Special Issue *Papers di diritto europeo* 67, 78.

3 On the 'traditional' recognition method, see P. Picone, 'Les méthodes de coordination entre ordres juridiques en droit international privé: Cours général de droit international privé' (1999) 276 *Recueil des Cours de l'Académie de droit international de La Haye* 9, 119–42; G. Rossolillo, *Mutuo riconoscimento e tecniche conflittuali*, Padua, Cedam, 2002; P. Picone, 'Diritto internazionale privato comunitario e pluralità di metodi di coordinamento tra ordinamenti' in P. Picone (ed.), *Diritto internazionale privato e diritto comunitario*, Padua, Cedam, 2004, p. 495 ff; P. Mayer, 'La Reconnaissance: Notions et Méthodes' in P. Lagarde (ed.), *La reconnaissance des situations en droit international privé*, Paris, Éditions A. Pedone, 2013, pp. 27–33; A. Davì, 'Il riconoscimento delle situazioni giuridiche costituite all'estero nella prospettiva di una riforma del sistema di diritto internazionale privato' (2019) 102(2) *Rivista di diritto internazionale* 319.

4 Case C-673/16, *Coman*, ECLI:EU:C:2018:385. For some comments on this judgment, see, e.g. S. Peers, 'Love wins in the CJEU: Same Sex Marriages and EU free movement law', *EU Law Analysis* (5 June 2018) <https://eulawanalysis.blogspot.com/2018/06/love-wins-in-cjeu-same-sex-marriages.html>; U. Belavusau and D. Kochenov, 'Same-sex Spouses: More Free Movement, but What about Marriage? Coman' (2020) 57(1) *Common Market Law Review* 227; J.-Y. Carlier, 'Vers un ordre public européen des droits fondamentaux – L'exemple de la reconnaissance des mariages de personnes de même sexe dans l'arrêt Coman' (2019) 117 *Revue trimestrielle des droits de l'homme* 203; A. Perelli, 'Matrimonio tra persone dello stesso sesso. Il caso Coman: un importante passo verso l'eguaglianza' (2018) 36(3) *DPCE Online* 753 <https://www.dpceonline.it/index.php/dpceonline/article/view/558/540>; G. Rossolillo, 'Corte di Giustizia, matrimonio tra persone dello stesso sesso e diritti fondamentali: il caso Coman', *SIDIBlog* (8 July 2018) <http://www.sidiblog.org/2018/07/08/corte-di-giustizia-matrimonio-tra-persone-dello-stesso-sesso-e-diritti-fondamentali-il-caso-coman/>; I. Marchioro, 'The free movement of same-sex registered partners in the light of the evolutive interpretation of Directive 2004/38/EC' in M.C. Baruffi and M. Ortino (eds.), *Trending topics in international and EU law: legal and economic perspectives*, Naples, Edizioni Scientifiche Italiane, 2019, pp. 203–20; E. Chiaretto, 'Libera circolazione dei coniugi dello stesso sesso nell'Unione Europea' (2018) 12 *La Nuova Giurisprudenza Civile Commentata* 1753, 1759–65.

5 Case C-490/20, *V.M.A. v. Stolichna obshtina, 'Pancharevo'*, ECLI:EU:C:2021:1008. For some comments on this judgment, see E. Gualco, 'Habemus Pancharevo – A new Chapter of the

In a nutshell, with these two decisions the Court has ruled that a family status (be it marital status or parenthood) legally acquired[6] in a first Member State must be recognised in another Member State for the purposes of the enjoyment of the rights drawn from EU citizenship, in particular the right to move and reside freely within the EU. As a result, even a Member State that does not permit, in its own legal order, the creation of non-traditional family bonds such as same-sex marriages, same-sex registered partnerships or parenthood in homoparental families is required to take all necessary steps to allow for these families to reside in its territory and to move freely throughout the EU. For instance, states might be required to issue travel documents that fully reflect the status acquired abroad or to accept that some third-country nationals must be considered family members of an EU citizen for the sake of the exercise of the rights stemming from Articles 20 and 21 of the Treaty on the Functioning of the European Union (TFEU), as well as from the Citizens' Rights Directive 2004/38 on the right of citizens of the EU and their family members to move and reside freely within the territory of the Member States.[7]

It is generally understood that this kind of functionally oriented recognition does not necessarily extend to all social, civil and succession aspects normally covered by 'full' recognition. This limitation marks the distance between the landmark rulings of the Court and the proposed EU Regulation aimed at introducing a comprehensive private international law of filiation, including

EU Citizenship Fairy-tale', *BlogDUE* (22 March 2022) <https://www.aisdue.eu/wp-content/uploads/2022/03/Gualco-BlogDUE.pdf>; J. Meeusen, see above n. 2; F. Maoli, 'La Corte di Giustizia si pronuncia sull'obbligo degli Stati membri di riconoscere il rapporto di filiazione tra una minore e due madri', *SIDIBlog* (17 January 2022) <http://www.sidiblog.org/2022/01/17/la-corte-di-giustizia-si-pronuncia-sullobbligo-degli-stati-membri-di-riconoscere-il-rapporto-di-filiazione-tra-una-minore-e-due-madri/>; A. Schillaci, 'Genitori in ogni paese: la Corte di Giustizia si pronuncia sulla tutela transnazionale delle famiglie arcobaleno nell'UE', *Diritti Comparati* (22 December 2021) <https://www.diritticomparati.it/genitori-in-ogni-paese-la-corte-di-giustizia-si-pronuncia-sulla-tutela-transnazionale-delle-famiglie-arcobaleno-nellue/>; A. Tryfonidou, 'The Cross-Border Recognition of the Parent-Child Relationship in Rainbow Families under EU Law: A Critical View of the ECJ's V.M.A. Ruling', *European Law Blog* (21 December 2021) <https://www.europeanlawblog.eu/pub/the-cross-border-recognition-of-the-parent-child-relationship-in-rainbow-families-under-eu-law-a-critical-view-of-the-ecjs-v-m-a-ruling/release/1>; A. Tryfonidou, 'The ECJ Recognises the Right of Rainbow Families to Move Freely between EU Member States: the V.M.A. Ruling' (2022) 47(4) *European Law Review* 534.

6 It is not fully clear what the Court means by a status 'legally' acquired in a Member State. For some thoughts on this topic, see I. Marchioro, 'Quali prospettive per il legislatore europeo dopo Coman e Pancharevo?' (2023) Special Issue 1 *Quaderni AISDUE* 404.

7 Consolidated Version of the Treaty on the Functioning of the European Union [2016] OJ C202/47. Council Directive 2004/38/EC of 29 April 2004 on the right of citizens of the Union and their family members to move and reside freely within the territory of the Member States [2004] OJ L158/77.

its (full) recognition and the creation of an EU Certificate of Parenthood.[8] This Regulation, proposed by the Commission and backed by the Parliament,[9] is currently blocked in a stalemate in the Council, with little hope of being approved.[10] However, interestingly, it contains a specific rule of coordination with the Treaty-based rights already affirmed by ECJ case law, which seems to imply that the proposed Regulation would serve, to a certain extent, more as a codification than the source of parenthood recognition obligations.[11] In this scenario, some scholars have felt that the effects of functionally oriented

---

[8] See 'Proposal for a Council Regulation on jurisdiction, applicable law, recognition of decisions and acceptance of authentic instruments in matters of parenthood and on the creation of a European Certificate of Parenthood', COM(2022) 695 final. For some comments on the proposal, see C. Budzikiewicz, K. Duden, A. Dutta, T. Helms and C. Mayer, 'The European Commission's Parenthood Proposal – Comments of the Marburg Group' (2023) 43 *Praxis des Internationalen Privat- und Verfahrensrechts* 425; C. Budzikiewicz, K. Duden, A. Dutta, T. Helms and C. Mayer (eds.), *The Marburg Group's Comments on the European Commission's Parenthood Proposal*, Cambridge, Intersentia, 2024; L. Válková, 'The Commission Proposal for a Regulation on the Recognition of Parenthood and other Legislative Trends affecting Legal Parenthood' (2022) 58 *Rivista di diritto internazionale privato e processuale* 854; R. Legendre, 'À propos de la proposition de Règlement européen en matière de filiation' (2023) 2 *Revue critique de droit international privé* 495; M.C. Baruffi, 'La proposta di Regolamento UE sulla filiazione: un superamento dei diritti derivanti dalla libera circolazione' (2023) 6 *Famiglia e diritto* 535; D. Danieli, 'La proposta di regolamento UE sul riconoscimento della filiazione tra Stati membri: alla ricerca di un equilibrio tra obiettivi di armonizzazione e divergenze nazionali', *SIDIBlog* (23 February 2023) <http://www.sidiblog.org/2023/02/23/la-proposta-di-regolamento-ue-sul-riconoscimento-della-filiazione-tra-stati-membri-alla-ricerca-di-un-equilibrio-tra-obiettivi-di-armonizzazione-e-divergenze-nazionali/>; L. Carpaneto, 'Filiazione, circolazione degli status e diritto internazionale privato: la nuova proposta di regolamento UE e orizzonti di sviluppo', *Aldricus* (9 January 2023) <https://aldricus.giustizia.it/2023/01/09/filiazione-circolazione-degli-status-e-diritto-internazionale-privato-la-nuova-proposta-di-regolamento-ue-e-orizzonti-di-sviluppo/>.

[9] See European Parliament legislative resolution of 14 December 2023, P9_TA(2023)0481.

[10] The Commission-proposed Regulation on filiation matters is (necessarily) based on Article 81(3) of the TFEU and requires unanimity in the Council, which is unlikely to be reached in the near future. Criticisms of the framework of the legislative procedure have already been expressed by Romania (document of 28 August 2023, no. 12458/23), the Czech Republic (document of 5 April 2023, no. 8112/23), Italy (document of 31 March 2023, no. 8017/23) and Portugal (document of 29 March 2023, no. 7884/23). The Netherlands have requested a detailed report on the number of cases occurring in the last five years in the EU involving the 'recognition of parental responsibility and rights of access, succession rights and name' as well as on any research tackling these issues without resorting to EU law (document of 31 March 2023, no. 8033/23). Spain, on the contrary, considers the proposal to be fully compliant with the EU principle of subsidiarity (document of 29 March 2023, no. 7892/23).

[11] See Article 2(1) of the said proposal (COM(2022) 695 final, above n. 8), according to which the 'Regulation shall not affect the limitations relating to the use of public policy as a justification to refuse the recognition of parenthood where, under Union law on free movement, Member States are obliged to recognise a document establishing a parent-child relationship issued by the authorities of another Member State for the purposes of rights derived from Union law'.

recognition, while not encompassing all the effects of ordinary full recognition, are, at the end of the day, not *that* limited.[12]

The aim of this chapter is to examine the consequences of the relevant ECJ decisions, investigating the actual obligations that Member States will need to fulfil to comply with the conclusions of the Court. To this purpose, it focuses on the case law of the ECJ to determine in what occasions, in what way and with which consequences the Court has extended the scope of application of the freedom to move and reside stemming from the Treaty and from Directive 2004/38. Further, it explores the substantive rights that come with the inclusion of 'new' types of family members in the scope of application of the Directive and discusses the applicability of the *Pancharevo* principle to parenthood deriving from surrogacy agreements.

SECTION II ECJ CASE LAW THAT EXTENDS THE SCOPE OF THE FREEDOM TO MOVE AND RESIDE FOR EU NATIONALS AND THEIR FAMILY MEMBERS

The case law of the ECJ extending the scope of application of EU legislation on the freedom to move and reside of EU nationals and their family members began before the introduction of Directive 2004/38. The Court took its first (bold) steps into the extensive interpretation of free movement and residence rights stemming from EU citizenship when it ruled on the scope of application of Article 18 of the Treaty establishing the European Community (TEC)[13] and Directive 90/364/EEC[14] in the well-known *Zhu and Chen* case.[15] Shortly thereafter it extended 'by analogy' the scope of application of Regulation (EEC)

---

12 F. Battaglia, 'La definizione di "coniuge" ai sensi della direttiva 38/20043: il caso Coman e Hamilton' (2018) *Ordine internazionale e diritti umani* 218; S. Penasa, 'Matrimonio tra persone dello stesso sesso e libertà di circolazione dei cittadini europei e dei loro familiari: osservazioni "a cerchi concentrici" sul caso Coman c. Romania della Corte di Giustizia' (2018) 3 *Diritto, Immigrazione e Cittadinanza* 14.

13 Consolidated Version of the Treaty establishing the European Community [2002] OJ C325/33.

14 Council Directive 90/364/EEC of 28 June 1990 on the right of residence [1990] OJ L180/26, which was in force until 29 April 2006.

15 Case C-200/02, *Zhu and Chen v. Secretary of State for the Home Department*, ECLI:EU:C:2004:639. On this case, see, e.g. B. Hofstötter, 'A cascade of rights, or who shall care for little Catherine? Some reflections on the Chen case' (2005) 30(4) *European Law Review* 548; A. Tryfonidou, 'C-200/02, *Kunqian Catherine Zhu and Man Lavette Chen v. Secretary of State for the Home Department*: Further Cracks in the "Great Wall" of the European Union?' (2005) 11(4) *European Public Law* 527.

1612/68[16] in *Eind*, based on the need to preserve the *effet utile* of Article 39 of the TEC and EU citizenship, intended as the fundamental status of nationals of Member States.[17]

Even before the introduction of EU citizenship itself, the Court had made an extensive reading of the residence rights of a former spouse of a migrant worker in *Singh*.[18] In that case, it again imposed the application by analogy of the relevant secondary law instruments, among them Directive 73/148/EEC on the abolition of restrictions on movement and residence for nationals of Member States.[19]

Since then, ECJ case law has continued to evolve in this respect. This case law can be divided into four types of case. The first concerns the situation of an EU national who has never circulated and yet demands residence rights for his/her family members under EU law. According to its wording, Directive 2004/38 does not apply to such situations.[20] Yet the Court has found that, in some circumstances, the family members of a 'static' EU national can claim a derived right to be admitted and to reside in the Member State of origin of that EU national.

The second type of case deals with the situation of third-country nationals who are parents of a minor possessing EU citizenship, when that child would be obliged to leave EU territory if the parent(s) were not allowed to stay or join the child, thus depriving the minor's EU citizenship of its effectiveness.

The third type of case involves the application of Directive 2004/38 to an EU citizen who has returned to his/her country of origin after having settled for some time in another Member State, and possibly becoming a dual national.

The final type of case involves the evolving and extensive interpretation of the very notion of 'family member' contained in the Directive, with a view to expanding its scope of application to new forms of families.

---

16 Council Regulation (EEC) 1612/68 of 15 October 1968 on freedom of movement for workers within the Community [1968] OJ L257/2.

17 Case C-291/05, *Minister voor Vreemdelingenzaken en Integratie v. R.N.G. Eind*, ECLI:EU:C:2007:771, especially paras. 32 and 37–39.

18 Case C-370/90, *Singh*, ECLI:EU:C:1992:296.

19 Council Directive 73/148/EEC of 21 May 1973 on the abolition of restrictions on movement and residence within the Community for nationals of Member States with regard to establishment and the provision of services [1973] OJ L172/14.

20 See Article 3(1) of Directive 2004/38, according to which the Directive 'shall apply to all Union citizens who move to or reside in a Member State other than that of which they are a national, and to their family members as defined in point 2 of Article 2 who accompany or join them'.

SECTION III
EXTENSIVE INTERPRETATION OF THE PROVISIONS OF THE TREATY

Looking at these four types of case and the rights that the Court has conferred upon the individuals involved, some notable differences stand out. One of these is that when the ECJ has judged cases of 'static' EU nationals, as in *McCarthy*,[21] *Dereci*[22] and, more recently, *Subdelegación del Gobierno en Ciudad Real*,[23] after stating that 'a principle of international law [...] precludes a Member State from refusing its own nationals the right to enter its territory and remain there for any reason',[24] it notes that, therefore, Directive 2004/38 'cannot apply to a Union citizen who enjoys an unconditional right of residence due to the fact that he resides in the Member State of which he is a national',[25] even in the case in which the EU national holds dual nationality, as in *McCarthy*. The family member of such an EU national, therefore, cannot rely on the Directive to claim derived residence rights in the EU.

And yet the Court has found that the status of an EU citizen under Article 20(1) of the TFEU confers certain rights that can be invoked even against the Member State of origin, in particular the right conferred by Article 21 of the TFEU to move and reside freely within the territory of the Member States.[26] Therefore, a family member must be allowed to join an EU national and reside with him/her if, otherwise, the EU national would be deprived of the genuine enjoyment of the rights conferred by his/her status as an EU citizen or of the exercise of the right to free movement and residence within the territory of the Member States. The Court states that it is up to the national referring court to verify if such a risk exists.

---

21 Case C-434/09, *Shirley McCarthy v. Secretary of State for the Home Department*, ECLI:EU:C:2011:277. See the comments by, e.g. P. Van Elsuwege, 'European Union citizenship and the purely internal rule revisited: Decision of 5 May 2011, Case C-434/09, *Shirley McCarthy v. Secretary of State for the Home Department*' (2011) 7 *European Constitutional Law Review* 308 and A. Wiesbrock, 'Disentangling the "Union citizenship puzzle?" The *McCarthy* case' (2011) 36(6) *European Law Review* 861.

22 Case C-256/11, *Dereci v. Bundesministerium für Inneres*, ECLI:EU:C:2011:734. For comments on *McCarthy* (above n. 21) and *Dereci*, see D. Kochenov, 'A real European citizenship: A new jurisdiction test: A novel chapter in the development of the Union in Europe' (2011) 18(1) *Columbia Journal of European Law* 56. For comments on these two judgments and on *Ruiz Zambrano* (see below n. 30), see A. Tryfonidou, 'Redefining the Outer Boundaries of EU Law: The *Zambrano, McCarthy* and *Dereci* trilogy' (2012) 18(3) *European Public Law* 493.

23 Case C-836/18, *Subdelegación del Gobierno en Ciudad Real v. RH*, ECLI:EU:C:2020:119.

24 *McCarthy*, above n. 21, para. 29.

25 Ibid., para. 34.

26 Ibid., above n. 21, para. 48 and *Dereci*, above n. 22, para. 63.

In these cases, the right to reside in an EU Member State is drawn directly from the Treaty and does not touch upon the applicability of Directive 2004/38. As a consequence, the only guarantee that is granted to those family members is that of being admitted in the Member State and being able to reside within it. The Court does not ask for the Member State to ensure that the entry and residence of the third-country national in question takes place under the same conditions as the entry and residence of a family member of an EU national within the meaning of the Directive. The Member States are therefore not obliged to issue a residence card according to the Directive, nor to guarantee, in general, the rights enshrined therein. Moreover, the right of entry is itself subject to proving that the risk for the EU national of being obliged to leave the country of origin is real and concrete,[27] a burden of proof that was not met, for instance, in either *McCarthy*[28] or in *Ymeraga e Ymeraga-Tafarshiku.*[29]

The second group of cases, regarding the derived residence rights of the parent of an EU minor, shares many similarities with the case of the 'static' EU citizen. The first judgment issued on this topic after Directive 2004/38 entered into force was *Ruiz Zambrano.*[30] That case actually lay at the crossroads between the first and second type of cases, since the EU minors involved in that case had never circulated. For the sake of the genuine enjoyment of the EU

---

27 P. Van Elsuwege, above n. 21, 314, affirms that 'the threshold to conclude that a measure deprives a Union citizen of the genuine enjoyment of his citizenship rights is rather high. Only in exceptional circumstances, such as situations where a citizen's residence in the Union or his status as citizen of the Union is at stake, EU citizenship law can be expected to apply to purely internal situations'.

28 On the other hand, once it is assessed that such a risk indeed exists, the effective enjoyment of the substance of the rights conferred by the status of EU citizenship requires that Member States are not allowed to reject an application for family reunification submitted from the third-country national on the sole grounds that the EU citizen does not have sufficient resources not to become a burden on the national social assistance system (see *Subdelegación del Gobierno en Ciudad Real*, above n. 23, paras. 48–49).

29 Case C-87/12, *Ymeraga e Ymeraga-Tafarshiku*, ECLI:EU:C:2013:291. In this decision, the Court also clarified that in a situation like that at hand, the behaviour of the Luxembourg authorities could not be scrutinised under the lens of the principles enshrined in the EU Charter of Fundamental Rights (Charter of Fundamental Rights of the European Union [2016] OJ C202/389), since the situation itself did not involve the implementation of EU law in the meaning of Article 51 of the Charter (see paras. 41–43).

30 Case C-34/09, *Gerardo Ruiz Zambrano v. Office national de l'emploi (ONEm)*, ECLI:EU:C:2011:124. For comments on this case, see P. Mengozzi, 'La sentenza *Zambrano*: prodromi e conseguenze di una pronuncia inattesa' (2011) 6(3) *Studi sull'integrazione europea* 417; R. Palladino, 'Il diritto di soggiorno nel "proprio" Stato membro quale (nuovo) corollario della cittadinanza europea?' (2011) 6(2) *Studi sull'integrazione europea* 331; R. Morris, 'European Citizenship and the right to move freely: internal situations, reverse discrimination and fundamental rights' (2011) 18 *Maastricht Journal of European and Comparative Law* 179. A. Tryfonidou (see above n. 22) argues (see 513ff) that in *McCarthy* (above n. 21) and *Dereci* (above n. 22) the Court has taken a step back from the findings of *Ruiz Zambrano*, in so much as it has demonstrated a limited understanding of the 'substance' of the rights to enter and reside. It appears that the Court only considers as relevant for the triggering of those rights the physical impossibility of living in a place

citizenship rights conferred on the children, the Court ruled that their father's residence in the Member State could not be denied, even though the Directive was not applicable. Furthermore, a work permit had to be issued in his favour, to allow him sufficient economic resources for his family.

This principle was later reiterated in *Alokpa and Moudoulou*,[31] which, echoing the findings of *Zhu and Chen*, included two different issues. In the first place, the ruling found that the right of an EU minor to reside in a host Member State when he/she does not have sufficient resources under Article 7(1)(b) of Directive 2004/38 must nonetheless be granted if such resources are provided by the non-EU parent.[32] If that is the case, then the non-EU parent must also be able to reside in the host state with the minor, whose right to residence would otherwise be deprived of its useful effect, even if that parent is not a 'family member' according to the Directive.[33] Secondly, the Court ruled that, even if the economic conditions under Article 7(1)(b) are not met, a right of residence might still be exceptionally recognised for a third-country national under Articles 20 and 21 of the TFEU if the EU citizen would otherwise be obliged to leave the territory of the EU altogether.

Again, in this case the right of residence is drawn directly from the Treaty, and the burden of proof of sufficient resources lies on the applicant. With regard to the risk that the EU national would be forced to leave the EU, the Court explained in *Chavez-Vilchez* that equally:

> the competent authorities of the Member State concerned [must] undertake, on the basis of the evidence provided by the third-country national, the necessary enquiries in order to be able to assess, in the light of all the specific circumstances, whether a refusal [of a right of residence] would have such consequences.[34]

If the Member State's authorities establish that the right of residence is indeed founded, this could prevail over opposing interests of the state, such as that of automatically refusing, for the sake of general prevention, a permit

without certain relatives (such as in the case of the minor in the case, who could not sustain himself without his parents) and not all the other conditions under which a person might *desire* to continue living in the EU.

31 Case C-86/12, *Adzo Domenyo Alokpa and Moudoulou v. Ministre du Travail, de l'Emploi et de l'Immigration*, ECLI:EU:C:2013:645.

32 In a recent judgment on Case C-93/18, *Ermira Bajratari v. Secretary of State for the Home Department*, ECLI:EU:C:2019:809, the Court delved deeper into this issue, ruling that a minor EU citizen has sufficient resources even when these resources derive from income obtained from the unlawful employment of his/her father, in this case, a third-country national without a residence card or work permit.

33 According to Article 2(2)(d) of Directive 2004/38, family members are 'the *dependent* direct relatives in the ascending line and those of the spouse or partner [...]' (emphasis added).

34 Case C-133/15, *H.C. Chavez-Vilchez and Others v. Raad van bestuur van de Sociale verzekeringsbank and Others*, ECLI:EU:C:2017:354, para. 78.

of stay to individuals who have been criminally convicted, as in the *Rendón Marín* case.[35]

Recently, ECJ case law seems to have taken a slight – but significant – detour in the case of *Commissioners for Her Majesty's Revenue and Customs*,[36] which again dealt with an EU minor and his non-EU parent and primary carer for whom the Directive did not apply. In that case, the Court did not simply rely on the provisions of the Treaty to find that the relative had a right of residence, but rather held that:

> the right of residence of more than three months and less than five years conferred by [...] directive [38/2004] on that minor Union citizen [...] extends, in order to ensure the effectiveness of that right of residence, to [the] parent by virtue of Article 21 TFEU.[37]

What may look like a nuance here might actually have relevant consequences: in this decision, the right of residence of the parent is not disconnected from the Directive and based on the Treaty alone; instead, Article 21 of the TFEU functions as a mechanism that appears to trigger the applicability of the Directive itself. This is coherent with the findings of the Court in the first part of the decision, where it assessed that the benefits that come with the acquisition by the EU citizen of permanent residence under Article 16(1) of the Directive – thus lifting the duty to fulfil the conditions of Article 7 – extend to the third-country national parent, pursuant to Article 21 of the TFEU.[38] Again, the provision of the Treaty does not confer a right on its own, but because it *extends* the applicability (one could say by analogy) of a provision contained (only) in the Directive. It will be interesting to observe if upcoming judgments will confirm this trend, which has its roots in *Singh* and *Eind*, to use Articles 20 and 21 of the TFEU not as standalone provisions, but rather as means to expand the applicability of the Directive to case law on the residence of non-EU parents.

---

35 Case C-165/14, *Alfredo Rendón Marín v. Administración del Estado*, ECLI:EU:C:2016:675. This case involved two minors, one of whom was a national of Spain, where he had always lived; hence, he was not a 'beneficiary' according to the wording of Directive 2004/38. His sister, however, was a Polish national living in Spain since birth, for whom the Directive was applicable. Their father, a Colombian national, had been rejected a permit of stay in Spain for the reason that he had a criminal record.

36 Case C-247/20, *VI v. Commissioners for Her Majesty's Revenue and Customs*, ECLI:EU:C:2022:177.

37 Ibid., para. 64.

38 Ibid., para. 59.

SECTION IV EXTENSIVE INTERPRETATION OF DIRECTIVE 2004/38

When shifting attention to the third type of cases, dealing with returning EU citizens, it can be observed that the Court's approach significantly diverges from the case law described so far. In *O.B.*,[39] the Court first states that:

> a third-country national who is a family member of a Union citizen cannot invoke, on the basis of [the] directive, a derived right of residence in the Member State of which that citizen is a national.[40]

However, it then adds a reminder that the residence of that EU citizen for a significant period of time in a host Member State together with a third-country national family member confers upon the latter a derived right of residence in the state of which the EU citizen is a national, when this national returns to his/her home country. If this were not the case:

> a worker who is a Union citizen could be discouraged from leaving the Member State of which he is a national in order to pursue gainful employment in another Member State [...].[41]

The foundation of such a right lies, once again, in Article 21 of the TFEU, yet in this case the Court expressly refers to Directive 2004/38 being applicable *by analogy*. As a result, the third-country national is not only entitled to a residence right under the provisions of the Treaty, but the finding also clarifies that the conditions of that residence 'should not, in principle, be more strict than those provided for by Directive 2004/38'.[42] Of course, the right is not unconditional, since it is subject to the fact that 'the residence of the Union citizen in the host Member State has been sufficiently genuine so as to enable that citizen to create or strengthen family life in that Member State', a condition that is left for the referring court to determine. Thus, Article 21(1) of the TFEU does not grant a general and absolute right, applicable solely because of circulation.[43] However, once the conditions for asserting that right are met, the applicant might be able to draw on a wide range of rights and benefits that

---

39 Case C-456/12, *O. v. Minister voor Immigratie, Integratie en Asiel and Minister voor Immigratie, Integratie en Asiel v. B.*, ECLI:EU:C:2014:135.

40 Ibid., para. 40.

41 Ibid., para. 46.

42 Ibid., para. 50.

43 Ibid., para. 51.

derive from the application of the Directive, and that go far beyond the mere right to entry and residence.

The same principle was applied in *Lounes* with reference to an EU national who had exercised her freedom of movement by settling in a host state, the nationality of which she later acquired by naturalisation, thus losing the quality of 'beneficiary' according to Directive 2004/38.[44] It was found that the Directive must apply by analogy to that individual, so that her husband could share his life with his European wife in her host Member State, which had also become her state of nationality.[45] In this case, again, the conditions for granting the derived residence right must not be stricter than those provided for by the Directive.

All these cases share the circumstance that the individuals involved can fully rely on their quality as 'family member' under the meaning of the Directive, applied 'by analogy'. This was indirectly confirmed by the recent judgment in *Chief Appeals Officer and others*, which presented a situation similar to that of *Lounes* (an EU national who had moved to another Member State and later acquired the nationality of that Member State).[46] On that occasion, the Court implied that the EU national's family member who resides in a Member State according to an analogical application of the Directive must also be considered as a family member following the application of Article 7(2) of Regulation 492/2011,[47] which protects a circulating worker from discrimination in access to social advantages, indirectly protecting his/her family members as well. The Court had already confirmed in a previous decision 'that the family members able to benefit indirectly from equal treatment under Regulation No 492/2011 are those family members within the meaning of Directive 2004/38',[48] since nothing suggests that the EU legislation intended to differentiate the

---

44 Case C-165/16, *Toufik Lounes v. Secretary of State for the Home Department*, ECLI:EU:C:2017:862. See comments by, e.g. V. Réveillère, 'Family rights for naturalized EU citizens: *Lounes*' (2018) 55(6) *Common Market Law Review* 1855; P.R. Polak, 'A Commentary on the *Lounes* Case and the Protection of EU Citizens' Rights Post-Brexit' (2018) 44 *Revista General de Derecho Europeo* 190.

45 It should be noted that in *Lounes*, above n. 44, the Court did not require that family life had been created and strengthened before the moment in which the Directive ceased to apply (i.e. the acquisition of new citizenship), distinguishing this case from that of a returning citizen who must have built his/her family life during the period of application of the Directive (i.e. before returning to his/her home country). On this point, see N. Lazzerini, 'Il diritto dei cittadini dell'Unione "circolanti" di condurre una normale vita familiare: stato dell'arte e prospettive' (2024) Special Issue 1 *Quaderni AISDUE* 303.

46 Case C-488/21, *GV v. Chief Appeals Officer and others*, ECLI:EU:C:2023:1013.

47 Council Regulation (EU) 492/2011 of 5 April 2011 on freedom of movement for workers within the Union [2011] OJ L141/1. Article 7(2) prescribes that an EU worker in a host Member State 'shall enjoy the same social and tax advantages as national workers'. On this topic, see D. O'Keeffe, 'Equal Rights for Migrants: the Concept of Social Advantages in Article 7(2), Regulation 1612/68' (1985) 5 *Yearbook of European Law* 93.

48 See Joined Cases C-401/15 to C-403/15, *Depesme and Kerrou*, ECLI:EU:C:2016:955, para. 51.

two categories. The 2023 *Chief Appeals Officer and others* ruling confirms that a family member 'by analogy' must also be considered a family member when the EU citizen exercises his/her right as a worker.

Lastly, there is the fourth type of ECJ decision, in which the Court has extended the notion of family members to adapt them to new conceptions of the family. The first judgment of this kind was the 2018 *Coman* case, in which the ECJ decided to overcome the uncertainties of the EU legislator, which, at the time the Directive was drafted, refrained from expressly attributing a gender-neutral connotation to the notion of 'spouse', thus including a same-sex spouse.[49] The Court, which in this case also applied the Directive by analogy (as Coman was an EU national returning to his Member State and seeking family reunification with his husband), ruled that:

> a Member State cannot rely on its national law as justification for refusing to recognise in its territory, for the sole purpose of granting a derived right of residence to a third-country national, a marriage concluded by that national with a Union citizen of the same sex in another Member State in accordance with the law of that state.[50]

It follows from this assumption that a same-sex marriage, in a situation that falls under the scope of application of the Directive, either directly or by analogy, must be recognised 'for the sole purpose of granting a derived right of residence'. This concise expression might be better rephrased with the wording 'for the purpose of exercising the rights and freedoms that descend from being a family member according to the Directive'.

In 2019, the Court ruled again on the notion of family members in the *SM* case[51] about a child placed under the Algerian kafala system (the provision for adoption or guardianship in Algerian law). On this occasion, the Court excluded that a child placed under kafala falls under the notion of 'direct descendant' of Directive 2004/38, for the reason that the placement does not create any parent–child relationship between them. However, the Court also ruled that the child qualifies as one of the 'other family members' within the

---

49 See 'Amended proposal for a Directive of the European Parliament and of the Council on the right of citizens of the Union and their family members to move and reside freely within the territory of the Member States', COM(2003) 199 final. See also J. Borg-Barthet, 'The Principled Imperative to Recognise Same-Sex Unions in the EU' (2012) 8(2) *Journal of Private International Law* 359.

50 *Coman*, above n. 4, para. 36.

51 Case C-129/18, *SM v. Entry Clearance Officer, UK Visa Section*, ECLI:EU:C:2019:248. For a comprehensive discussion, see C. Peraro, 'L'istituto della kafala quale presupposto per il ricongiungimento familiare con il cittadino europeo: la sentenza della Corte di giustizia nel caso "S.M.C. Entry Clearance Officer"' (2019) 55 *Rivista di diritto internazionale privato e processuale* 319.

meaning of Article 3(2)(a) of the Directive and therefore enjoys the – relatively limited – advantages that go with it.[52]

The second milestone in the extension of the notions of Directive 2004/38 to new family structures is found in the 2021 *Pancharevo* case. This decision tackled the matter of the recognition in Bulgaria of a birth certificate issued in Spain, indicating two mothers (a Bulgarian and a UK national) as parents of a minor. The judgment was based on the assumption that the minor is a Bulgarian national; however, the decision also addressed, although very briefly, the hypothesis that baby Sara might later be found not to be an EU national (as the biological mother was not revealed).[53] In the case that the minor is an EU national, the Court relied on the obligation stemming from Article 4(3) of the Directive[54] to conclude that a Member State is obliged to issue a passport to its own national, the child of a same-sex couple whose birth certificate was legally drawn up in a host Member State, regardless of the fact that the state's own national law requires that a birth certificate is drawn up before an identity card or passport can be issued.[55] Moreover, the mothers of the EU child must:

> pursuant to Article 21 TFEU and Directive 2004/38, [...] be recognised by all Member States as having the right to accompany that child when her right to move and reside freely within the territory of the Member States is being exercised.[56]

In the case that the minor is not an EU national, family unity would still be protected under EU law, due to the presence of the Bulgarian mother. Her wife and her child would have to be considered, respectively, as the spouse and the direct descendant of an EU national 'for the purposes of the exercise of the rights conferred in Article 21(1) TFEU and the secondary legislation relating thereto'.[57]

The principles of *Pancharevo* were reiterated in 2022 in the *Rzecznik Praw Obywatelskich* case[58] in a situation in which all the individuals involved possessed EU nationality. From this case law it can be inferred that in a

---

52 Unlike the other family members, who possess a full – though derived – right to entry and residence, the Directive prescribes that the host Member State is merely obliged to 'facilitate' the entry and residence of the 'other family members' according to Article 3.

53 The nationality of the child was not clear because the identity of the biological mother of the baby was never revealed. It should be noted that the judgment of the Court adopted a different perspective from that of the Opinion of the Advocate General, whose arguments were equally divided between the two hypotheses of baby Sara having or not having Bulgarian citizenship.

54 Article 4(3) of Directive 2004/38 prescribes that 'Member States shall, acting in accordance with their laws, issue to their own nationals, and renew, an identity card or passport stating their nationality'.

55 See *Pancharevo*, above n. 5, para. 45.

56 Ibid., para. 48.

57 Ibid., para. 68.

58 Case C-2/21, *Rzecznik Praw Obywatelskich v. K.S. and Others*, ECLI:EU:C:2022:502.

situation in which the child is an EU national but the parent is not – a case that has not yet been presented to the attention of the Court – that minor, whose filiation cannot be denied for the purpose of the freedom to move and reside, will benefit from the findings of ECJ case law on the residence rights of a third-country parent of an EU minor according to the Treaty.

SECTION V THE PRACTICAL OUTCOMES OF THESE JUDGMENTS AND THE CORRESPONDING OBLIGATIONS OF MEMBER STATES

To draw some initial conclusions, the practical outcomes of the judgments described above seem to differ depending on the type of case. The family members of the static EU citizen hold a derived right to entry and residence which: (i) is drawn from the Treaty; (ii) does not imply the application of Directive 2004/38; and (iii) is subject to the existence of a real risk that the EU national be obliged to leave EU territory (with the burden of proof on the applicant). The same applies to the case of a non-EU parent of an EU minor, although the recent case of *Commissioners for Her Majesty's Revenue and Customs* may cast new light on this subject, as has been discussed.

In the case of an EU national returning to his/her Member State of origin and in the case of a citizen who has acquired the nationality of the host Member State, the derived residence right of the family member also descends from the Treaty, since the Directive is not applicable per se. And yet in these circumstances the Court expressly refers to the Directive being applicable *by analogy*, with some notable consequences. Only in these decisions – unlike in those mentioned above – is it clarified that the entry and residence of the family members involved must be under the same conditions as the entry and residence of a family member under Directive 2004/38. The returning citizen, though, must still prove that family life was created and strengthened during a genuine residence in the host Member State in order to be protected.

Finally, in the cases in which the Court extended the very notion of family member, it clearly applied the Directive as such. These rulings leave no doubt that the same-sex spouse of an EU national, or his/her direct descendant born through medically assisted procreation or surrogacy (as will be explained in Section IV), are, respectively, the spouse and the direct descendant under the Directive. According to the Court, those family members must be recognised as such for the purpose of the exercise of the right to move and reside freely within the territory of the Member States. That right, however, is surrounded by other rights and benefits that come with the application of the Directive, which complete the set of duties that Member States are required to comply with, so that the obligation to recognise a same-sex marriage or homoparentality does not end with the mere issuance of a residence permit.

This implies a range of obligations for the Member States. First of all, these family members will be entitled to a specific type of permit of stay (rather than being generically allowed to reside in a Member State), namely a 'residence card of a family member of a Union citizen', created by the Directive. The issuance of this specific title of residence includes a number of guarantees: (i) the card shall be issued within six months from the date of application;[59] (ii) a certificate proving the application for the residence card shall be issued immediately;[60] (iii) the card is valid for five years and its validity is not affected by temporary absences not exceeding six months in a year;[61] (iv) under some conditions, the family member retains the right of residence even in the event of death or departure of the EU citizen and in the event of divorce, annulment of marriage or termination of registered partnership;[62] (v) expiry of the identity card or passport does not constitute grounds for expulsion from the host Member State;[63] and (vi) decisions restricting the free movement of these subjects are subject to the procedural safeguards contained in the Directive.[64] Plus, the family members who have resided legally for a continuous period of five years in the host Member State acquire, like their EU relatives, the right of permanent residence, which is not subject to the conditions prescribed for a residence shorter than five years.[65] Under some circumstances, the right of permanent residence can be acquired even before five years.[66]

Secondly, a family member under the Directive can extend his/her qualification to other relatives of his/her own. According to Article 2(2) (c) and (d) of the Directive, the notion of family member also includes the direct descendants of the spouse or partner of the EU national, as well as the dependent direct relatives in the ascending line of the spouse or partner. That means, for instance, that the children of a same-sex spouse of an EU citizen from a previous relationship will be entitled to a residence card under the Directive.

---

59 See Article 10(1) of the Directive 2004/38. In practice, however, this deadline is rarely respected. On the duty to respect this deadline, see Case C-246/17, *Diallo*, ECLI:EU:C:2018:499, paras. 32–43.

60 See Directive 2004/38, Article 10(1).

61 See ibid., Article 11, which specifies that the validity of the residence card is not affected by an absence 'for compulsory military service or by one absence of a maximum of twelve consecutive months for important reasons such as pregnancy and childbirth, serious illness, study or vocational training, or a posting in another Member State or a third country'.

62 See ibid., Articles 12 and 13.

63 See ibid., Article 15(2).

64 See ibid., Article 15(1).

65 See ibid., Article 16. This right is crystallised in a permanent residence card, under Article 20.

66 See ibid., Article 17.

Thirdly, as the ECJ has highlighted on several occasions, the residence card 'has a declaratory, as opposed to a constitutive, character'.[67] This means that the granting of such a permit is not intended as:

> a measure giving rise to rights, but as a measure by a Member State serving to prove the individual position of a national of another Member State with regard to provisions of European Union law,[68]

namely a certification of rights that already exist for the person concerned. In addition to this, possession of a valid residence card exempts the family members of the EU national from the visa requirement when they move throughout the EU.[69] The same exemption applies to holders of a permanent residence card.[70]

Most importantly, all family members falling under the meaning stipulated in the Directive are protected by Article 24, which requires equal treatment between them and the nationals of the host Member State. As emerges in Article 24(2), the equal treatment rule expressly extends to social assistance and to maintenance aid for studies, two fields in which Member States have a limited power of derogation.[71]

As regards the non-discrimination principle, this is embodied in other rules, which, in turn, apply to EU nationals and to their family members. As previously mentioned,[72] family members under the Directive benefit from the provision contained in Article 7(2) of Regulation 492/2011 protecting EU workers (and thus, indirectly, their family members) from discrimination in access to social advantages available in the host Member State. The non-discrimination principle is further detailed[73] in Article 4 of Regulation 883/2004,[74] imposing

---

67 See *O.B.*, para. 60

68 See Case C-325/09, *Secretary of State for Work and Pensions v. Maria Dias*, ECLI:EU:C:2011:498, para. 48, and *Diallo*, above n. 59, para. 48.

69 See Article 5(2) of Directive 2004/38.

70 This clarification is needed because Article 5 of Directive 2004/38 expressly refers to the residence card alone. However, the ECJ has made it clear that an interpretation of that provision consistent with the context and the objectives of the legislation of which it forms a part necessarily includes the permanent residence card as well. See Case C-754/18, *Ryanair Designated Activity Company*, ECLI:EU:C:2020:478.

71 The host Member State is not obliged to grant access to social assistance during the first three months of residence or during the longer period provided for in Article 14(4)(b). In addition, the maintenance aid for studies to individuals other than workers, the self-employed, persons who retain such status and members of their families can be delayed until the acquisition of permanent residence.

72 See *Depesme and Kerrou*, above n. 48.

73 See Case C-535/19, *A (Soins de santé publics)*, ECLI:EU:C:2021:595, para. 40.

74 Council Regulation (EC) 883/2004 of 29 April 2004 on the coordination of social security systems [2004] OJ L166/1.

equal treatment in a number of branches of social security, as specified in Article 3(1) of the Regulation.[75]

It follows from these considerations that a Member State is not in fact compelled to acknowledge a certificate of a same-sex marriage or a birth certificate indicating two mothers for the sole purpose of granting right of residence. If the EU national or the family member decide to apply for a benefit such as universal credit or a family unity allowance (both of which have been considered as social assistance benefits under EU law),[76] for instance, the competent public welfare institution of the host state (or of the state of origin of the returning citizen to whom the Directive applies by analogy) must verify the composition of the family unit on presentation of these certificates, the validity of which it will not be in a position to question. The same goes if the EU national's relative needs to prove his/her quality as a family member for the purpose of accessing medical care,[77] and so on.

In this regard, it must be noted that the Directive itself specifies that the possession of a family member residence card or of a certificate attesting the submission of an application for such a card:

> may under no circumstances be made a precondition for the exercise of a right or the completion of an administrative formality, as entitlement to rights may be attested by any other means of proof.[78]

Moreover, the presentation of these certificates benefit from all simplifications prescribed by Regulation (EU) 2016/1191.[79] As a result, it is easy to imagine that these certificates, which some Member States refuse to

---

75 These social branches include sickness benefits, maternity and equivalent paternity benefits, invalidity benefits, old-age benefits, survivors' benefits, benefits in respect of accidents at work and occupational disease, death grants, unemployment benefits, pre-retirement benefits, and family benefits.

76 With regard to the UK's universal credit, see Case C-709/20, *CG v. The Department for Communities in Northern Ireland*, ECLI:EU:C:2021:602; with regard to the Italian family allowance, see Case C-302/19, *Istituto Nazionale della Previdenza Sociale (Prestations familiales pour les titulaires d'un permis unique)*, ECLI:EU:C:2020:957 and Case C-303/19, *Istituto Nazionale della Previdenza Sociale (Prestations familiales pour les résidents de longue durée)*, ECLI:EU:C:2020:958. For the notion of social assistance, see the well-known Case C-333/13, *Dano*, ECLI:EU:C:2014:2358, in which the Court describes this as 'all assistance schemes established by the public authorities […] to which recourse may be had by an individual who does not have resources sufficient to meet his own basic needs and those of his family and who by reason of that fact may, during his period of residence, become a burden on the public finances of the host Member State […]' (para. 63).

77 Which, under some conditions, does fall under the scope of application of Regulation 883/2004: see *A (Soins de santé publics)*, above n. 73, para. 36.

78 Article 25(1) of Directive 2004/38.

79 Council Regulation (EU) 2016/1191 of 6 July 2016 on promoting the free movement of citizens by simplifying the requirements for presenting certain public documents in the European Union [2016] OJ L200/1.

recognise despite being obliged to recognise for the exercise of the right to move and reside of the individuals concerned, will reach the various branches of the public administration of the host state, which will necessarily have to deal with them. The 'functionally oriented' obligation to recognise these certificates will thus require a substantial adaptation capacity on the side of the Member State compelled to recognise these certificates.

In addition to all this it should be noted that on multiple occasions the Court has held that the authorities of a Member State are not allowed to refuse to recognise the name of an EU national who exercised his/her right of free movement, since that refusal is likely to hinder the exercise of the right to move and reside freely in the territory of the Member States.[80] It can be assumed, therefore, that in the case of a returning citizen who has made a same-sex marriage abroad and changed his/her name accordingly, the obligation to recognise that marriage for the purposes of the freedom of circulation will also require the Member State of that EU national to modify its national civil registries in order to update them to the new name of its national. This operation may be quite tricky if the marriage certificate that justifies the modification of the name is not contextually transcribed into these registries.[81] The same applies to the situation of a minor, who must be registered in the Member State of his/her nationality with the name acquired in the Member State where the birth certificate was legally drawn up, even if that name is the combination of the names of two mothers or two fathers.

All in all, it seems fair to say that the consequences of the Court's decisions, however much one may share the spirit of protection of the rights of individuals that the Court wished to impose, are undeniably very impactful on the Member States.

---

80 This principle was pronounced: with reference to the situation of the national of a Member State who had acquired a name in another Member State of which he was also a national, which conflicted with the internal rules of the first Member State (see Case C-148/02, *Garcia Avello*, ECLI:EU:C:2003:539); with reference to the situation of a national of a Member State who had acquired a given name in the state of residence that was not recognised in the state of citizenship (Case C-353/06, *Grunkin und Paul*, ECLI:EU:C:2008:559); and with reference to the situation of an EU national whose name was modified in the Member State of origin but not recognised in the state of residence of which he was also a national (Case C-541/15, *Freitag*, ECLI:EU:C:2017:432).

81 This case is currently pending before the ECJ: Pending Case C-713/23, *Wojewoda Mazowiecki*.

SECTION VI
THE IMPACT OF *PANCHAREVO* ON THE RECOGNITION OF PARENTHOOD RESULTING FROM SURROGACY

Following this overview of the range of rights arising from '*Pancharevo* type' recognition, what can be ascertained about this jurisprudence in reference to whether these principles can also be applied with respect to surrogacy? In the great majority of EU Member States, surrogacy is not legal or, at least, not legally accepted. Still, some Member States do allow it, which could mean that the intentional parents of a child born through surrogacy and registered as the son or daughter of these parents in one Member State could ask for the recognition of that birth certificate in another Member State.[82] It might well happen that the birth certificate drawn up in a third country is recognised in one Member State, which poses the problem of its successive recognition in a second Member State, i.e. of its intra-European circulation.

The European Court of Human Rights (ECtHR) has delivered several decisions[83] and one opinion on this topic.[84] According to the ECtHR, contracting states are obliged to recognise the parenthood relationship between the intentional parents and the child born abroad through surrogacy; however, they remain free to choose the form of such recognition, which might occur through inscription in national civil registries or through adoption.

While Member States are not obliged to fully recognise these certificates, they may be obliged to provide at least functionally oriented recognition. The extension of the *Pancharevo* principle to births occurring through surrogacy, however, is not obvious. It has been challenged by some scholars who have argued that surrogacy would conflict with the values of the Member States that do not allow it to the extent that it would constitute a legitimate cause for

---

82 Surrogacy is legal in Greece and Cyprus; it is not penalised and therefore de facto practised in Belgium, the Netherlands and the Czech Republic. See F. G'Sell, 'La légalisation de la maternité pour autrui à l'étranger: exemples de droit comparé' (2017) 7 *Droit, Sciences et Technologies* 93 and G. Schamps and J. Sosson (eds.), *La gestation pour autrui: vers un encadrement?*, Brussels, Larcier, 2013. See also the Council of Europe, 'Maternité de substitution: Addendum aux réponses au questionnaire sur l'accès à la procréation médicalement assistée (PMA) et sur le droit à la connaissance de ses origines pour les enfants nés après PMA', DH-BIO/INF (2016) 4 Addendum (30 November 2021) <https://rm.coe.int/inf-2016-4-addendum-update-october-2021-f-/1680a5655f> and the *Direction de l'initiative parlementaire et des délégations* (of the French Senate), 'Note sur la gestation pour autrui', LC 327 (October 2023) <https://www.senat.fr /lc/lc327/lc327.pdf>.

83 The most well-known decisions are *Mennesson v. France*, no. 65192/11, ECtHR, 26 June 2014; *Labassée v. France*, no. 65941/11, ECtHR, 26 June 2014; and *Paradiso and Campanelli v. Italy*, no. 25358/12, ECtHR, 24 January 2017.

84 *Advisory opinion concerning the recognition in domestic law of a legal parent-child relationship between a child born through a gestational surrogacy arrangement abroad and the intended mother*, no. P16-2018-001, ECtHR, 10 April 2019.

restriction of the freedom of movement established by EU law in the form of an overriding reason of general interest.[85] Yet there are three arguments that could be made to support that *Pancharevo* should apply irrespective of the reproductive techniques used and, therefore, to surrogacy.

The first is a literal argument. Nowhere in *Pancharevo*, nor in the later case of *Rzecznik Praw Obywatelskich*, does the Court dwell on the description of the material circumstances of the birth of the minor involved, or on the type of reproductive technique used. Indeed, it is quite the opposite: in *Rzecznik Praw Obywatelskich*, the Court argued that 'the Spanish authorities lawfully established that there was a parent-child relationship, biological or legal, between S.R.S.-D. and her two parents',[86] thus showing its indifference to the origin of that relationship.

The second – and most relevant – argument is logical. In *Pancharevo*, the Court extensively addresses the issue of the possible violation of public policy and of the national identity of Bulgaria, concluding that the mere obligation to issue an identity card or a passport to a child whose birth certificate designates two persons of the same sex as her parents, and to recognise the parent–child relationship in the context of the child's exercise of her rights to move and reside in the EU, 'does not undermine the national identity or pose a threat to the public policy of that Member State'.[87] Indeed:

> Such an obligation does not require the Member State […] to provide, in its national law, for the parenthood of persons of the same sex, or to recognise, for purposes other than the exercise of the rights which that child derives from EU law, the parent-child relationship […].[88]

The Court's reasoning on the alleged violation of public policy and the national identity of Bulgaria did not focus on the extent of the possible undermining of that Member State by homoparentality, but rather on the incidence of the obligations it imposes on its legal order. These consequences remain identical irrespective of the events leading to the drawing up of a birth certificate in a Member State. Hence, it seems logical to conclude that a Member State required to grant recognition to a homoparental filiation for the sole exercise of the rights to move and reside will not be allowed to investigate the circumstances of the birth, which are relevant only to full recognition of all its civil effects.

Lastly, a systematic argument can also be made, based on the consistency of the conduct of EU institutions taken as a whole. The proposed but deadlocked

85 See E. di Napoli, G. Biagioni, O. Feraci, R. Calvigioni and P. Pasqualis, above n. 2.
86 See *Rzecznik Praw Obywatelskich*, above n. 58, para. 42.
87 See *Pancharevo*, above n. 5, para. 56.
88 Ibid., para. 57.

Regulation on parenthood indicates that it shall apply, if it is adopted, 'irrespective of how the child was conceived or born and irrespective of the child's type of family'.[89] The aim of the EU legislation is to introduce a system of private international law that leads to the full recognition of parenthood, including that resulting from surrogacy. *A fortiori*, then, it is not surprising that the Court requires its *Pancharevo*-type recognition to also apply to parenthood through surrogacy. Of course, one could argue that recognition under the proposed Regulation remains subject – unlike functionally oriented recognition – to the possibility of invoking the limits of public policy. However, in the text of the proposal, those limits appear to be massively watered down.[90] All evidence thus suggests that in the future, children born through surrogacy will be able to benefit from the judgments of the Court of Justice.

---

89 Recital 21 of the 'Proposal for a Council Regulation on jurisdiction, applicable law, recognition of decisions and acceptance of authentic instruments in matters of parenthood and on the creation of a European Certificate of Parenthood', COM(2022) 695 final, above n. 8.

90 See ibid., Article 22.

CHAPTER 5
EUROPEAN VALUES AND THE SCOPE OF EU CITIZENSHIP LAW: LOGICAL AVOIDANCE OR MUTUAL INFLUENCE?

Mathieu Rouy*

SECTION I
INTRODUCTION

The aim of this chapter is to analyse the existing or the potential relationship between the scope of EU citizenship and European values. The study of this relationship can be seen as both obvious and complex. Obvious, because these two concepts are naturally linked. The very idea of citizenship refers to belonging to a community, which is itself connected to certain shared values. The relationship between European citizenship and values can be seen in Article 3(5) of the Treaty of the European Union (TEU):[1] 'In its relations with the wider world, the Union shall uphold and promote its values and interests and contribute to the protection of its citizens'.

However, studying the scope of EU citizenship through the lens of European values is also complex for different reasons. One is manifest: the European Court of Justice (ECJ) has never referred to the values enshrined in Article 2 of the TEU when defining the scope of EU citizenship provisions. Moreover, the scope of European citizenship and of European values is quite different. The first is theoretically limited, although the second is potentially unlimited.[2] Whereas most EU citizenship provisions only apply to nationals of a Member State who can demonstrate a link with EU law, Article 2 of the TEU seems to be applied even if the infringement has no connection with EU law. There is

* PhD in EU Law, Research fellow at EDIEC, Jean Moulin Lyon 3 University.

1 Consolidated Version of the Treaty on European Union [2008] OJ C115/13.

2 On the scope of Article 2 of the TEU, see L.D. Spieker, *EU Values Before the Court of Justice: Foundations, Potential, Risks*, Oxford, Oxford University Press, 2023, p. 64.

thus a risk of restricting the scope of Article 2 of the TEU by linking it to the more limited European citizenship provisions.

Yet there may be added value in examining the area of citizenship in light of European values. Values are both a foundation (Article 2 of the TEU) and an objective of the EU (Article 3 of the TEU). They could therefore be seen as an argument for a certain interpretation of the scope of European citizenship[3]. While the aim of this chapter is not to provide an explicit and autonomous criterion for this scope, it seeks to explore whether EU values can constitute a principle guiding, even implicitly, the delimitation of European citizenship.

Section II looks at how a reading of the Court of Justice's case law reveals a historical avoidance of European values when defining the scope of EU citizenship. Yet as investigated in Section III, it seems possible to detect, in various judgments, a potential influence of European values on the delimitation of EU citizenship.

SECTION II
EU VALUES AND THE SCOPE OF EU CITIZENSHIP: A HISTORICAL AVOIDANCE

Despite the links sometimes claimed between European citizenship and values, the ECJ has tended to avoid these, preferring a purely functionalist approach to the scope of EU citizenship.

§ 1. THE CLAIMED LINKS WITH VALUES IN THE DEFINITION OF EU CITIZENSHIP

Values have sometimes been linked to EU citizenship in defining the scope of EU law, both by various Advocates General and in different doctrinal proposals. Firstly, references to European values can be found in multiple Opinions of Advocates General to interpret EU law and have in common that they link fundamental rights (which are among the values listed in Article 2 of the TEU) and European citizenship in order to justify a broader vision of the field of EU law.

For example, in the context of the free movement of workers, in 1993 Advocate General Jacobs considered that a worker moving to another Member

[3] Thus, the ECJ has recently invoked Article 10(1) TEU, which gives concrete form to the value of democracy referred to in Article 2 TEU, in its broad interpretation of the scope of Article 22 TFEU. See, Case C-808/21, *Commission v. Czech Republic*, ECLI:EU:C:2024:962, para 161 and Case C-814/21, *Commission v. Poland*, ECLI:EU:C:2024:963, para 158.

State should be treated according to a common code of fundamental values: 'he is entitled to say "civis europeus sum" and to invoke that status in order to oppose any violation of his fundamental rights'.[4] The Advocate General's Opinion is of interest; although it does not make the violation of a fundamental right or value a trigger for the application of EU law, it would potentially have the effect of greatly increasing the scope of the latter. Once a national had made use of his or her freedom of movement, it would allow him or her to invoke an infringement of a fundamental right, irrespective of the finding of a possible obstacle to freedom of movement, and even against a national measure that does not constitute an obstacle to freedom of movement.

This idea was further developed by Advocate General Poiares Maduro in the 2008 *Centro Europa 7* case:[5] 'Protection of the "common code" of fundamental rights [...] constitutes an existential requirement for the EU legal order'.[6] Further:

> serious and persistent violations which highlight a problem of systemic nature in the protection of fundamental rights in the Member State at issue, would, [...] qualify as violations of the rules on free movement, by virtue of the direct threat they would pose to the transnational dimension of European citizenship and to the integrity of the EU legal order.[7]

Like Advocate General Jacobs's Opinion, that of Advocate General Poiares Maduro would have the potential effect of greatly extending the scope of EU law by making it possible, in certain circumstances, to invoke the infringement of a fundamental right independently of any obstacle to freedom of movement.

Nevertheless, these two Opinions do not call into question the need to circulate as a condition for the activation of citizens' rights. This issue was key in the *Ruiz Zambrano* case.[8] In that case, the Court had to rule on the recognition of a right of residence for the parents of EU citizens who had never lived outside their country of birth. Without giving her Opinion in its entirety here,[9] Advocate General Sharpston used different reasons to argue for a decorrelation between the protection offered by EU law and the exercise of mobility by an EU citizen. The necessity to protect fundamental rights had a central place in her argumentation. In particular, she questioned the possibility of invoking the 'fundamental right to family life [enshrined in European Union law] independently of any other provision of [that] law'.[10] Indeed, the

4 Opinion of AG Jacobs, Case C-168/91, *Konstantinidis*, ECLI:EU:C:1992:504, para. 46.
5 Opinion of AG Poiares Maduro, Case C-380/05, *Centro Europea 7*, ECLI:EU:C:2007:505.
6 Ibid., para. 19.
7 Ibid., para. 22.
8 Case C-34/09, *Ruiz Zambrano*, ECLI:EU:C:2011:124.
9 Opinion of AG Sharpston, Case C-34/09, *Ruiz Zambrano*, ECLI:EU:C:2010:560.
10 Ibid., para. 151.

Advocate General argued that the application of fundamental rights should no longer be subordinate to the applicability of EU law, but 'rather on *the existence and scope of a material EU competence*',[11] even if the competence has not been exercised. The main reason was axiological and linked to Article 2 of the TEU. After quoting Article 2, the Advocate General stated that:

> In a European Union founded on fundamental rights and the rule of law, protection should not depend on the legislative initiative of the institutions and the political process. Such contingent protection of rights is the antithesis of the way in which contemporary democracies legitimise the authority of the State.[12]

These examples illustrate how different Advocates General have invoked – directly or indirectly – European values in order to change the interpretation of the scope of EU law, particularly in the context of the protection of the fundamental rights of European citizens, and to overcome the 'purely internal rule'.

These Opinions have been supplemented by various doctrinal proposals. The most well-known is that made in 2012 to 'reverse' the *Solange* ruling.[13] This sought to link 'the substance of rights' settled in the *Ruiz Zambrano* case to the essence of fundamental rights and Article 2 of the TEU.[14] In this sense, a violation of the essence of fundamental rights committed by a Member State, even outside the scope of the Charter of Fundamental Rights of the European Union (CFR),[15] could constitute a violation of EU citizenship and thus be brought within the scope of EU law. This argument proposed to 'overturn' the *Solange* case.[16] Taking up the ruling of the German Constitutional Court in the *Solange* case, fundamental rights would not be reviewed outside the scope of EU law as long as it could be presumed that the essence of these rights was guaranteed. However, this ruling could be rebutted if it were shown that the national legal order did not adequately protect fundamental rights, particularly in the case of systemic violations. This proposal has not been taken up in

---

11 Ibid., para. 163.

12 Ibid., para. 165.

13 See below n. 15 and A. von Bogdandy, M. Kottman, C. Antpöhler, J. Dickschen, S. Hentrei and M. Smrkolj, 'Reverse *Solange* – Protecting the Essence of Fundamental Rights against EU Member States' (2012) 49(2) *Common Market Law Review* 489.

14 Many authors have argued for fundamental rights to be included in the substance of EU citizens' rights: see, e.g. M. van den Brink, 'EU Citizenship and EU Fundamental Rights: Taking EU Citizenship Rights Seriously?' (2012) 39(2) *Legal Issues of Economic Integration* 273. The opposite position is taken in M. van den Brink, 'EU citizenship and (fundamental) rights: Empirical, normative, and conceptual problems' (2019) 25 *European Law Journal* 21. More generally, see A. Yong, *The Rise and Decline of Fundamental Rights in EU Citizenship*, Oxford, Hart Publishing, 2019.

15 Charter of Fundamental Rights of the European Union [2016] OJ C202/389.

16 See BVerfG, Order of 28 May 1974, 2 BvL 52/71, *Solange I*; Order of 22 October 1986, 2 BvR 197/83, *Solange II*.

ECJ case law and has been criticised by other authors.[17] The main criticism is that it does not fit the strict vision of the 'substance of rights' of EU citizens, which seems to refer only to the rights in Article 20 of the Treaty on the Functioning of the European Union (TFEU).[18] Moreover, it would run the risk of calling into question the allocation of authority between the EU and the Member States and would entail an undue extension of the scope of EU law. Considering these criticisms and given developments in case law, an amended proposal was presented in 2019, still based on reversing the *Solange* model, but no longer on Article 20 of the TFEU.[19] Other authors have sought to improve on this by arguing for the establishment of a principle of non-regression, which would justify the application of the CFR even in purely internal situations.[20]

§2. THE IGNORED LINKS WITH VALUES IN THE DEFINITION OF EU CITIZENSHIP

Despite the occasional links between European citizenship and values evoked by different Advocates General and certain authors, the Court has never referred to these when interpreting the scope of application. Rather, the broadening of the scope of EU citizenship has been justified by the desire to protect or promote the effectiveness of the objectives of EU law and the useful effect of the rights attached to EU citizenship. The following observations on three types of cases are not exhaustive but aim to illustrate the approach taken by the ECJ in defining the scope of EU citizenship provisions. What these three examples have in common is that they demonstrate the Court's flexible approach to the requirement of a cross-border element based on functionalist considerations.

Among the most obvious illustrations are the cases following the *Ruiz Zambrano* ruling.[21] In these cases, the Court found that EU law could apply in

---

17 K. Lenaerts and J.A. Gutiérrez-Fons, 'Epilogue on EU citizenship: Hopes and Fears' in D. Kochenov (ed.), *EU Citizenship and Federalism: The Role of Rights*, Cambridge, Cambridge University Press, 2017, pp. 751–81; L.D. Spieker, see above n. 2, p. 192.

18 Consolidated Version of the Treaty on the Functioning of the European Union [2016] OJ C202/47.

19 A. von Bogdandy and L.D. Spieker, 'Countering the judicial silencing of critics: Article 2 TEU values, reverse *Solange*, and the responsibilities of national judges' (2019) 15(3) *European Constitutional Law Review* 391.

20 D. Kostakopoulou, 'Justice, individual empowerment and the principle of non-regression in the European Union' (2021) 46(1) *European Law Review* 92.

21 There is a plethora of case law related to this, but see, e.g. Case C-434/09, *McCarthy*, ECLI:EU:C:2011:277; Case C-256/11, *Dereci*, ECLI:EU:C:2011:734; Case C-133/15, *Chavez-Vilchez*, ECLI:EU:C:2017:354; Case C-82/16, *K.A.*, ECLI:EU:C:2018:308; Case C-836/18, *Subdelegación del Gobierno en Ciudad Real*, ECLI:EU:C:2020:119; Joined Cases C-451/19 and C-532/19, *Subdelegación del Gobierno en Toledo*, ECLI:EU:C:2022:354; and Case C-459/20, *Staatssecretaris van Justitie en Veiligheid*, ECLI:EU:C:2023:499.

the state of nationality of an EU citizen, even if the citizen has never exercised his or her freedom of movement. This ruling allows a citizen's family members to be granted right of residence if the EU citizen is obliged to leave the territory of the EU as a whole. The ECJ specified that this application was justified in order to avoid the loss of the enjoyment of citizens' rights. But it is important to note that in these cases, a major element of the justification of the ECJ is governed by the argument of not undermining the effectiveness of EU citizenship status and of Article 20 of the TFEU.

In the *Lounes* case,[22] the Court found that a national of a Member State who has resided in another Member State before acquiring nationality in the latter cannot result in the inapplicability of EU law and the refusal of the right of residence. According to Article 3(1) of Directive 2004/38,[23] this text does not apply in the citizen's state of nationality. Otherwise, the Directive must be applied by analogy via Article 21 of the TFEU. For the Court:

> a national of one Member State who has moved to and resides in another Member State cannot be denied that right merely because he subsequently acquires the nationality of the second Member State in addition to his nationality of origin, otherwise the effectiveness of Article 21(1) TFEU would be undermined.[24]

Moreover:

> if the rights conferred on Union citizens by Article 21(1) TFEU are to be effective, citizens in a situation such as Ms Ormazabal's must be able to continue to enjoy, in the host Member State, the rights arising under that provision, after they have acquired the nationality of that Member State in addition to their nationality of origin and, in particular, must be able to build a family life with their third-country-national spouse, by means of the grant of a derived right of residence to that spouse.[25]

Again, the justification of the ECJ is principally based on functionalist considerations and the goal of ensuring the effectiveness of citizens' rights.

More recently, the *Generalstaatsanwaltschaft Berlin* case[26] concerned the situation of a national of one Member State (Romania) residing in another Member State (Germany) who had acquired Romanian nationality when he was already residing in Germany. The ECJ confirmed the established principle

---

22 Case C-165/16, *Lounes*, ECLI:EU:C:2017:862.

23 Council Directive 2004/38/EC of 29 April 2004 on the right of citizens of the Union and their family members to move and reside freely within the territory of the Member States [2004] OJ L158/77.

24 *Lounes*, above n. 21, para. 53.

25 Ibid., para. 60.

26 Case C-398/19, *Generalstaatsanwaltschaft Berlin*, ECLI:EU:C:2020:1032.

that 'by virtue of having Union citizenship, a national of a Member State residing in another Member State is entitled to rely on Article 21(1) TFEU'.[27] Above all:

> The fact that [a] Union citizen acquired the nationality of a Member State and, therefore, Union citizenship, only at a time when he or she was already residing in a Member State other than that of which he or she subsequently became a national[28]

is not such as to render EU citizenship inapplicable. The contrary interpretation 'would undermine the effectiveness' of the status of EU citizenship.[29]

Other examples could be given, but the key element of these different solutions remains the enlistment of effectiveness and a pragmatic vision of the cross-border element. In other words, if the Court of Justice has declared EU citizenship law applicable, even in apparent purely internal situations, this has had seemingly nothing to do with the objective of protecting or promoting European values. The Court has usually avoided these implications and focused on purely functionalist considerations linked to the protection of EU objectives and, more specifically, to the effectiveness of EU citizenship. The interpretation of the Court is thus a 'consequentialist' approach. The applicability of EU law is determined primarily by the aim of ensuring or avoiding an 'effect' rather than by a formal interpretation of the applicability criteria, in particular the cross-border element. In a way, the ECJ considers the scope of application as a tool to effectively construct the status of EU citizen, rather than to protect European values.

Three important points should be made. Firstly, the ECJ's functionalist approach is, of course, not limited to the case of EU citizenship. It is more broadly linked to the teleological approach that has governed ECJ rulings, particularly when it interprets the scope of EU law.[30] Competition law and data protection are two other major illustrations of the broad interpretation of the scope of EU law justified by the aim to guarantee the effectiveness of EU legislation.[31]

Secondly, this pragmatic and functionalist approach leads to fragmentation of the field of application by multiplying the hypotheses of applicability of EU law, and to a dilution of this by contributing to its casuistic character, which makes it very difficult to clearly delineate the scope of EU citizenship.

---

27 Ibid., para. 30.

28 Ibid., para. 31.

29 Ibid.

30 K. Lenaerts and J.A. Gutiérrez-Fons, *Les méthodes d'interprétation de la Cour de justice de l'Union européenne*, Brussels, Bruylant, 2020.

31 More broadly, see T. Marzal, 'Le champ d'application territorial du droit de l'Union européenne' in L. Clément-Wilz (ed.), *Le rôle politique de la Cour de justice de l'Union européenne*, Brussels, Bruylant, 2018, pp. 101–20.

Finally, a functionalist approach is not always beneficial to the citizen. The considerations related to the objectives of Directive 2004/38 may result in a narrow vision of the scope of application.[32] This is particularly true in consideration of the scope of equal treatment. Thus, in the *Dano* ruling,[33] the Court of Justice limited the personal scope of equal treatment to citizens with lawful residence based on Directive 2004/38.[34] The Court held that to allow citizens without right of residence to claim the right to equal treatment in respect of social benefits:

> would run counter to an objective of the directive, set out in recital 10 [...], namely preventing Union citizens who are nationals of other Member States from becoming an unreasonable burden on the social assistance system [...].[35]

Here, the enlistment of the objective of the law as set out in the preamble to the Directive leads to a narrower scope of application. This forms part of a teleological interpretation that:

> can also serve to highlight the objectives pursued by the Union legislator, in order to prevent the Court from interpreting the Union act in question beyond those objectives, on pain of overstepping the line separating the judicial from the political.[36]

Yet despite the functionalist interpretation of the scope of EU citizenship law, there is a growing emphasis on fundamental rights in the Court's delimitation of the scope of EU citizenship. For example, Articles 7 and 24 of the CFR occupy a central, if ambivalent, place in ECJ case law, particularly in the context of assessing the relationship of dependence that makes it possible to determine whether a citizen is obliged to leave the territory of the Union.[37]

---

32 K. Lenaerts and J.A. Gutiérrez-Fons, above n. 29, p. 59.

33 Case C-333/13, *Dano*, ECLI:EU:C:2014:2358.

34 On this point, see N. Nic Shuibhne, '"What I tell you three times is true": Lawful residence and equal treatment after *Dano*' (2016) 23(6) *Maastricht Journal of European and Comparative Law* 908.

35 *Dano*, above n. 32, para. 74.

36 K. Lenaerts and J.A. Gutiérrez-Fons, above n. 29, p. 69 (translation by M. Rouy).

37 See, e.g. *Chavez-Vilchez*, above n. 20, para. 70. On the evaluation of the dependency relationship in ECJ case law, see F. Ristuccia, 'Ties that bind and ties that compel: dependency and the *Ruiz Zambrano* doctrine' (2023) 60(5) *Common Market Law Review* 1227.

The Court has also increased its references to the social integration of the citizen.[38] For example in *Lounes*, the Court found that:

> the rights conferred on a Union citizen by Article 21(1) TFEU, including the derived rights enjoyed by his family members, are intended, amongst other things, to promote the gradual integration of the Union citizen concerned in the society of the host Member State.[39]

As such:

> it would be contrary to the underlying logic of gradual integration that informs Article 21(1) TFEU to hold that such citizens, who have acquired rights under that provision as a result of having exercised their freedom of movement, must forgo those rights – in particular the right to family life in the host Member State – because they have sought, by becoming naturalised in that Member State, to become more deeply integrated in the society of that State.[40]

But this has often been seen as an instrumentalisation and a further illustration of the functionalist interpretation of the scope of application. These elements are often mentioned to reinforce the aim of promoting the effectiveness of EU objectives and are not protected per se. However, it is worth asking whether ECJ case law shows a broader evolution of the scope of application of EU law, characterised by an (implicit) influence of European values.

SECTION III
EU VALUES AND THE SCOPE OF EU CITIZENSHIP: A POTENTIAL INFLUENCE

Recent case law seems to demonstrate that the enlistment of fundamental rights and the concrete situation of the citizen in the definition of the scope of application of EU law is no longer totally instrumental. This may reveal a more concrete influence of values on citizenship. This section examines signs of this new vision of the scope of application and considers its consequences.

---

38 On this point, see S. Barbou des Places, 'The Integrated Person in EU Law' in L. Azoulai, S. Barbou des Places and E. Pataut (eds.), *Constructing the Person in EU Law: Rights, Roles, Identities*, Oxford, Hart Publishing, 2016, pp. 179–202.

39 *Lounes*, above n. 21, para. 56.

40 Ibid., para. 58.

§ 1. THE SIGNS OF A NEW VISION OF THE SCOPE OF EU CITIZENSHIP LAW

Recent rulings suggest that the scope of citizenship is no longer restricted to a purely functionalist interpretation. Clearly, the latter has not disappeared, but, in parallel, ECJ case law shows a more ontological dimension. Some authors have argued that ECJ case law reveals an 'integrity approach' to the scope of application.[41] This implies an important paradigm shift. This line of thinking argues that the applicability of EU law is justified in case law 'not as resulting from the EU's functional needs, but because of the nature of the EU as a bound community, concretely localized'[42] and defined by certain values. This idea may be transposed to the case of EU citizenship. Indeed, the applicability of EU citizenship law seems to be increasingly justified by the citizen's place in the community of belonging that constitutes the EU, and by the goal of protecting the citizen as well as this community of belonging. In this reading, EU values play an implicit but major role. While the influence of European values is principally found in the definition of the scope of Article 20 of the TFEU, these values seem to be increasingly important in other areas of EU citizenship law. Three main examples illustrate this: the territory of the EU, the doctrine of the substance of rights, and the vulnerability of EU citizens.

I. VALUES AND THE TERRITORY OF THE EU

One of the main points made by the ECJ in the *Ruiz Zambrano* case to justify the applicability of EU law in circumstances that appear purely internal is to avoid a situation in which citizens would have to leave the territory of the EU. This idea was reinforced in the *Chavez-Vilchez* case, in which the Court found concretely a 'right to stay within the territory of the European Union'.[43] The Court has also recently added that the consequences for a citizen of being prevented from entering a state within the territory must be regarded as analogous to those flowing from being compelled to leave this territory.[44]

This interesting argument should not be underestimated. Usually, the territory of the EU refers to the scope of application of the EU, which is

[41] T. Marzal, 'From World Actor to Local Community: Territoriality and the Scope of Application of EU Law' in L. Azoulai (ed.), *European Union Law and Forms of Life: Madness or Malaise?*, Hart Publishing, forthcoming; T. Marzal, 'The territorial reach of European Union law: a private international law enquiry into the European Union's spatial identity' (2024) 73(1) *International & Comparative Law Quarterly* 29.

[42] T. Marzal, 'From World Actor to Local Community: Territoriality and the Scope of Application of EU Law', above n. 40.

[43] *Chavez-Vilchez*, above n. 20, paras. 42 and 44.

[44] *Staatssecretaris van Justitie en Veiligheid*, above n. 20.

defined objectively as the sum of the territories of the Member States. But here, the concept of 'territory of the Union' seems to be something different, independent from the geographical territories of the Member States. In fact, it should be understood in a metaphorical sense, representing a common community of values.[45] The consequence of this is important. According to L. Azoulai:

> leaving European territory means not only leaving Europe in the geographical sense, it also means leaving a community of ideals and values, it means being deprived of a certain mode of existence corresponding to the standards of European society.[46]

In other words, it is because an EU citizen is part of a community of belonging bound by certain values and materialised by the territory of the EU that he or she must be protected by EU law from being forced to leave this territory or being prevented from entering it.

This reading is also illustrated by the case law relating to the extradition of citizens to a third country. In *Petruhhin* and subsequent judgments,[47] the Court of Justice found that the extradition of a citizen of a Member State could be interpreted with regard to Articles 18 and 21 of the TFEU. Although the right to remain in the EU is not expressly mentioned, the idea seems to be the same: to prevent EU citizens from being forced to leave this territory and its community of values. This is directly apparent in the comments of ECJ President Lenaerts in one of his articles on this line of case law:[48]

> The EU is much more than its internal market. It aims to establish a European area of shared values, such as respect for democracy, fundamental rights, and the rule of law [...]. The feeling of freedom and security could be threatened when a Union

---

45 On this point, see L. Azoulai, 'Transfiguring European Citizenship: From Member State Territory to Union Territory' in D. Kochenov (ed.), *EU Citizenship and Federalism: The Role of Rights*, Cambridge, Cambridge University Press, 2017, pp. 178–203; N. Nic Shuibhne, 'The "territory of the Union" in EU Citizenship Law: charting a route from parallel to integrated narratives' (2019) 38(1) *Yearbook of European Law* 267; H. Kroeze, 'EU citizenship and family reunification: the evolving concept of a European Union territory' in D. Kostakopoulou and D. Thym (eds.), *Research Handbook on Union Citizenship Law and Policy: Navigating Challenges and Crises*, Cheltenham, Edward Elgar Publishing, 2022, pp. 165–83.

46 L. Azoulai, above n. 44, p. 181.

47 Case C-182/15, *Petruhhin*, ECLI:EU:C:2016:630; Case C-191/16, *Pisciotti*, ECLI:EU:C:2018:222; Case C-247/17, *Raugevicius*, ECLI:EU:C:2018:898; Case C-897/19 PPU, *I.N.*, ECLI:EU:C:2020:262; *Generalstaatsanwaltschaft Berlin*, above n. 25; Case C-237/21, *Generalstaatsanwaltschaft München*, ECLI:EU:C:2022:1017.

48 K. Lenaerts, 'La dimension extérieure de la citoyenneté de l'Union dans le contexte de l'extradition' in E. Bribosia, N. Joncheray, A. Navasartian and A. Weyembergh (eds.), *L'Europe au Kaléidoscope: Liber Amicorum Marianne Dony*, Brussels, Éditions de l'Université de Bruxelles, 2019, pp. 442–55.

> citizen who has exercised his or her right to free movement is forced to leave the territory of the Union and, consequently, this area of shared values.[49]

With the reference to EU territory, the definition of the scope of application of EU citizenship becomes not purely functionalist but linked to the aim of protecting the citizen's place in a community based on certain values.

II. VALUES AND THE SUBSTANCE OF RIGHTS OF EU CITIZENSHIP

More than the reference to the 'territory of the Union', the formula relating to the deprivation of the effective enjoyment of the substance of rights attached to the status of EU citizen has been noted and questioned by many observers.[50] Two main questions can reasonably be raised. On the one hand, the criterion of the substance of rights involves a clarification of the content of the rights enshrined in this status. On the other, it is necessary to clarify the degree of deprivation of the enjoyment of these rights that is likely to trigger protection under Article 20 of the TFEU. The rulings in case law illustrate a narrow conception of the criterion of the substance of these rights. The deprivation of the effective enjoyment of rights attached to the status of citizen has been found only in 'very specific situations', when the citizen is forced 'to leave the territory of the Union taken as a whole'. In fact, the Court of Justice's interpretation of the criterion of the substance of rights can reasonably be described as 'minimalist'.[51] Moreover, the Court has explicitly linked the deprivation of the essential rights attached to the status of citizen to the deprivation of the potential exercise of freedom of movement. This is explicitly stated in the *Iida* case, in which the Court found that the situations in which Article 20 of the TFEU is intended to apply are intrinsically linked to 'the

---

49 Ibid., p. 441 (translation by M. Rouy).

50 See, e.g. K. Hailbronner and D. Thym, 'Case C-34/09, *Gerardo Ruiz Zambrano v Office national de l'emploi (ONEm)*' (2011) 48 *Common Market Law Review* 1253, 1256: 'given the autonomy of the substance of rights benchmark, its material scope is crucial for the immediate impact of the judgement *Ruiz Zambrano*'. See also D. Kochenov, 'The right to have *what* rights? EU citizenship in need of clarification' (2013) 19 *European Law Journal* 502; M. van den Brink, 'The origins and the potential federalising effects of the substance of rights test' in D. Kochenov (ed.), *EU Citizenship and Federalism: The Role of Rights*, Cambridge, Cambridge University Press, 2017, pp. 85–106. More recently, see H. Kroeze and P. Van Elsuwege, 'Revisiting *Ruiz Zambrano*: A Never Ending Story?' (2021) 23(1) *European Journal of Migration and Law* 1; M. van den Brink, 'Is it time to abolish the substance of EU Citizenship rights test?' (2021) 23(1) *European Journal of Migration and Law* 13.

51 M. van den Brink, 'The origins and the potential federalising effects of the substance of rights test', above n. 49, p. 86.

freedom of movement of a Union citizen'.[52] In other words, the protection offered by Article 20 of the TFEU appears to be justified above all by the goal of protecting the (future) prospect of a citizen exercising his or her freedom of movement, which would be rendered impossible by his or her departure from EU territory.[53] Consequently, the criterion of the substance of rights, which in principle is limited to the rights listed in Article 20(2) of the TFEU, seems in practice to be limited to the protection of freedom of movement within EU territory.

This idea is open to criticism, and a 'positive' interpretation of the substance of rights, detached from the sole obligation to leave EU territory, seems possible.[54] This is based on the idea that if the substance of rights can only be based on those explicitly mentioned in Article 20(2) of the TFEU, it must take into account all of those rights. Moreover, the fact that the substance of citizens' rights is based on Article 20(2) of the TFEU does not prevent other provisions of the Treaty or the CFR from being taken into account. Indeed, it is possible to understand the substance of rights as a more substantial criterion, linked to a core of rights that would allow citizens to live in dignified conditions associated with the substance of a European identity.[55]

III. VALUES AND THE VULNERABILITY OF AN EU CITIZEN

A reading of ECJ case law also shows that the vulnerability of a citizen is increasingly, if often implicitly, taken into account as a justification for the applicability of EU law. It is no longer simply a question of making EU law applicable in order to avoid a citizen being subject to the legal order of a third country, but of ensuring that someone who is apparently outside the scope of EU law is nevertheless protected by it due to his or her vulnerability. The

---

52 Case C-40/11, *Iida*, ECLI:EU:C:2012:691, para. 72.

53 S. Reynolds, 'Exploring the "intrinsic connection" between free movement and the genuine enjoyment test: reflections on EU citizenship after *Iida*' (2013) 38(3) *European Law Review* 376; P.J. Neuvonen, 'EU citizenship and its "very specific" essence: *Rendón Marín* and *CS*' (2017) 54 *Common Market Law Review* 1201, 1210–11: 'it appears more as a revised version of the older test, according to which "any limitation on EU citizens' rights to free movement and residence fall within the scope of EU law", than as a new test as to what it takes for EU citizenship to be de facto effective for its holder. [...] Although the rights to free movement and residence seem to form the protected core of EU citizenship rights in "very specific situations"'.

54 A. Bouveresse and A. Iliopoulou-Penot, 'Introductory remarks: Defending the added value of European citizenship in the face of persisting criticism' in A. Bouveresse, A. Iliopoulou-Penot and J. Rondu (eds.), *La citoyenneté européenne, quelle valeur ajoutée? European Citizenship: what added value?*, Brussels, Bruylant, 2023, pp. 11–36, pp. 30–31.

55 Ibid.

vulnerability of a citizen may therefore serve as another key to understanding certain interpretations of the Court of Justice.[56]

Again, the paradigmatic illustration is the *Ruiz Zambrano* case. To trigger the application of a right of residence in EU territory, the Court specified that the relationship between the EU citizen and the member of his family asking for residence in the citizen's state of nationality must be defined by a relationship of dependency.[57] Behind this condition of dependence, it is ultimately the citizen's vulnerability that justifies his or her need to be protected by EU law.[58] The consideration is in some ways 'ethical'[59] and may refer to the goal of ensuring the dignity of citizens set out in Article 2 of the TEU. This idea could explain the otherwise problematic distinction between minor and adult citizens in the *Ruiz Zambrano* case. In the *K.A.* case, the Court held that the adult spouse of a citizen is not, in principle, in a situation of dependence.[60] Barring exceptional considerations, an adult citizen and adult family member cannot, therefore, benefit from this case law, unless they can demonstrate that he or she is in a situation of vulnerability.

Beyond this single case of the right of residence based on Article 20 of the TFEU, the consideration of the vulnerability of citizens as a determining factor for their protection by EU law can also be seen in the *CG* judgment.[61] This case confirmed and refined the principles of the *Dano* case ruling,[62] in which a citizen whose residence is based solely on national law, and not on Directive 2004/38, cannot benefit from equal treatment on the basis of Article 24. However, contrary to the previous ruling, the Court found that the CFR is applicable in a situation when an EU citizen has exercised his or her freedom of movement. It held that Article 1 of the CFR requires a Member State:

> to ensure that a Union citizen who has made use of his or her freedom to move and to reside within the territory of the Member States, who has a right of residence on

---

56 On this idea, see E. Dubout, 'La vulnérabilité saisie par la Cour de justice de l'Union européenne' in L. Burgorgue-Larsen (ed.), *La vulnérabilité saisie par les juges en Europe*, Paris, Pedone, 2014, pp. 31–58, p. 54.

57 F. Ristuccia, above n. 36.

58 D. Sarmiento, 'EU Citizenship as an autonomous legal concept of EU law' in A. Bouveresse, A. Iliopoulou-Penot and J. Rondu (eds.), *La citoyenneté européenne, quelle valeur ajoutée? European Citizenship: what added value?*, Brussels, Bruylant, 2023, pp. 39–60, p. 48.

59 E. Dubout, 'La primauté du droit de l'Union et le passage au pluralisme constitutionnel: Réflexions autour de l'arrêt *M.A.S. et M.B.*' (2018) 3 *Revue trimestrielle de droit européen* 563.

60 *K.A.*, above n. 20, para. 78.

61 Case C-709/20, *CG v. The Department for Communities in Northern Ireland*, ECLI:EU:C:2021:602.

62 For a critical analysis, see, e.g. C. O'Brien, 'The great EU citizenship illusion exposed: equal treatment rights evaporate for the vulnerable' (2021) 6 *European Law Review* 801; M. Haag, 'The *coup de grâce* to the Union citizen's right to equal treatment: *CG v. The Department for Communities in Northern Ireland*' (2022) 59(4) *Common Market Law Review* 1081.

the basis of national law, and who is in a vulnerable situation, may nevertheless live in dignified conditions.[63]

The difference in reasoning with the *Dano* judgment is symptomatic of a certain change of approach with regard to the delimitation of the scope of the CFR. Whereas Ms Dano's difficult economic situation was assessed negatively, making it possible to demonstrate the EU citizen's lack of integration in her host state and justifying the inapplicability of both Article 24 of Directive 2004/38 and the CFR, the analysis of Ms CG's situation is 'more in the realm of *emotion*'.[64] This is particularly true regarding the reference to the vulnerable situation of EU citizens and their children.

Thus, values seem at times to influence the definition of the scope of application, in parallel to the conventional functionalist interpretation. In certain cases, the applicability of EU citizenship is justified, not only to promote the effectiveness of the status and of the objectives of EU law, but also to protect fundamental values. This idea seems to have gradually permeated the case law relating to citizenship; the consequences of this new vision need to be considered.

§2. THE POTENTIAL CONSEQUENCES OF A NEW VISION OF THE SCOPE OF EU CITIZENSHIP

I. TOWARDS AN AUTONOMOUS SCOPE OF APPLICATION?

The emergence of a new vision of the scope of EU citizenship has two main advantages. First, its potential to contribute to the autonomous scope of application of EU citizenship regarding national law and EU internal market law. While this status was originally linked to the possession of nationality in a Member State and to the exercise of freedom of movement, the influence of values allows a more autonomous status, beyond nationality and independent of mobility. This would make it possible to minimise the impact of nationality and mobility, and thus, the scope of application via the Member State, and the influence of the internal market. The field of application can have a protective function in that the citizen is attached to the EU legal order not because he or she is perceived as an agent in the service of the EU's objectives, but more fundamentally because the values enshrined in the EU require such protection.

63 *CG*, above n. 60, para. 89.

64 M. de Walsche and P. Dupont, 'La citoyenne dans la jurisprudence de la Cour de justice de l'Union européenne' in A. Bouveresse, A. Iliopoulou-Penot and J. Rondu (eds.), *La citoyenneté européenne, quelle valeur ajoutée? European Citizenship: what added value?*, Brussels, Bruylant, 2023, pp. 211–48, p. 226 (emphasis added, translation by M. Rouy).

In making EU law applicable to citizens, the ECJ seems to be trying to correct certain strict conditions to avoid leaving out situations considered alarming in the event of the non-applicability of EU law. In this way, vulnerability is used to compensate for certain blind spots in the scope of EU law. In a purely internal situation, the citizen cannot, in principle, benefit from the protection offered by EU law, but the very nature of the status of citizen justifies taking into account his or her possible vulnerability and offering a minimum level of protection, therefore legitimising a departure from the cross-border element as a criterion linking the EU citizen to EU law. Similarly, in the context of equal treatment, while residence on the basis of national law alone does not bring a person within the scope of Article 24 of Directive 2004/38, here too the citizen's vulnerable situation requires national authorities to guarantee his or her dignity and has the effect of bringing him or her within the scope of Article 1 of the CFR.

Thus, beyond the arguments based on the promotion of effectiveness, it is in fact the protection of the very essence of what constitutes European citizenship that seems to guide the scope of the protection it offers. In other words, the applicability of EU law is ultimately justified less by the aim to promote a concrete objective than by the preservation of an abstract ideal. Beyond the mere perspective of the scope of application, this new approach contributes to giving substance and autonomy to the status of citizen, going beyond transnational status to become a genuine supranational citizenship. This kind of citizenship would encompass not only a right to free movement, but also a right to enjoy the community of values anywhere within the EU.[65]

II. TOWARDS A UNIFORM SCOPE OF APPLICATION?

Second, this new vision also reinforces a more uniform interpretation of the scope of EU citizenship. This responds to certain limitations of the functionalist approach, which splinters the field of application of citizenship into a multitude of hypotheses that are not necessarily consistent. The traditional functionalist approach is also characterised by a casuistic jurisprudence that can be explained by the diffuse and evolving nature of the objectives linked to the establishment of European citizenship. In contrast, the new approach is more abstract and makes it possible to give individual case law a more holistic perspective. This is reflected in the extent to which the aim to maintain the presence of EU citizens in the territory of the Union and to take into account their vulnerability is

---

[65] S. Coutts, 'The shifting geometry of Union citizenship: a supranational status from transnational rights' (2019) 21 *Cambridge Yearbook of European Legal Studies* 318.

found not only in Article 20 of the TFEU but also, progressively, in other provisions relating to European citizenship.

Similarly, the idea of protecting the citizen and the community that the European Union represents would constitute, beyond the case of European citizenship, a source of unity for the scope of EU law more generally. Indeed, certain links can be found in other areas of EU law. To take just one example in personal data protection, in the *Schrems* and *Schrems II* judgments,[66] the Court of Justice annulled two Commission Decisions authorising the transfer of data to the United States on the grounds that the latter did not provide an equivalent level of protection of personal data to that provided in the EU. While this case law has often served to illustrate the extraterritorial dimension of EU law on the protection of personal data:

> such a reading, however, does not fit the reasoning followed by the Court, which chose to focus on the values on which the EU is said to be founded, rather than consider the territorial reach of its legislation or the regulatory goals that it pursues.[67]

More specifically, beyond the objectives pursued by EU law and its effectiveness, it is ultimately the nature of the EU and the values on which it is founded that dictate that a transfer of personal data to third countries must not undermine the fundamental values of the Union.[68] If the transfer of such data to a third country could seriously undermine these values, the authorities of the Member States must be able to oppose it. As in the case of EU citizenship, it is, to some extent, the goal of preserving the integrity of EU law that justifies their intervention.[69] A similar comparison can be made with the broad interpretation of the scope of EU law in relation to the protection of values based on Article 19 of the TEU. Although this jurisprudence is quite different from that on citizenship, the two tend to show 'a growing convergence in the formation of a consistent set of supra-primary rules of EU law touching on existential matters that comprise the Union's very identity',[70] the protection of which requires a partial emancipation from the traditional interpretation of the scope of EU law.

---

66 Case C-362/14, *Schrems*, ECLI:EU:C:2015:650; Case C-311/18, *Schrems II*, ECLI:EU:C:2020:559.

67 T. Marzal, 'The territorial reach of European Union law: a private international law enquiry into the European Union's spatial identity', above n. 40, 45.

68 T. Marzal, 'From World Actor to Local Community: Territoriality and the Scope of Application of EU Law', above n. 40, p. 21.

69 For a broader comparison between EU citizenship law and personal data protection law, see A. Iliopoulou-Penot, 'The construction of a European digital citizenship in the case law of the Court of Justice of the EU' (2022) 59 *Common Market Law Review* 969.

70 D. Sarmiento, above n. 57, p. 53.

III. TOWARDS A PARADOXICAL DELIMITATION?

The new vision of the scope of EU citizenship, based more on European values, also has some drawbacks. The principal of these is that this reading is profoundly paradoxical. Firstly, the values of Article 2 of the TEU are both universal and relative: they are universal because they are protected and recognised not just by the European Union and its Member States, but more widely; they are relative because they are increasingly contested by certain Member States. This undermines the idea that they could delimit a community of belonging and its insiders and outsiders.

Secondly, while the prospect of associating values and scope certainly improves the protection of citizens offered by EU law, so far this remains exceptional, concerns only vulnerable citizens, and offers them only minimal protection. While the various case rulings have the advantage of bringing within the scope of EU law nationals who might be perceived as on the fringes of the EU legal order, in fact this is justified only in fairly limited circumstances. This may seem logical: it is precisely because of their exceptional nature that situations that appear to be outside EU law are drawn into its scope. Yet rather than extending the overall scope of beneficiaries of the protection offered by European citizenship, the protection of its essence at best makes it possible to correct certain rigidities in that scope.

Moreover, the protection afforded to the citizen seems minimal by nature, which again undermines the importance of the potential redefinition of the contours of the status of citizen. Bringing EU citizens within the scope of EU law, justified by the essence of European citizenship, does not offer them real substantive rights, but rather protection of a procedural nature. For example, in *CG*, the Court of Justice did not in any way allow the applicant to benefit from equal treatment in terms of social benefits, but simply enshrined the obligation of the host state to ensure that the refusal of the social benefit did not result in undignified living conditions. The situation is doubly paradoxical. It means on the one hand that a citizen 'who has meagre personal resources, or material assistance from his family, even of minor importance, cannot therefore invoke Union law against such a refusal'.[71] On the other, by basing their protection not on Article 18 of the TFEU but on the CFR, nationals who have no resources and are economically inactive ultimately appear to be better protected by the CFR than by their status as citizens. The added value of the status of citizen is thereby reduced.[72]

---

[71] J. Rondu, 'Les droits fondamentaux, enrichissement ou dilution du statut de citoyen?' in A. Bouveresse, A. Iliopoulou-Penot and J. Rondu (eds.), *La citoyenneté européenne, quelle valeur ajoutée? European Citizenship: what added value?*, Brussels, Bruylant, 2023, pp. 293–310, p. 308 (translation by M. Rouy).

[72] Ibid., p. 307.

It should be added that this new vision does not seem capable of correcting the casuistic nature of the Court of Justice. By way of illustration, in *CG*, the Court refers to the children of an EU citizen as being 'particularly vulnerable', whereas the EU citizen herself is considered to be merely 'vulnerable'.[73] If the vulnerability of the citizen appears to justify the protection of the latter by EU law, the level of vulnerability may be able to modulate the degree of this protection, contributing to the casuistic dimension of the delimitation of the scope of application. Ultimately, while extending the scope of application governed by the integrity of the citizen's status or the citizen's vulnerability has certain advantages, it remains intrinsically paradoxical. Limited in terms of its beneficiaries, and minimal in terms of the protection it offers, it seems only marginally capable of renewing the scope of EU citizenship law.

SECTION IV
CONCLUSION

Citizenship of the European Union and the values enshrined in Article 2 of the TEU are, naturally, linked. However, the influence of the latter in defining the scope of EU citizenship is debatable. Despite the links often drawn by the Advocates General and academics, the Court of Justice has never explicitly mentioned Article 2 of the TEU in its case law on EU citizenship. The scope of this jurisprudence remains focused on the aim of ensuring the effectiveness of the status of EU citizenship. Nevertheless, a close reading of the case law shows that although values are not a formal criterion of the scope of citizenship, they seem to have an important influence. This can be seen in criteria such as the territory of the Union, the substance of rights, or the consideration of vulnerability. The applicability of EU law is no longer triggered solely to ensure the effectiveness of the status of citizen, but also to protect the citizen as well as European values. This increases the autonomy and uniformity of the scope of application, even if this new approach contains certain paradoxes.

[73] *CG*, above n. 60, para. 91.

CHAPTER 6
EU CITIZENS' PLACE IN THE PROCESS OF CONCRETISING THE VALUE OF DEMOCRACY

Félicie REMLINGER*

Abstract

Mirroring the development of standards relating to the rule of law, the EU is creating tools to concretise the value of democracy enshrined in Article 2 of the Treaty on European Union (TEU). This process occurs within the Court of Justice's case law and the European Democracy Action Plan framed by the European Commission. It mainly focuses on safeguarding the electoral process and guaranteeing press freedom and pluralism. This chapter aims to analyse the place of EU citizens in the process of concretising democracy. While EU citizens are put at the centre of the narrative of this concretisation, it can be argued that they do not have the decisive word in the definition of the democratic standards being developed. However, they can play a central role in making these democratic standards effective by implementing them.

SECTION I
INTRODUCTION

Although until recently European Union (EU) institutions have focused primarily on protecting the rule of law, a movement has been initiated towards concretising the value of democracy enshrined in Article 2 of the Treaty on European Union (TEU).[1] In this process, there are recurring references to the protection of citizens, as if to justify the EU's intervention on this question.

* Félicie Remlinger (remlinger.felicie@gmail.com) is a PhD student at Paris-Panthéon-Assas University (Centre of European Law) under the direction of Professor Anastasia Iliopoulou-Penot. This chapter benefitted from fruitful exchanges within the Amsterdam Centre for European Law and Governance (University of Amsterdam), as it was written during a research stay there.

1 Consolidated Version of the Treaty on European Union [2016] OJ C202/13.

Before assessing the role EU citizens play in the process, an overview of the main issues surrounding this concretisation is of value.

Since the Lisbon Treaty, there has been debate among academics on the normative potential of Article 2 of the TEU.[2] To some extent, the Court of Justice settled the issue by considering that values are not mere political statements: Article 2 of the TEU contains legally binding obligations for the Member States that can be implemented through other Treaty provisions or secondary legislation giving concrete expression to values.[3] Still, many questions about the justiciability of these values remain. Can Article 2 of the TEU be invoked as a standalone provision?[4] What are the provisions 'giving concrete expression' to it? This statement does, however, give a method to define and implement common values, which this chapter will refer to as 'concretisation'. Initiated with a clear focus on the rule of law,[5] this approach is now being extended to the value of democracy in two main areas: the safeguarding of the electoral process and the protection of media freedom and pluralism.

Regarding the scope of concretisation, this appears to be multilayered, between the EU as a democratic space and Member States' legal orders. The concretisation of the value of democracy takes place in the Court of Justice's case law and the European Democracy Action Plan framed by the European

2 For a general overview, see L.D. Spieker, 'Doctrine: The Judicial Applicability of Article 2 TEU' in L.D. Spieker, *EU Values Before the Court of Justice: Foundations, Potential, Risks*, Oxford, Oxford University Press, 2023, p. 33.

3 Case C-156/21, *Hungary v. European Parliament and Council of the European Union*, ECLI:EU:C:2022:97, paras. 232 and 159; Case C-157/21, *Poland v. European Parliament and Council of the European Union*, ECLI:EU:C:2022:98, paras. 264 and 195. On secondary legislation, see K. Lenaerts, 'On checks and balances: the Rule of Law within the EU' (2023) 29(2) *Columbia Journal of European Law* 25, 27.

4 Pending Case C-769/22, introduced on 19 December 2022, *European Commission v. Hungary*; see M. Bonelli and M. Claes, 'Crossing the Rubicon? The Commission's use of Article 2 TEU in the Infringement Action on LGBTIQ+ Rights in Hungary' (2023) 30(1) *Maastricht Journal of European and Comparative Law* 3; K. Barley and Q. Weinzierl, 'Op-Ed: "Fulfilling the Lisbon Treaty's promise: The Article 2 TEU Values for the First Time in Court" by Katarina Barley and Quirin Weinzierl', *EU Law Live* (14 September 2023) <https://eulawlive.com/op-ed-fulfilling-the-lisbon-treatys-promise-the-article-2-teu-values-for-the-first-time-in-court-by-katarina-barley-and-quirin-weinzierl/>. See more recently after the hearing before the Court of Justice: L. Kaiser, A. Knecht and L.D. Spieker, 'European Society Strikes Back. The Member States Embrace Article 2 TEU in Commission v Hungary', *Verfassungsblog* (26 November 2024) < https://verfassungsblog.de/european-society-strikes-back/>.

5 See Case C-64/16, *Associação Sindical dos Juízes Portugueses (ASJP)*, ECLI:EU:C:2018:117 and Council Regulation (EU) 2020/2092 of 16 December 2020 on a general regime of conditionality for the protection of the Union budget (the Conditionality Regulation) [2020] OJ L433I/1.

Commission[6] and implemented primarily through harmonisation of the internal market.[7] These initiatives taken at EU level are meant to address the democratic backsliding in some Member States,[8] digitalisation and the development of new technology. As a consequence, the standards that are developed concern broader checks and balances in a democratic society.[9] They apply to national authorities, but also to private operators: for example, online platforms can both create new forms of risks to democracy (e.g. the manipulation of social behaviour with artificial intelligence systems, disinformation) and facilitate Member States' non-compliance with this value (e.g. retention of personal data,[10] influence over electoral processes).[11]

What about EU citizens? The aim of this chapter is to assess the role they play in the process of concretising the value of democracy. This question is relevant because there is a 'mismatch' between the importance of values as part of the EU's 'identity'[12] and the absence of a clear competence for EU institutions to uphold them through new mechanisms.[13] Concretisation has been developed to address this gap by enabling EU institutions to rely on existing Treaty provisions or legal bases for legislation to define standards opposable to Member States and private stakeholders that threaten democracy.

The EU, however, needs legitimate grounds to act. The protection of nationals in Member States is a promising constitutional prospect since they

6 'Communication from the Commission to the European Parliament, the Council, the European Economic and Social Committee and the Committee of the Regions on the European Democracy Action Plan', COM(2020) 790 final (3 December 2020).

7 See below Section II.§2.

8 In particular Hungary and Poland, but not only: see M. Claes, 'Safeguarding a rule of law culture in the Member States: Engaging national actors' (2023) 29(2) *Columbia Journal of European Law* 214, 214–15 and 217.

9 See A. von Bogdandy, 'Principles of a systemic deficiencies doctrine: How to protect checks and balances in the Member States' (2020) 57(3) *Common Market Law Review* 705, 706.

10 For example, Council Directive 2002/58/EC of 12 July 2002 concerning the processing of personal data and the protection of privacy in the electronic communications sector [2022] OJ L201/37 applies to national authorities because they call on private operators to collect connection data to safeguard national security: Joined Cases C-511/18, C-512/18 and C-520/18, *La Quadrature du Net and Others*, ECLI:EU:C:2020:791, paras. 87–104, and see more recently Joined Cases C-793/19 and C-794/19, *SpaceNet*, ECLI:EU:C:2022:702, para. 48.

11 See, e.g. M. Brkan, 'The regulation of data-driven political campaigns in the EU: from data protection to specialized regulation' (2022) 41 *Yearbook of European Law* 348.

12 *Hungary v. European Parliament and Council of the European Union*, above n. 3, para. 127 and *Poland v. European Parliament and Council of the European Union*, above n. 3, para. 145.

13 M. Bonelli, 'Constitutional Language and Constitutional Limits: The Court of Justice Dismisses the Challenges to the Budgetary Conditionality Regulation' (2022) 7(2) *European Papers* 507, 521. See also J. Wouters, 'Revisiting Art. 2 TEU: A True Union of Values?' (2020) 5(1) *European Papers* 255, 260.

are also EU citizens.[14] Although they are not mentioned in Article 2 of the TEU, the respect of this provision in all Member States would ultimately be to their benefit. Section II of this chapter shows how this is reflected in the narratives developed in the Court of Justice's case law and the European Democracy Action Plan. Nevertheless, from a representative and participatory democracy point of view, it appears that the EU's intervention is not the result of a direct (or institutional) choice of EU citizens, as examined in Section III. Section IV discusses how individuals can nonetheless have a decisive role in using the developed democratic standards against national authorities and private platforms by implementing them. This would represent the true empowerment of EU citizens in the concretisation of the value of democracy, although it is subject to strong limitations.

SECTION II THE NARRATIVE DEVELOPED AROUND PROTECTING EU CITIZENS BY CONCRETISING THE VALUE OF DEMOCRACY

In November 2023, Didier Reynders, European Commissioner for Justice in charge of protecting the rule of law, wrote to Spain's government to ask for precisions about the Amnesty Law for the Catalan pro-independence leaders. This legislative step, now adopted, was due to a political compromise intended to enable Pedro Sánchez to form a government after the July 2023 elections. The letter from Reynders only asked for details about the temporal, personal and material scope of the envisaged law[15] without expressing legal concerns (even though it could have raised issues regarding democracy and the rule of law).[16] It is of interest that Didier Reynders affirmed that his letter followed

14 See A. von Bogdandy, above n. 9, 713. See also J.-W. Müller, 'Should the EU protect Democracy and the Rule of Law inside Member States?' (2015) 21(2) *European Law Journal* 141, 145.

15 It takes place in a particular context since the Commission is playing a mediation role in the renewal of the Spanish Council for the Judiciary that has been raising rule of law concerns for a while due to a strong political polarisation: M. Díez Sarasola, 'EU's Involvement in the Renewal of the Spanish Council of the Judiciary: The European Commission's New Role as an Intermediary in the Internal Constitutional Affairs of the Member States', *Verfassungsblog* (19 February 2024) <https://verfassungsblog.de/renewal-of-the-judiciary/>.

16 See G.M. Teruel Lozano, 'Rule of Law Eroded: Unpacking the Catalan Amnesty Law', *Verfassungsblog* (6 December 2023) <https://verfassungsblog.de/rule-of-law-eroded/>. See also N. Torbisco Casals and N. Krisch, 'The Spanish Amnesty, the Conflict with Catalonia, and the Rule of Law', *Verfassungsblog* (20 March 2024) < https://verfassungsblog.de/the-spanish-amnesty-the-conflict-with-catalonia-and-the-rule-of-law/>.

public concerns brought to the attention of the Commission, 'including by a large number of citizens'.[17]

This precision can be interpreted as part of a broader approach of EU institutions to legitimise their intervention to concretise the value of democracy through the stated goal of protecting EU citizens. Below, the chapter will examine Court of Justice case law and the European Democracy Action Plan put forward by the Commission to assess how this idea of protection serves as a narrative in judicial and legislative discourse.

§ 1. THE NON-LEGAL ARGUMENT IN COURT OF JUSTICE CASE LAW

Two lines of Court of Justice case law hold interesting features that have both paved the way and could further influence the definition of the value of democracy based on a narrative of protecting EU citizens.

I. NATIONAL CITIZENS ARE ALSO EUROPEAN CITIZENS

The first line of case law began in 2019 through *Junqueras*[18] in which the Court of Justice showed its willingness to apply the logic of *ASJP*[19] to the value of democracy to review national situations that fall under the scope of EU law. In this judgment, the Court assessed the useful effect of elections to the European Parliament by considering that the Member of European Parliament's (MEP's) status (and subsequent immunity)[20] is obtained simultaneously with their election by direct universal suffrage. No matter, then, that the Spanish Constitution requires an additional formality to give effect to this election, and no matter that the competence of the Member States to organise the elections is at stake: this competence has to be exercised with due respect to EU law and the obligation for MEPs to be elected by direct and universal suffrage. According to the Court, this legally binding obligation is a direct consequence of the principle of representative democracy enshrined in Article 10 of the TEU, which gives concrete expression to the

---

17 Ibid., although the number of actors expressing concerns about this law was very significant.

18 Case C-502/19, *Junqueras*, ECLI:EU:C:2019:1115. For an overview of the legal implications and practical consequences of the case, see V. Torre de Silva, 'Enlarging the Immunities of European Parliament's Members: The *Junqueras* Judgment' (2021) 22(1) *German Law Journal* 85.

19 See *ASJP*, above n. 5.

20 Under the Protocol (No 7) on the privileges and immunities of the European Union [2012] OJ C326/266.

value of democracy.[21] Interestingly, this top-down normative approach is reinforced by a non-legal argument based on the protection of EU citizens: the composition of the European Parliament:

> must reflect faithfully and completely the free expression of choices made by the citizens of the European Union, by direct universal suffrage, as regards the persons by whom they wish to be represented during a given term […].[22]

This formulation appears as an obiter dictum, since the Court neither mentions nor protects the right to vote of EU citizens as enshrined in the Charter of Fundamental Rights, which was not at stake here despite its large scope of application.[23]

The breakthrough of combining Articles 2 and 10(1) of the TEU led to a creative 'legal fiction'[24] that could be transformed into a substantial normative narrative. Coming back to the logic of combining Articles 2 and 19(1) of the TEU, elaborated on in *ASJP*,[25] one might note that just as national judges are also European judges, national citizens are also EU citizens under Article 20 of the Treaty on the Functioning of the European Union (TFEU).[26] This double logic can open a lot of scenarios regarding the concretisation of democracy, by assessing if EU citizens' rights under the Treaties or the national electoral process are safeguarded within the Member States. The Grand Chamber of the Court of Justice heavily relies on this logic in recent judgments, in which concretisation of Article 2 of the TEU by representative democracy appears both for the interpretation of Article 22 of the TFEU and for the interpretation of national identity within the meaning of Article 4(2) TEU.[27]

---

21 See *Junqueras*, above n. 18, para. 63.

22 Ibid., para. 83.

23 Charter of Fundamental Rights of the European Union [2016] OJ C202/389. See below n. 61.

24 A. von Bogdandy and L.D. Spieker, 'Transformative constitutionalism in Luxembourg: How the Court can support democratic transitions' (2023) 29(2) *Columbia Journal of European Law* 65, 91.

25 See *ASJP*, above n. 5.

26 Consolidated Version of the Treaty on the Functioning of the European Union [2016] OJ C202/47. See, e.g. M. Schuler, 'Op-Ed: "A vague response to a vague law: The Commission's infringement procedure against Hungary's Defence of Sovereignty Bill" by Miriam Schuler', *EU Law Live* (16 February 2024) <https://eulawlive.com/op-ed-a-vague-response-to-a-vague-law-the-commissions-infringement-procedure-against-hungarys-defence-of-sovereignty-bill-by-miriam-schuler/>.

27 Case C-808/21, *European Commission v. Czech Republic*, ECLI:EU:C:2024:962 and Case C-814/21, *European Commission v. Republic of Poland*, ECLI:EU:C:2024:963. Both judgments provide that national measures preventing mobile EU citizens from joining a political party in the Member State in which they reside are counter to the equality of all citizens to vote and stand as candidates at municipal and European Parliament elections.

An infringement procedure launched by the European Commission can be mentioned that might lead the Court to apply these legal narratives. The Polish Lex Tusk[28] created an administrative committee to assess and decide whether individuals should be deprived of the right to hold public office on the basis that they acted under Russian influence to the detriment of public interest between 2007 and 2022. Among other issues related to the rule of law, this legislation could lead to the elimination of political opponents, as developed in the Venice Commission's opinion on this law.[29] A candidate running for election may be subject to an examination by the State Commission and be deprived of their right to stand for election for ten years if they have been found to have acted under Russian influence. Furthermore, a candidate could be stigmatised by the proceedings and conceived as an enemy of the state, leading to significant effects on their career and eroding the democratic process and pluralism in the political landscape.

The Commission opened an infringement procedure, considering that this law unduly interferes with the democratic process, and invokes, among others, the violation of Articles 2 and 10 of the TEU.[30] Suppose this infringement procedure progressed to the Court: in that case, it may rely on Article 10(1) of the TEU to consider that the law violates the principle of representative democracy (concretising Article 2 of the TEU) by preventing or making it difficult for candidates to compete in European elections. It could also extend its oversight to national elections by applying the logic offered by A. von Bogdandy and L.D. Spieker: EU citizens are also represented, in the European Union, in the two Councils whose composition is dependent on national elections. According to these authors: 'A government cannot be "democratically accountable" at the European level if its domestic accountability is weak'.[31]

This logic could also be applied in another infringement procedure launched against Hungary, with even more potential, since in this procedure the European Commission invokes a broad range of EU law violations. In the letter of formal notice sent in February 2024 (in INFR(2024)2001), the Commission considers that the Hungarian Defence of Sovereignty Bill

---

28 Polish law creating the State Committee for the Examination of Russian Influence on Internal Security between 2007 and 2022. It entered into force in May 2023.

29 Venice Commission, 'Urgent opinion on the law on the State Commission to investigate Russian influence on the internal security of the Republic of Poland in the period of 2007–2022 and on the draft law amending that law', CLP-PI(2023)021 (26 July 2023), paras. 64 and 65.

30 Letter of formal notice sent to Poland on 8 June 2023 in INFR(2023)2088.

31 A. von Bogdandy and L.D. Spieker, see above n. 24, 83. See also J. Cotter, 'To everything there is a season: instrumentalising Article 10 TEU to exclude undemocratic Member State Representatives from the European Council and the Council' (2022) 47(1) *European Law Review* 69.

violates 'the democratic values of the Union, the principle of democracy and the electoral rights of EU citizens' inter alia. The new Sovereignty Protection Office (SPO) that Hungary's bill sets up will have broad authority to protect 'constitutional identity', including by carrying out investigations against individuals or legal entities and publishing reports on its findings, without any legal remedy against these interventions.

In this case, in addition to the normative grounds and narrative prospects evoked regarding the Polish Lex Tusk, other provisions of EU law could be found to be violated if the case was brought before the Court, including some based on the protection of EU citizens. The SPO could prevent or dissuade EU citizens from using their right to participate in a European Citizens' Initiative, enshrined in Article 11(4) of the TEU, or the broader informal right to contact EU institutions (for example, by submitting a complaint to the European Commission concerning a possible infringement of EU law).[32] The bill also enables the SPO to investigate individuals and entities who contribute to the European Commission's annual Rule of Law Reports, which violates Article 11 of the TEU.[33]

Finally, in addition to this focus on electoral and participatory rights, a more ambitious approach could be developed related to EU values. Some aspects of the law could be subject to Article 10(3) of the TEU or Article 2 of the TEU itself as, even though they do not have a clear European dimension, they undermine the very existence of liberal democracy. Indeed, by implying that foreign interests are behind every critical position, the Hungarian Defence of Sovereignty Bill protects the position of the government on Hungarian sovereignty and could, therefore, silence anyone, including individuals.[34] This echoes the proposal of A. von Bogdandy and L.D. Spieker to consider that Article 10(3) of the TEU not be limited to democratic participation in the EU ('the democratic life of the Union presupposes a democratic life in the Member States'), which could translate the value of democracy into a judicial obligation ensuring the right of individuals to assess democratic standards within the Member States.[35]

---

32 Amnesty International and Hungarian Helsinki Committee, 'Hungary's Act on the protection of national sovereignty in breach of EU law' (8 February 2024), pp. 1, 7.

33 Ibid.

34 See M. Schuler, above n. 26.

35 See A. von Bogdandy and L.D. Spieker, above n. 24, 83–84. See also L.D. Spieker, 'Top-Down Review' in L.D. Spieker, *EU Values Before the Court of Justice: Foundations, Potential, Risks*, Oxford, Oxford University Press, 2023, pp. 183, 201.

II. EU CITIZENS AS PART OF A BROADER DEMOCRATIC SOCIETY AT EU LEVEL

The Court has also developed a promising narrative regarding the protection of the democratic society overall. This line of case law, introduced in cases dealing with MEP immunity,[36] has quickly spread to online media and communication. It is based on the iterative assumption that:

> Freedom of expression, as an essential foundation of a pluralist, democratic society reflecting the values on which the Union, in accordance with Article 2 TEU, is based, constitutes a fundamental right guaranteed by Article 11 of the Charter [...].[37]

This formulation contributes to the Court's argument that the general and indiscriminate retention of personal connection data, even for reasons of national security, cannot prevail in a democratic society. It is also used to assess what is not acceptable in a democratic society: for example, freedom of expression cannot cover discriminatory remarks based on sexual orientation made on the radio by a lawyer stating that he would never hire, nor work with, homosexual persons.[38]

In these cases, the underlying idea is to protect EU citizens against the feeling of being monitored when using digital platforms[39] and against the feeling of discrimination when hearing public statements based on sexual orientation.[40] It could extend to having access to an opposition radio station, with the recent infringement procedure launched by the Commission against Hungary.[41]

---

36 Case C-163/10, *Patriciello*, ECLI:EU:C:2011:543.

37 Ibid., para. 31. The Court even goes further by considering that freedom of expression is a value implicitly enshrined in Article 2 of the TEU: Joined Cases C-203/15 and C-698/15, *Tele2 Sverige*, ECLI:EU:C:2016:970, para. 93. See D. Kochenov and M. Klamert, 'Article 2 TEU' in M. Kellerbauer, M. Klamert and J. Tomkin (eds.), *The EU Treaties and Charter of Fundamental Rights: A Commentary*, 1st ed., Oxford, Oxford University Press, 2019, p. 22. See also, more recently, Case C-633/22, *Real Madrid v. Le Monde*, ECLI:EU:C:2024:843.

38 Case C-507/18, *Associazione Avvocatura per i diritti LGBTI*, ECLI:EU:C:2020:289, para. 48.

39 *La Quadrature du Net and Others*, above n. 10, paras. 186–87; Opinion of AG Villalón, Joined Cases C-293/12 and C-594/12, *Digital Rights Ireland*, ECLI:EU:C:2013:845, para. 72.

40 In the absence of any prohibition of discrimination on grounds of sexual orientation in Italian or EU law, the protection works only against statements that are not hypothetically linked to the employer's recruitment policy under Council Directive 2000/78/EC of 27 November 2000 establishing a general framework for equal treatment in employment and occupation [2000] OJ L303/16, but the Court indicated to the national court to take into account the public character of the statements to 'take the perspective of the potential victim of discrimination': V. Passalacqua, 'Homophobic Statements and Hypothetical Discrimination: Expanding the Scope of Directive 2000/78/EC' (2020) 16(3) *European Constitutional Law Review* 513, 523.

41 Pending Case C-92/23, *Commission v. Hungary*. See also the so-called infringement action based on Article 2 of the TEU as a self-standing plea in Pending Case C-769/22, *Commission v. Hungary*, where the Court could also rely on this iterative narrative of protecting democratic

The action, based on Article 11 of the Charter inter alia, deals with decisions of the Hungarian media regulatory authorities and the legislation on which those decisions are based, by which Klubrádió, a commercial radio station operating in Hungary, was deprived of the possibility of broadcasting its programming on the analogue terrestrial FM frequency and thus, according to the Commission's application, of reaching 'large sections of the Hungarian population'.

This infringement procedure on media freedom illustrates a more general approach by the European Commission to defend the value of democracy within the European Democracy Action Plan through the independence of media and fairness of elections.

§2. REFERENCES TO EU CITIZENS AS A LEITMOTIF IN THE EUROPEAN DEMOCRACY ACTION PLAN

The European Democracy Action Plan (hereafter Plan), presented in December 2020 by the Commission,[42] aims to uphold the value of democracy,[43] in particular through the concretisation of freedom of expression as enshrined in Article 11 of the Charter. This Plan, and some of the legislative initiatives applying it, echo the case law discussed above, in which freedom of expression is conceived as an essential pillar of a democratic society founded on Article 2 of the TEU.[44] It could mark a rupture in EU material law's traditional methods and enhance European digital citizenship,[45] in particular since it intervenes

society through freedom of expression since the Commission mentioned Article 11 of the Charter of Fundamental Rights in the provisions that could be infringed upon: S. Okunrobo, 'Case C-769/22: A further step in the protection of the fundamental rights within the European Union?', *European Law Blog* (17 May 2023) <https://www.europeanlawblog.eu/pub/case-c-769-22-a-further-step-in-the-protection-of-the-fundamental-rights-within-the-european-union/release/1>.

42 COM(2020) 790 final, above n. 6. It was recently supplemented by the 'Communication from the Commission to the European Parliament, the Council, the European Economic and Social Committee and the Committee of the Regions on Defence of Democracy', COM(2023) 630 final (12 December 2023).

43 C. Ladenburger, Y. Marinova and J. Tomkin, 'Institutional Report' in A. Kornezov (ed.), *The XXX FIDE Congress in Sofia: Mutual Trust, Mutual Recognition and the Rule of Law*, vol. 1, Sofia, Congress Publications, 2023, pp. 67, 123–24.

44 For example, under the SLAPP Directive (see below n. 50), a matter of public interest covered by the protection of 'public participation' encompasses activities aimed at protecting the values enshrined in Article 2 of the TEU, including the protection of democratic processes against undue interference, in particular by fighting disinformation (Article 4(2)(e) of the SLAPP Directive).

45 A. Iliopoulou-Penot, 'The construction of a European Digital Citizenship in the case law of the Court of Justice of the EU' (2022) 59(4) *Common Market Law Review* 969. See also B. Bertrand, 'L'Europe et le numérique: de la politique numérique à la citoyenneté numérique européenne?' (2021) 2 *Revue trimestrielle de droit européen* 245.

in a context in which Member States do not have a pre-existing constitutional corpus on digital matters.[46]

To name but a few, the Plan includes the Digital Services Act (DSA),[47] the Artificial Intelligence Act (AI Act),[48] the European Media Freedom Act (EMFA)[49] and the Directive on Strategic Lawsuits against Public Participation (SLAPP).[50] Relying on internal market harmonisation, these acts assess media and online content and try to provide for free and plural content creation, without manipulation or disinformation from the state or private companies or individuals. The rapid diffusion of hate content or AI-manipulated content online,[51] the arbitrary suppression of content by social media platforms, and abusive cross-border judicial pursuits of journalists are all types of practices created or facilitated by the rise of powerful private online platforms.[52] They should be covered by the Plan put forward by the Commission, in which each regulation is intertwined with the others in terms of name,[53] substantive action[54] or logic.[55]

Thus, however important it is to enable EU citizens to make informed electoral choices, this legislation goes far beyond elections by trying to create,

---

46 B. Bertrand, above n. 45.

47 European Parliament and Council Regulation (EU) 2022/2065 of 19 October 2022 on a Single Market For Digital Services [2022] OJ L277/1.

48 European Parliament and Council Regulation (EU) 2024/1689 of 13 June 2024 laying down harmonised rules on artificial intelligence [2024] OJ L2024/1689, 12.7.2024.

49 European Parliament and Council Regulation (EU) 2024/1083 of 11 April 2024 establishing a common framework for media services in the internal market [2024] OJ L2024/1083, 17.4.2024.

50 European Parliament and Council Directive (EU) 2024/1069 of 11 April 2024 on protecting persons who engage in public participation from manifestly unfounded claims or abusive court proceedings [2024] OJ L2024/1069, 16.4.2024. See recital 15 and Article 4(3) of the Directive for a definition of 'Slapps'.

51 See, e.g. P. Nemitz, 'Democracy through law: The Transatlantic Reflection Group and its manifesto in defence of democracy and the rule of law in the age of "artificial intelligence"' (2021) 29(1-2) *European Law Journal* 1.

52 Part of the power to regulate public expression has been transferred from the states to the platforms: C. Broyelle, 'Le Media Freedom Act: Comment protéger les médias de l'emprise des plateformes' (2023) 6 *Revue du droit public* 1470, 1471; see further A. Iliopoulou-Penot, 'La Constitution numérique européenne' (2023) 3 *Revue française de droit administratif* 945, 946 and 953.

53 'Acts' is an unusual term in EU legislation and is more accessible for EU citizens and other actors involved.

54 For example, 'when it comes to the dissemination of media content in the online environment, the European Media Freedom Act proposal builds on the horizontal framework established by the Digital Services Act' (see COM(2023) 630 final, above n. 42, p. 14); Article 34 of Regulation (EU) 2022/2065 (DSA) requires providers of very large online platforms to diligently identify 'systemic risks' stemming from their service, including the use of algorithmic systems, for civic discourse and electoral processes or for the exercise of fundamental rights.

55 The layered approach of the AI Act is connected to the risks of AI systems while the DSA is focused on the size of online platforms: A. Iliopoulou-Penot, above n. 52, 950.

across the internal market, a space of healthy expression and information. The reference to common values and Article 11 of the Charter could ultimately enable the Court of Justice to enhance the importance of this protection through interpretation.

The SLAPP Directive, also part of the Plan, interestingly echoes these considerations and the jurisprudential prospects previously outlined. Firstly, in its first recitals[56] it reiterates common values and the rights of EU citizens to participate in the democratic life of the Union:[57] it reflects the narratives that could give concrete expression to the value of democracy, linking the constitutional and legislative approaches. Secondly, it underlines that:

> Journalists play an important role in facilitating public debate and in the imparting and reception of information, opinions and ideas. They should be able to conduct their activities effectively and without fear to ensure that citizens have access to a plurality of views in European democracies. Independent, professional and responsible journalism, as well as access to pluralistic information, are key pillars of democracy. [...][58]

Overall, all these elements illustrate the stated objective of the European Democracy Action Plan to uphold democratic values by strengthening the resilience of EU democracies in the face of challenges, addressing the areas in which our systems and citizens are most vulnerable.[59]

In short, EU citizens play a role in the process of defining the value of democracy, at least as a legitimising argument to flesh out EU intervention: they are present in the substantive definitions that the Court of Justice and the legislature give to the value of democracy. This is consistent with the fact that national citizens are also EU citizens who should benefit from the defence of the value of democracy.[60] Ultimately, these considerations build an interesting narrative to justify EU intervention. The question that is not addressed by this observation is whether or not EU citizens are also involved in the process driving this development of democratic standards. Does it represent yet another top-down way for EU institutions to fill the gap between Article 2 of the TEU and their limited competences to uphold it? As stated above, it appears that

---

56 Recitals 2 and 3 of the SLAPP Directive.

57 Article 10(3) of the TEU.

58 Recital 8 of the SLAPP Directive.

59 COM(2023) 630 final, above n. 42, p. 9. See also the Speech by Commission President Ursula von der Leyen in the European Parliament Plenary of 27 November 2019, in which she stated that the European Union 'is not only about parties and politics, rules or regulations, markets or currencies. It is ultimately – and above all else – about people and their aspirations. It is about people standing together. For their liberty, for their values, simply for a better future', available <https://ec.europa.eu/commission/presscorner/detail/en/SPEECH_19_6408>.

60 A. von Bogdandy, see above n. 9, 713.

EU citizens did not trigger most of the cases that have led (or could lead) the Court of Justice to develop this narrative. Nevertheless, this is not so evident for the legislature's intervention on this matter.

SECTION III EU CITIZENS' RESIDUAL PLACE IN THE INSTITUTIONAL FRAMEWORK TO PROTECT THE VALUE OF DEMOCRACY

None of the cases in Section II were brought before the Court of Justice by an EU citizen. This can happen, of course, and such cases can also lead to ambitious judgments.[61] However, most of the value-centred rulings have been triggered by national courts through preliminary references or by the Commission according to Article 258 of the TFEU. This leads one to turn to the concretisation of the value of democracy through legislative standards as the most promising, if disappointing, avenue for the involvement of EU citizens in this process.

§ 1. REPRESENTATIVE DEMOCRACY IN ACTION?

As underlined in the introduction of this chapter (Section I), the Court of Justice affirmed that Article 2 of the TEU can be implemented through secondary legislation.[62] This method of intervention seems more legitimate from a democratic point of view and vis-à-vis Member States since it results in a common understanding of democratic standards.[63] Having said that, the

61 For example, Case C-650/13, *Delvigne*, ECLI:EU:C:2015:648: the Court applied Article 39(2) of the Charter in a purely internal situation considering that this right was designed primarily to impose specific obligations on the Member States contrary to other fundamental rights enshrined in the Charter, which is supported by the fact that this right 'mirrors' Article 14(3) of the TEU and Article 1(3) of the Electoral Act of 1976. As a consequence, the scope of the Charter is almost irrelevant. This analysis of the case is found in S. Platon, 'The Right to Participate in the European Elections and the Vertical Division of Competences in the European Union' in N. Cambien, D. Kochenov and E. Muir (eds.), *European Citizenship under Stress: Social Justice, Brexit and Other Challenges*, Leiden, Brill Nijhoff, 2020, p. 364, pp. 370–76.

62 See above n. 3.

63 E. Muir, P. Van Nuffel and G. De Baere, 'The EU as a guardian of the rule of law within its Member States' (2023) 29(2) *Columbia Journal of European Law* 1, 21 and 23; T.V. Olsen, 'Why and How Should the European Union Defend its Values?' (2023) 29 *Res Publica* 69, 73–74; T. Tridimas, 'Wreaking the wrongs: Balancing rights and the public interest the EU way' (2023) 29(2) *Columbia Journal of European Law* 185, 198; A. von Bogdandy, see above n. 9, 715.

Union's legitimacy to impose democratic standards within the Member States strongly depends on its respect for the value of democracy,[64] and there has been an iterative criticism of the Union's 'democratic deficit',[65] although this is not a subject that will be tackled here. Rather, focus will be on the following question: have EU citizens influenced or triggered EU legislative intervention to concretise the value of democracy?

From a representative democracy point of view, some legislative initiatives studied here stem partially from,[66] or adhere more closely to,[67] European Parliament Resolutions according to Article 225 of the TFEU. However, the references to these Resolutions are quite elusive, underlining once again the fact that the European Parliament does not have the right to initiate legislation at the EU level.[68] Although it is a co-legislator, the European Parliament did not directly trigger the legislative concretisation of the value of democracy.

What about participatory democracy? Since *Van Gend en Loos* in 1963,[69] it has frequently been pointed out that the EU owes its specificity in international public law to the fact that individuals are as much subjects of the EU as Member States. The TEU itself provides that 'Every citizen shall have the right to participate in the democratic life of the Union'.[70] The Court, however, on the occasion of a judgment on the European Citizens' Initiative, underlined

---

64 See T.V. Olsen, above n. 63; J.-W. Müller, above n. 14, 146.

65 See, e.g. J.H.H. Weiler, '*Van Gend en Loos*: The individual as subject and object and the dilemma of European legitimacy' (2014) 12(1) *International Journal of Constitutional Law* 94, 98–103. It echoes interestingly with Section IV of this chapter.

66 The AI Act protects ethical principles as specifically requested by the European Parliament in its Resolution of 20 October 2020 with recommendations to the Commission on a framework of ethical aspects of artificial intelligence, robotics and related technologies (2020/2012(INL)) [2021] OJ C404/63. It does not rely on other resolutions adopted in the area of AI, although the Commission mentions them in the explanatory memorandum attached to the proposal: 'Proposal for a Regulation of the European Parliament and of the Council laying down harmonised rules on Artificial Intelligence (Artificial Intelligence Act) and amending certain Union legislative acts', COM(2021) 206 final (21 April 2021).

67 Recital 5 of the SLAPP Directive refers to the European Parliament's Resolution of 11 November 2021 on strengthening democracy and media freedom and pluralism in the EU: the undue use of actions under civil and criminal law to silence journalists, NGOs and civil society (2021/2036(INI)) [2022] OJ C205/2. The explanatory memorandum attached to the EMFA proposal ('Proposal for a regulation of the European Parliament and of the Council establishing a common framework for media services in the internal market (European Media Freedom Act) and amending Directive 2010/13/EU', COM(2022) 457 final (16 September 2022)) mentions European Parliament Resolutions calling upon the Commission to take action to lift barriers on the functioning of the internal media market and promote pluralism and independence in that market, but still, the proposal and the regulation adopted do not refer to them.

68 See European Parliament Resolution of 22 November 2023 on proposals of the European Parliament for the amendment of the Treaties (2022/2051(INL)), p. 5.

69 Case 26/62, *Van Gend en Loos v. Nederlandse Administratie Der Belastingen*, ECLI:EU:C:1963:1.

70 Article 10(3) of the TEU.

that instruments of participatory democracy merely complement the principle of representative democracy.[71] As a consequence, participatory tools do not aim to shake up the pre-existing institutional balance of power between EU institutions.[72] Two tools of participatory democracy offer an illustration and potential solutions to this issue: the European Citizens' Initiative (ECI) and the Conference on the Future of Europe.

§2. THE EUROPEAN CITIZENS' INITIATIVE

This mechanism, created by the Lisbon Treaty, that enables one million EU citizens to present a legislative proposal before the European Commission and the European Parliament,[73] while ostensibly promoting participatory democracy, has been highly criticised. From the beginning, the parameters of the tool were not designed to give a strong voice to citizens in the decision-making process.[74] Its failure has been illustrated by the great number of Commission Decisions refusing to register some proposals, considering that they were outside the scope of its competence to offer a legislative act of the Union. The disappointment has grown as the few ECI proposals that were registered and collected enough statements of support have not led to actual legislation. However, the effectiveness of the mechanism with a view to its stated objectives is not the focus here (even though this has played a role in the disinterest of EU citizens for this tool).[75] For a start, it must be noted that most of the proposals do not reach the end of the procedure because they do not collect enough statements of support,[76] which indicates that the failure of the tool must also be analysed through the lack of interest of EU citizens for Union debates, and not only through a procedural lens.

With a view to the protection of common values, there are some points of interest in the General Court and Court of Justice case law. First of all, Member

---

71 Case C-418/18 P, *Puppinck*, ECLI:EU:C:2019:1113, para. 65 (with a reference to *Junqueras*, above n. 18).

72 *Puppinck*, above n. 71, para. 63. See also A. Alemanno, 'Europe's Democracy Challenge: Citizen Participation in and Beyond Elections' (2020) 21(1) *German Law Journal* 35, 37–38.

73 Article 11(4) of the TEU, implemented in Council Regulation (EU) 211/2011 of 16 February 2011 on the citizens' initiative [2011] OJ L65/1 and Council Regulation (EU) 2019/788 of 17 April 2019 on the European Citizens' Initiative [2019] OJ L130/55.

74 M. Dougan, 'What are we to make of the Citizens' Initiative?' (2011) 48(6) *Common Market Law Review* 1807. On Regulation 2019/788, see A. Parol, 'The European Citizens' Initiative Reform: Does it Matter?' (2020) 40(1) *Review of European and Comparative Law* 67.

75 R. Tinière, 'L'initiative citoyenne européenne à l'épreuve de la régulation du marché' in E. Carpano and G. Marti (eds.), *Démocratie et marché dans l'Union européenne*, Brussels, Bruylant, 2021, pp. 119, 120.

76 On 9 January 2025, 118 initiatives were registered with 66 that did not collect enough support and 27 that were withdrawn by the organisers.

States began to participate as observers in some of the disputes opposing the organisers of the ECI and the Commission.[77] Romania also contested before the General Court and the Court of Justice two decisions on the registration of ECIs dealing with regional minorities.[78] How has it come about that Member States have become interested in this tool whose effectiveness is contested? These cases concern the competence of the Commission to make a legislative proposal, so more generally the principle of conferral: the interest of Member States in some proposals thus underlines the potential of the debate that could be triggered by the success of an ECI.

This becomes all the more interesting as there are some ECI proposals that deal with democracy and the rule of law within the Member States. However, these proposals did not achieve the public support needed to be presented to the European Parliament and to trigger a response by the European Commission, be it because their legal bases did not meet the criteria of the procedure[79] or because they were too national centred to collect enough statements of support among EU citizens.[80]

The purpose of the ECI is to enhance democracy at the institutional level of the EU by giving a voice to citizens in the decision-making process. If these proposals were strongly conducted across the Union, this could be the

77 See, e.g. Case T-611/19, *Comité de ciudadanos de la iniciativa v. Commission*, ECLI:EU:T:2021:340, with the observations of Spain in support of the Commission.

78 'Minority SafePack – One million signatures for diversity in Europe' led to Case T-391/17, *Romania v. Commission*, ECLI:EU:T:2019:672 and Case C-899/19 P, *Romania v. Commission*, ECLI:EU:C:2022:41; 'Cohesion policy for the equality of the regions and sustainability of the regional cultures' led to Case T-495/19 *Romania v. Commission*, ECLI:EU:T:2021:781 and Case C-54/22 P, *Romania v. Commission*, ECLI:EU:C:2024:164. In both cases, Romania contested the registration of the proposals by the Commission, but the rulings dismissed its actions and appeals. The former ECI did not receive enough statements of support but the latter is going to be presented before the Commission because it collected enough support.

79 For example, the ECI 'Derecho de la UE, derechos de la minorías y democratización de las instituciones españolas' was not registered because the Commission considered that it implicitly invited it to examine the situation in Spain regarding the movement for independence in Catalonia in the light of the rule of law framework and to take measures in this regard if necessary. This decision was confirmed by the General Court in *Comité de ciudadanos de la iniciativa v. Commission*, above n. 77, para. 75. See, for another example, Commission Decision (EU) 2019/569 of 3 April 2019 on the proposed citizens' initiative entitled 'Respect for the rule of law within the European Union' [2019] OJ L99/39, para. 7.

80 For example, 'Stop corruption in Europe as its root' (the initiative, registered, explicitly referred to Bulgaria and Romania); 'Respect for the rule of law within the European Union' (this initiative referred to Poland, Hungary, Romania, and asked for the legislative simplification of Article 7 of the TEU's enforcement). See by analogy some ECIs triggered by Brexit and focused on the EU citizens' status (e.g. 'Permanent European Union Citizenship' or 'Retaining European Citizenship'): all of them were registered by the Commission but did not collect enough support. For an analysis, see N. Athanasiadou, 'The European Citizens' Initiative in Times of Brexit' in N. Cambien, D. Kochenov and E. Muir (eds.), *European Citizenship under Stress, Social Justice, Brexit and Other Challenges*, Leiden, Brill Nijhoff, 2020, pp. 387–412, p. 408.

occasion to discuss the value of democracy through the lens of competence in the European institutions. Transparency and accountability[81] would also require the Commission to state what has been done and what could be done to implement this value. Furthermore, it is likely that the European Commission and European Parliament would use such ECI proposals as democratic input to support their legal and political actions.[82] This has been seen with the Conference on the Future of Europe which represents, to date, the best example of EU citizens' involvement in the definition of the value of democracy.

§3. THE CONFERENCE ON THE FUTURE OF EUROPE

A 'hybrid' form of representative, participative and deliberative democracy,[83] the Conference on the Future of Europe (CoFoE), held between April 2021 and May 2022, was[84] (and remains)[85] an interesting event in terms of the representative power of EU citizens and the awareness of the participating panels about EU matters.[86] Two aspects were particularly promising in this event and the final report[87] concerning the protection of the value of democracy. From a substantive point of view, the protection of values was

81 Article 10(1)(c) of Regulation 211/2011; Article 15(2) of Regulation 2019/788.

82 This could particularly have been the case for the ECI 'European Initiative for Media Pluralism' which was registered by the Commission but did not collect enough statements of support. The legal bases and normative objectives were very similar to the Media Freedom Act. See also S. Gozi, 'La Conférence sur l'avenir de l'Europe: Analyse juridique de la plus grande expérience démocratique du continent' (2022) 1 *Revue du droit de l'Union européenne* 171, 182–83. The author explains how the role of the European Parliament could be enhanced to implement successful proposals, with a hybrid representative and participatory approach.

83 C. Spector, 'La Conférence sur l'avenir de l'Europe, un exercice démocratique?' (2021) 3 *Revue des affaires européennes* 463, 464.

84 'Future of Europe, Special Eurobarometer 500 Report' (October–November 2020): in a joint survey of the European Commission and the European Parliament, three out of four respondents agreed that the CoFoE would represent significant progress for democracy in the EU (p. 9).

85 The focus here is not on the potential of this event from the point of view of an institutional realisation of democracy in the Union. On this point, see A. Alemanno, 'Unboxing the Conference on the Future of Europe and its democratic raison d'être' (2020) 26(5–6) *European Law Journal* 484; M. Steuer, 'To End Sleepwalking: The Constitutional Potential of the Conference on the Future of Europe' in F. Horák and K. Řepa (eds.), *European Constitutionalism and the Virus of Distrust*, Leges, Prague 2022, p. 57. On the potential of the Citizens' Panels: G. Abels, A. Alemanno, B. Crum, A. Demidov, D. Hierlemann, A. Renkamp, and A. Trechsel (eds.), *Next level citizen participation in the EU: Institutionalising European Citizens' Assemblies*, Gütersloh, Bertelsmann Stiftung, 2022.

86 C. Spector, above n. 83.

87 Conference on the Future of Europe, 'Report on the final outcome' (May 2022) <https://www.europarl.europa.eu/resources/library/media/20220509RES29121/20220509RES29121.pdf>.

directly taken into consideration by the panels (Proposal 25) including through the lens of the reform of the internal market to address the digitalisation and protect media pluralism (Proposal 27).

From a procedural point of view, the parameter that is the most relevant is the fact that it was organised outside the scope of the Treaties with an inter-institutional agreement.[88] The outcome was set to be very open depending on what was agreed to be necessary by EU citizens, be it through legislative steps or Treaty reform.[89] However, the principles governing EU legislative action – subsidiarity and proportionality – were very present in the joint declaration creating the event[90] and the official answers to the final report made by the European Commission[91] and the European Council.[92] Despite the resolutions of the European Parliament to this effect,[93] the CoFoE did not trigger a revision of the treaties.[94] From this point of view, its official follow-up was disappointing.[95]

Yet a more informal implementation of the CoFoE can be found in actions taken by European institutions under the European Democracy Action Plan, based on the example of the EMFA. In recital 6 of its proposal, the Commission

---

88 Joint Declaration of the European Parliament, the Council and the European Commission on the Conference on the Future of Europe Engaging with citizens for democracy – Building a more resilient Europe [2021] OJ C91I/1.

89 U. von der Leyen, 'A Union that strives for more: My agenda for Europe', p. 19 <https://commission.europa.eu/document/download/063d44e9-04ed-4033-acf9-639ecb187e87_en?filename=political-guidelines-next-commission_en.pdf>.

90 Joint Declaration, above n. 88: 'We, the Presidents of the European Parliament, the Council and the European Commission want citizens to join the conversation and have their say on the future of Europe. We hereby jointly commit to listen to Europeans and to follow up on the recommendations made by Conference, in full respect of our competences and the subsidiarity and proportionality principles enshrined in the European Treaties'.

91 'Communication from the Commission to the European Parliament, the European Council, the Council, the European Economic and Social Committee and the Committee of the Regions, Conference on the Future of Europe: Putting Vision into Concrete Action', COM(2022) 404 final (17 June 2022).

92 'Conclusions of the European Council', EUCO 24/22 (24 June 2022). This institution considered that around 95% of the proposals could be implemented in the current framework of the Treaties without Treaty reform: see para. 11 of the note accompanying the table of assessment (<https://data.consilium.europa.eu/doc/document/ST-16054-2023-INIT/fr/pdf>).

93 European Parliament Resolution of 4 May 2022 on the follow-up to the conclusions of the Conference on the Future of Europe, 2022/2648(RSP) [2022] OJ C465/109, para. 15; see 2022/2051(INL), above n. 68.

94 This was expected due to the very drafting of the joint declaration: A. Alemanno, above n. 85, 492; F. Fabbrini, 'The Conference on the Future of Europe: Process and prospects' (2020) 26(5–6) *European Law Journal* 401, 405–06. However, proposals from the final report have surely influenced the discussions on the Union's reform: see O. Costa, D. Schwarzer, P. Berès, G. Gressani, G. Marti, F. Mayer, T. Nguyen, N. von Ondarza, S. Russack, F. Tekin, S. Vallée and C. Verger, 'Sailing on High Seas: Reforming and Enlarging the EU for the 21st Century: Report of the Franco-German working group on EU institutional reform', Paris-Berlin (18 September 2023), p. 11.

95 See, contra, A. Alemanno, above n. 85, 486–87.

refers to the CoFoE and its Proposal 27 to state the will of citizens for EU intervention.[96] This reference was maintained in the first reading of the European Parliament proposal.[97] This use of the Conference suggests that it is part of the broader narrative described earlier, as these references do not appear to be politically decisive or normatively important for the adoption of the Act and the concretisation of the value of democracy.

Firstly, the European Democracy Action Plan seems to be implementing Proposal 27 on media pluralism but not Proposal 25 dealing with the protection of common values. This is confirmed by an assessment issued by the Council linking proposals and related specific measures implementing them,[98] in which Proposal 25 is mainly reduced to upholding the rule of law.[99] By contrast, the Council links Proposal 27 with the European Democracy Action Plan and the different initiatives taken to implement it, including the Media Freedom Act.[100] Thus, the CoFoE is not used for a value-based approach concerning democracy.

Secondly, it is difficult to know which has come first, the CoFoE's proposal or the political programme. Certain factors favour the second option as they indicate that the CoFoE merely confirmed a pre-existing political will of the European Commission.[101] In 2021, President von der Leyen mentioned the Commission's plan to deliver a Media Freedom Act in 2022, before the start of the CoFoE.[102] In the State of the Union Address of the following year, she mentioned the Act without any reference to the CoFoE, even though the final report had been already released. This is at odds with the recital of the legislative proposal mentioning the CoFoE as one of the sources justifying EU intervention to harmonise certain aspects of national rules related to media services through the internal market. Thus, overall, despite its importance for EU democracy, the CoFoE does not appear to have led to a direct involvement of EU citizens in the definition of the value of democracy. The role of EU citizens in concretising Article 2 of the TEU is to be found elsewhere.

---

96 Recital 8 of the EMFA (Regulation (EU) 2024/1083 of 11 April 2024 establishing a common framework for media services in the internal market).

97 For example, the European Parliament's first position issued on the proposal of the Commission in October 2023: 'With its position adopted today, Parliament responds to demands of citizens put forward in the conclusions of the Conference of the Future of Europe, notably in proposal 27 […]': 'Media Freedom Act: MEPs tighten rules to protect journalists and media outlets', *European Parliament* (3 October 2023) <https://www.europarl.europa.eu/news/en/press-room/20230929IPR06111/media-freedom-act-meps-tighten-rules-to-protect-journalists-and-media-outlets>.

98 'Proposals and related specific measures contained in the report on the final outcome of the Conference on the Future of Europe: Updated assessment', 16054/23 ADD 1 (7 December 2023).

99 Ibid., pp. 174–75.

100 Ibid., pp. 184–85.

101 'Sailing on High Seas: Reforming and Enlarging the EU for the 21st Century', above n. 94, p. 25.

102 U. von der Leyen, '2021 State of the Union Address', *European Commission* <https://ec.europa.eu/commission/presscorner/detail/ov/SPEECH_21_4701>.

As shown in this section, EU citizens have not, so far, had a clear and direct voice in the legislative concretisation of the value of democracy. However, it is possible to consider that they play a decisive role in the implementation of the democratic standards developed: individuals could be involved in the concretisation at a later stage of the process.

SECTION IV
EU CITIZENS CAN INFLUENCE THE IMPLEMENTATION OF DEMOCRATIC STANDARDS

While a commitment to common democratic values is apparent in the European Democracy Action Plan, the latter is also concerned with economic security. This is illustrated by the following statement on the EMFA:

> Press freedom is threatened worldwide, including in Europe: the murder in Malta, threats to press freedom in Hungary and many other examples clearly prove that. The European Media Freedom Act is our answer to this threat and a milestone in European legislation. It values and protects the double role of media as businesses and as guardians of democracy.[103]

The EU's response to the rise of online platforms and new forms of AI algorithms seems appropriate since online content and media services circulate in the internal market.[104] As a consequence, the binding safeguards created by these Acts can tackle the current threats to democracy only to the extent the latter also represent distortions to the internal market or judicial cooperation.[105] Furthermore, this intervention originated from the need to preserve the internal market's attractiveness for these economic stakeholders.[106] This economic approach does not fit the narrative on protecting the value of democracy as developed in Section II. It is, however, in line with the limited competence of the EU to act directly on common values, which implies a functional intervention.[107] This is why legislation tries to create rights opposable

---

[103] S. Verheyen (Rapporteur from the Culture and Education Committee on the EMFA) in the plenary debate of March 2024.

[104] See the explanatory memorandum in the proposal for the AI Act (COM(2021) 206 final, above n. 48), 'Subsidiarity', para. 2.2.

[105] C. Ladenburger, Y. Marinova and J. Tomkin, above n. 43.

[106] A. Iliopoulou-Penot, above n. 52, 947; e.g. the proposal for the AI Act underlines the 'Union interest to preserve the EU's technological leadership and to ensure that Europeans can benefit from new technologies developed and functioning according to Union values, fundamental rights and principles' (COM(2021) 206 final, above n. 48, para. 1.1).

[107] J. Wouters, above n. 13, 260–61.

to platforms.[108] In other words, the internal market becomes a meeting point for platform regulation and protection of democratic standards by these platforms and national authorities. This allows a space where EU citizens could be associated with the process of concretising the value of democracy.

§ 1. EU CITIZENS AS INDIVIDUALS

As discussed in Section II, the legislative steps taken under the European Democracy Action Plan represent an agreement between EU institutions and Member States to implement the value of democracy through secondary legislation on specific legal points. Yet they also show that EU citizenship is still more economic than political.[109] This requires a semantic shift in the argument to refer to EU citizens as individuals, as the democratic standards that could be sought by EU citizens are market-based. In terms of the EMFA, individuals are 'recipients of media services' or 'users' of platforms: essentially, they are consumers in the internal market.

Such an approach can present some advantages. For example, one does not necessarily need to be a national of a Member State (and subsequently an EU citizen) to benefit from the legislation. This is illustrated by the SLAPP Directive, which applies to any 'natural or legal person':[110] it encompasses the fact that any person can participate in public debate and be subject to abusive lawsuits. With the rise of online platforms, and in particular social media, content produced by a third-country national could be seen in several Member States, thus implying the jurisdiction of their courts. As an example, one could take the case of a climate activist who uses public flight data to trace the private jet journeys of public figures and then publishes this information on social media. This may fall within the definition of 'matters of public interest' protected under the SLAPP Directive, which includes the environment and the climate.[111] Under EU rules of private international law, if this person is domiciled in a Member State, he or she may be sued for defamation in another Member State where the harmful event occurred.[112] In defamation cases, the Court considers that the claimant can initiate proceedings in the place of publication.[113] Concerning digital publication, the potential for lawsuits is

[108] A. Iliopoulou-Penot, above n. 52, 953. On the EMFA, see C. Broyelle, above n. 52, 1472.

[109] V. Michel, 'Citoyenneté et marché' in E. Carpano and G. Marti (eds.), *Démocratie et marché dans l'Union européenne*, Brussels, Bruylant, 2021, pp. 105–18.

[110] SLAPP Directive, Recital 9.

[111] Ibid., Article 4(2)(a).

[112] Article 7(2) of Council Regulation (EU) 1215/2012 of 12 December 2012 on jurisdiction and the recognition and enforcement of judgments in civil and commercial matters [2012] OJ L351/1 (Brussels Ia Regulation).

[113] Case C-68/93, *Shevill/Presse Alliance*, ECLI:EU:C:1995:61, paras. 29–30.

limited only by the number of Member States.[114] The Directive thus intervenes to avoid abusive lawsuits that could be triggered by powerful private interests against content producers such as in the case of a climate activist, while preserving the right to defend one's right to private life through legal recourse. This hypothetical example demonstrates how this legislation could be used by individuals as a functionalist defence of democratic standards.

§2. FUNCTIONALIST DEFENCE

It is not new to argue that individuals could be empowered in protecting their rights following a functionalist logic. Fundamental rights were first introduced under the form of general legal principles to ensure the primacy of European law.[115] These fundamental rights have always been counterbalanced with the fundamental freedoms of the internal market.[116] Initiatives taken under the European Democracy Action Plan could rely on this logic. In this regard, the choice of the instrument is crucial since it could enable individuals to invoke rights opposable to Member States.[117] Except for the SLAPP Directive, Regulations 'shall have general application', 'be binding in [their] entirety and [be] directly applicable in all the Member States'.[118] Not all the provisions of a Regulation have a complete direct effect of course, but the national judge must always interpret the relevant provisions in conformity with EU law.

In the case of direct effect, individuals could be involved in the implementation of the democratic standards these legislations stand for.[119] This is in line with the ruling in *Van Gend en Loos* according to which:

> The vigilance of individuals concerned to protect their rights amounts to an effective supervision in addition to the supervision entrusted by Articles 169 and 170 to the diligence of the Commission and of the Member States.[120]

---

114 L. Gay, 'Les procédures-bâillons: une menace démocratique? L'état du droit' (2023) 413 *Légipresse* 209, 273. This author nuances this by pointing out that this does not apply to claims for damages.

115 Case 11/70, *Internationale Handelsgesellschaft*, ECLI:EU:C:1970:114.

116 For example, Case C-112/00, *Schmidberger*, ECLI:EU:C:2003:333; Case C-36/02, *Omega*, ECLI:EU:C:2004:614.

117 C. Broyelle, above n. 52, 1472.

118 Article 288 of the TFEU.

119 For example, Article 16(1) of Regulation 2022/2065 (DSA): users can notify providers of hosting services of the presence of what they consider to be illegal content; Article 85 of the AI Act provides the right for any natural or legal person to lodge a complaint with a market surveillance authority.

120 *Van Gend en Loos v. Nederlandse Administratie Der Belastingen*, above n. 69. Infringement actions and actions before a national judge are the traditional tools for the implementation of EU law: M. Blauberger and R.D. Kelemen, 'Can courts rescue national democracy? Judicial safeguards against democratic backsliding in the EU' (2017) 24(3) *Journal of European Public Policy* 321, 322. See also J.H.H. Weiler, above n. 65, 96.

Here, the idea of citizens' empowerment put forward in the European Democracy Action Plan is consistent with the choice of instrument made by the Commission. While the Plan is linked to economic concerns, it also grants individuals the possibility to participate in its effectiveness. The EMFA, in particular, provides for the right of recipients of media services to have access to a plurality of editorially independent media content.[121] Taking this right further compared to the original proposal of the Commission,[122] the Regulation obliges the Member States to ensure that framework conditions are in place in line with this Regulation to safeguard this right to the benefit of free and democratic discourse.

Thus, the functionalist logic underpinning the legislative acts at stake can benefit the implementation of the value of democracy since it gives a basis for private claims before national courts.[123] By invoking these rights, individuals can participate in the effective application of democratic standards. In case of doubt on their direct effect or interpretation, the national court could refer to the Court of Justice by application of Article 267 of the TFEU,[124] which would also provide for their uniform application across Member States.[125] It could also enable the Court to interpret them as part of a digital citizenship status[126] and to connect them further with Article 2 of the TEU.[127] Yet such an approach is dependent on the effective utilisation of these democratic standards by individuals: they must have a culture of the rule of law and liberal democracy for legal rules to prevail.[128] And they cannot act alone.

§ 3. SYSTEMIC LIMITS

Not all infringements of common values can be addressed through individual rights, as these need a basis for private litigation. The development of democratic standards can partially remedy this, but substantial limitations remain: for example, systemic deficiencies cannot always be addressed through

121 Article 3 of the EMFA.

122 The proposal more vaguely referred to the 'rights' of recipients of media services 'to receive a plurality of news and current affairs content produced with respect for editorial freedom of media service providers, to the benefit of the public discourse'.

123 See M. Blauberger and R.D. Kelemen, above n. 120, 328.

124 It is, however, up to the national judge to decide to use Article 267 of the TFEU; parties can only underline a point of EU law that could benefit from further interpretation. Moreover, private parties have a secondary role in the procedure: they can only present observations but do not decide on the formulation of the preliminary references. See the role of preliminary references in this specific context: M. Blauberger and R.D. Kelemen, above n. 120, 327.

125 J.H.H. Weiler, above n. 65, 97.

126 A. Iliopoulou-Penot, above n. 52, and B. Bertrand, above n. 45.

127 See E. Muir, P. Van Nuffel and G. De Baere, above n. 63, 22–23.

128 M. Claes, above n. 8, 219–20. See also T.V. Olsen, above n. 63, 76.

individual rights.[129] As a result, all the stakeholders in European society must be included in the protection of the value of democracy.[130]

This is particularly relevant when considering the intertwined nature of common values. These 'overlap' with each other: freedom of expression is a fundamental right enabling democracy;[131] AI systems can pose threats both to justice and democratic processes.[132] As a consequence, the protection of one common value relies on the respect of the others. As demonstrated by J.-W. Müller, an intervention focused exclusively on the rule of law is not coherent.[133] That author further argues that limiting the debate to the rule of law paves the way to considering 'illiberal democracies' democracies that are legitimated by electoral majority. However:

> A political system with regular elections, but clear limits on media freedom, on election campaigning, and on autonomous activity by civil society is not on the road to being an illiberal democracy; it is on the road to not being a democracy at all.[134]

In other words, to allow the concretisation of the value of democracy, individuals must have efficient access to a judge who is independent and impartial.[135] If the national judge is prevented from making preliminary references due to national political pressure[136] or because he or she does not meet the criteria of jurisdiction under Article 267 of the TFEU,[137] the Regulations and national legislation transposing the Directives will not

---

129 A. von Bogdandy, above n. 9, 715–20. See also M. Blauberger and R.D. Kelemen, above n. 120, 328–29; K.L. Scheppele, 'What can the European Commission Do When Member States Violate Basic Principles of the European Union? The Case for Systemic Infringement Actions', *Verfassungsblog* (November 2013) <https://verfassungsblog.de/wp-content/uploads/2013/11/scheppele-systemic-infringement-action-brussels-version.pdf>.

130 M. Claes, above n. 8, 219–20. See also K.L. Scheppele and R.D. Kelemen, 'Defending Democracy in EU Member States: Beyond Article 7 TEU' in F. Bignami (ed.), *EU Law in Populist Times: Crises and Prospects*, Cambridge, Cambridge University Press, 2020, pp. 413–56, p. 431.

131 T.L. Boekestein, 'Making do with what we have: on the interpretation and enforcement of the EU's founding values' (2022) 23 *German Law Journal* 431, 442.

132 Recital 61 of the AI Act, above n. 48.

133 J.-W. Müller, above n. 14, 142–43. Nor is it relevant to focus exclusively on the protection of fundamental rights: C. Antpöhler, J. Dickschen, S. Hentrei, M. Kottman, M. Smrkolj and A. von Bogdandy, 'Reverse Solange – Protecting the Essence of Fundamental Rights against EU Member States' (2012) 49(2) *Common Market Law Review* 489.

134 J.-W. Müller, above n. 14, 143. See also A. von Bogdandy, above n. 9, 738.

135 For example, the Hungarian Sovereignty Bill does not provide judicial remedies for individuals and entities that face investigations from the SPO.

136 For example, the draft version of the Spanish Amnesty Law was designed to prevent (to some extent) Spanish judges from making preliminary references under Article 267 of the TFEU, by expressly excluding conduct that affect the 'financial interests of the EU' from their scope: G.M. Teruel Lozano, 'Rule of Law Eroded: Unpacking the Catalan Amnesty Law', *Verfassungsblog* (12 June 2023) <https://verfassungsblog.de/rule-of-law-eroded/>.

137 Case C-718/21, *Krajowa Rada Sądownictwa*, ECLI:EU:C:2023:1015.

necessarily be interpreted uniformly.[138] This presupposes that Member States respect the judgment finding an infringement of EU law,[139] and that judicial dialogue between national courts and the Court of Justice be maintained.[140]

So the legislative steps taken at EU level to protect the value of democracy by implementing it through different standards can only work if EU citizens can invoke individual rights before the national judge (effectiveness); the national judge can eventually ask for an interpretation of these rights (uniformity) which could lead the Court of Justice to reinforce these rights by linking them to Article 2 of the TEU by way of interpretation (systemic constitutional impact) in the spirit of the texts.[141]

This is all the more important since values may compete with each other.[142] The implementation of the SLAPP Directive, for example, will necessitate a coherent balance across the Member States between the right to access a court and freedom of expression. For example, to avoid a journalist or another person facing abusive lawsuits it will be up to the national court or tribunal seised, if asked by the defendant, to assess whether or not a claim (e.g. of defamation) is abusive.[143] A balance between the two fundamental rights at stake could benefit from further interpretation in specific cases and a uniform approach in all Member States. It is welcome, in this regard, that the burden of proof be imposed on the claimant,[144] although the admissibility of proof could be subject to different interpretations.

SECTION V
CONCLUSION

In assessing the role of EU citizens in the concretisation of the value of democracy, there is a strong narrative in the Court of Justice case law and the European Democracy Action Plan as regards upholding this value for their protection. However, while this narrative is promising, it is mostly a top-down approach – these initiatives were not directly triggered by representative and participatory mechanisms. Nevertheless, the development of democratic standards by EU legislation could empower individuals. The latter can ask for the respect of their rights before a national judge, be it

---

138 For example, *Hungary v. European Parliament and Council of the European Union*, above n. 3, para. 233; J.H.H. Weiler, above n. 65, 97.

139 M. Claes, above n. 8, 222.

140 M. De Walsche, 'The ambivalent notion of "court or tribunal" in the context of the Rule of law crisis' (2023) 4 *Revue des affaires européennes* 927.

141 See Section II.§1 and C. Ladenburger, Y. Marinova and J. Tomkin, above n. 43, p. 125.

142 T.V. Olsen, above n. 63, 73.

143 SLAPP Directive, Articles 6(1)(b) and 11.

144 Ibid., Article 12.

against national authorities or powerful private interests, in particular online platforms. The narrative developed by the Court of Justice and academics could offer constitutional perspectives for the interpretation of these rights in case of preliminary references. Although subject to limitations, this approach offers the possibility of connecting individuals to the process of concretising democracy: not at the stage of the definition of democratic standards, but in their implementation.

Is this in keeping with the logic of *Van Gend en Loos* or in contradiction to it? Katarina Barley and Quirin Weinzierl[145] consider that *Van Gend en Loos* achieved the first foundational promise of the original Treaties: the establishment of a common market based on 'four freedoms'. The new promise made by the Lisbon Treaty would be to uphold the common values enshrined in Article 2 of the TEU, as they define the very identity of the European Union as a common legal order.

[145] K. Barley and Q. Weinzierl, above n. 4.

CHAPTER 7
THE LITIGIOUS PATH: A NEW FORM OF CITIZEN APPROPRIATION OF EU VALUES?

Ninon FORSTER*

Abstract

Citizens are increasingly making use of their right to take legal action to protect their rights and challenge state or European Union policies that they consider to be contrary to the values protected by Article 2 of the Treaty on European Union (TEU). While litigation has always been a means of contesting public authority, this judicial appropriation of values shows something about the way in which citizens understand their belonging to the European Union. Litigation can contribute to strengthening European identity, as the use of these norms, with their specific normativity, changes the role of the European Court of Justice. However, the invocation of these norms cannot be said to create an actio popularis, as the rules of litigation limit – although they do not eliminate – the legal scope of the values used to settle certain disputes.

SECTION I
INTRODUCTION

Going to court can be viewed as a powerful civic duty.[1] Litigation is a unique form of civic participation that empowers citizens to assert their interests or those of a group, and in doing so, to contribute to the general interest in a

* Professor of Public Law, Polytechnic University of Hauts-de-France.

[1] F. SAINT-BONNET, 'La citoyenneté juridictionnelle. Le prétoire préféré à l'agora' (February 2022) *JusPoliticum*, no. 27, <https://www.juspoliticum.com/articles/La-citoyennete-juridictionnelle-Le-pretoire-prefere-a-l-agora>; P. NOREAU, 'Le droit comme vecteur politique de la citoyenneté. Cadre d'analyse pour l'étude des rapports collectifs entre majorité et minorités' in M. COUTU, P. BOSSET, C. GENDREAU and D. VILLENEUVE (eds.), *Droits fondamentaux et citoyenneté: une citoyenneté fragmentée, limitée, illusoire?*, Montreal, Thémis, 2000, pp. 323–62, p. 346.

distinct manner from exercising political rights, which are the traditional mainsprings of citizenship.[2] By asserting their or others' interests, citizens act for the community, in the conviction that a particular cause – asserting a right, deploring ignorance, denouncing inaction, inciting for an issue to be taken up – contributes to serving the general interest.[3] This empowerment is evident in European citizens today who use the values of the European Union (EU) – via legal rules with singular normativity – to protect their rights and an idealised model of European society to which they aspire.

The judicial route is an essential tool for protecting the legal and political systems of the EU. The EU is highly integrated, legally speaking, which affects the relationship between the EU and its Member States, between the Member States themselves, and with individuals and citizens. As a 'Union of law',[4] the EU provides a legal framework for the actions of both national and supranational public authorities. As there is no fully developed political community, the law becomes the guide for membership in the EU. Since the *Van Gend en Loos* case,[5] individuals have played a crucial role in ensuring that both the Member States and the EU respect the rights and obligations conferred upon them by the EU.

Although the right to take legal action is not directly tied to citizenship,[6] individuals holding EU citizenship can leverage this right to support their attachment to certain EU values protected by EU Treaties. The case law refers to these values, which mainly manifest in the Court of Justice's response to the invocation of subjective rights. These rights are inherent in the fundamental status of EU citizenship, which, in turn, is founded on the values of the EU (values such as democracy and equality, which are the very essence of EU citizenship).[7] Invoking these rights:

> contributes to the promotion of the economic, social, cultural and linguistic dimensions of European citizenship in the Member States and thus contributes to the realisation of the Union's values.[8]

---

2 I. Fassassi, 'Droit d'agir en justice et citoyenneté aux Etats-Unis' (February 2022) *JusPoliticum*, no. 27, <https://www.juspoliticum.com/articles/Droit-d-agir-en-justice-et-citoyennete-aux-Etats-Unis>.

3 F. Saint-Bonnet, above n. 1.

4 Since the *Les Verts* ruling, the Court has recognised that the EU constitutes a 'community of values', describing the Treaty on European Union (TEU) (see below n. 11) as a 'constitutional charter of a community based on the rule of law', Case 294/83, *Parti écologiste 'Les Verts' v. European Parliament*, ECLI:EU:C:1986:166.

5 Case 26/62, *Van Gend en Loos*, ECLI:EU:C:1963:1.

6 Unlike in the United States: I. Fassassi, above n. 2.

7 Democracy is enacted through the right to vote and to stand for election, the principle of participation and the European Citizens' Initiative (ECI).

8 L. Potvin-Solis, 'Valeurs communes et citoyenneté européenne: quels progrès pour l'identité de l'Union devant la Cour de justice?' in L. Potvin-Solis (ed.), *Les valeurs communes dans l'Union européenne*, Brussels, Bruylant, 2014, pp. 119–54, p. 134 (translation by N. Forster).

Fundamental rights can also be invoked independently of EU citizenship and help to reinforce the value of the rule of law and respect for human rights, which are central to any democratic society. In these cases, individuals, alone or collectively, have highlighted their membership of the EU, particularly in relation to their Member State, but also in relation to the EU itself, contributing to the protection of a certain model of society.

A valuable study by Laurence Potvin-Solis has shown how case law establishes a connection between values, citizenship and the identity of the EU.[9] The aim of this chapter is not to repeat her arguments, but to focus on the way and the reason citizens appropriate the values of the EU by invoking them before a national court or the European Court of Justice (ECJ). These appropriations take place in cases in which citizens expressly invoke values in support of arguments they raise before the Court. This chapter will examine ECJ case law in this respect, and the reasons why citizens can claim these values as their own. Such an exploration is crucial to understand citizens' adoption of EU values, a process that shapes the very fabric of the EU.

Case law demonstrates that an increasing number of citizens affected by or opposed to the policies pursued by either the EU or Member States are taking the issue to court. As such, the courtroom is becoming a platform for citizens to voice their concerns, especially when the political chambers at national or supranational levels do not allow them to express their demands.[10] This use of the right to take legal action is not new or specific to EU law and can be seen as inherent in the principle of the separation of powers and the existence of judicial review. The uniqueness of these applications is that they are based directly on the values protected by Article 2 of the Treaty on European Union (TEU),[11] standards whose legal nature and justiciability raise questions.

The postulation that these values have a legal nature is now supported by the majority of academic writers,[12] but is not unanimously shared;[13] some have

---

9 Ibid., pp. 119–64.

10 Ibid., p. 134.

11 Consolidated Version of the Treaty on European Union [2016] OJ C202/13.

12 A. von Bogdandy and L.D. Spieker, 'Protecting Fundamental Rights Beyond the Charter: Repositioning Reverse *Solange* Doctrine in Light of the CJEU's Art. 2 TEU Case Law' in M. Bobek and J. Adams-Prassl (eds.), *The EU Charter of Fundamental Rights in the Member States*, Oxford, Hart Publishing, 2020, pp. 525–46, pp. 533–34; P. Zinonos, *Identité(s) transnational(s) de l'Union européenne: Analyse juridique pour un système de protection effective des droits*, Brussels, Bruylant, 2023, p. 117; R. Baratta, 'La "Communauté de valeurs" dans l'ordre juridique de l'Union européenne' in F. Peraldi-Leneuf (ed.), *Les valeurs de l'Union européenne*, Paris, Pedone, 2020, p. 91; L.D. Spieker, *EU Values before the Court of Justice: Foundations, Potential, Risks*, Oxford, Oxford University Press, 2023, p. 40.

13 D. Kochenov and L. Pech, 'Monitoring and enforcement of the rule of law in the EU: Rhetoric and reality' (2015) 11(3) *European Constitutional Law Review* 512, 520.

questioned its appropriateness.[14] Even if this assumption is established, several questions arise. What benefit does the citizen have in using values before the Court? What are the effects of invoking values on the role of the Court? And most importantly, how does the litigious use of values contribute to defining the relationship between individuals and the institutions of the European political systems they belong to, i.e. the bond of citizenship?[15]

Litigants often use values as a strategy to protect their rights, but the legal appropriation of values is also a means for citizens to participate in the definition and protection of the fundamental principles in the development of the European political community by using their capacity as litigants. As examined in Section II, the use of values is therefore a strategy that makes it possible to objectify the protection of citizens' rights. However, as will be clear in Section III, the effectiveness of this strategy is limited by the rules that govern litigation, as well as the role of courts in European society.

SECTION II
THE OBJECTIFICATION OF THE PROTECTION OF CITIZENS' RIGHTS THROUGH VALUES

An analysis of case law reveals that citizens are increasingly using the rhetoric of values to contest the legality of certain EU and national regulations.[16] This language did not originate with citizens but was inspired by a line of reasoning that has been developed by the Court of Justice since the mid-2010s. The Court has used values as an additional legal argument alongside fundamental rights when reviewing the legal legitimacy of political choices. This use of values expands the scope of the protection of fundamental rights, giving it a dimension related to the very existence of the European legal order and the EU itself. While the use of values has often only been implicit in the arguments of litigants, the Court of Justice has transcended this, paving the way for directly invoking values to protect an ideal European society.

---

14 R. Ogien, 'Les "valeurs morales" contre les droits' (2007) 6 *Raison publique* 47. This author argues that in democratic societies, there are solid reasons for favouring the immanent human language of rights, freedoms and consent over the transcendent, quasi-religious, paternalistic language of 'moral values'.

15 S. Platon, 'La citoyenneté dans ses rapports avec la démocratie participative et la démocratie directe en droit de l'Union européenne' (2015) 27 *Politeia* 283.

16 C. Perelman and L. Olbrechts-Tyteca (eds.), *Traité de l'Argumentation: La nouvelle Rhétorique*, 6th ed., Brussels, Éditions de l'université de Bruxelles, 2008, pp. 1–740.

§ 1. THE DEVELOPMENT OF THE RHETORIC OF VALUES BY THE COURT OF JUSTICE

The argument for protecting European values has long been made implicitly by litigants through the guise of fundamental rights.[17] Several cases are representative of this trend. Firstly, litigation concerning public services[18] and EU citizenship[19] provides an opportunity to establish a link between respect for the principle of equality and protection of EU values. Secondly, litigation concerning restrictive measures makes it possible to establish a link between respect for the value of the rule of law and respect for the right to access an independent and impartial tribunal or the right to defence,[20] without the applicants having initially invoked them. Thirdly, the same applies to disputes relating to the execution of a European arrest warrant, where the Court interprets the rules governing the operation of the arrest warrant in light of the protection of human dignity as a fundamental right protected by the Charter of Fundamental Rights (CFR), which 'enshrines one of the fundamental values of the Union and its Member States'.[21] The risk of harm to human dignity thus makes it possible to enshrine the national court's power to refuse to execute an arrest warrant, thereby overturning the presumption that fundamental rights

---

[17] Although this has mainly been carried out by EU institutions and in particular by the European Commission: for example, Case C-791/19, *Commission v. Poland*, ECLI:EU:C:2021:596; Case C-619/18, *Commission v. Poland*, ECLI:EU:C:2019:531; and Case C-192/18, *Commission v. Poland*, EU:C:2019:924.

[18] Case F-61/06, *Cathy Sapara*, ECLI:EU:F:2008:98, para. 107; Case T-275/17, *Michela Curto*, ECLI:EU:T:2018:479, para. 81; Case T-253/18, *VY*, ECLI:EU:T:2019:488, para. 59.

[19] For example, Case C-85/96, *Martínez Sala*, ECLI:EU:C:1998:217, para. 33; Case C-184/99, *Grzelczyk*, ECLI:EU:C:2001:458, para. 33; Case C-456/02, *Trojani*, ECLI:EU:C:2004:488, para. 40; Case C-212/06, *Gouvernement de la Communauté française et Gouvernement Wallon*, ECLI:EU:C:2008:178; and Case C-673/16, *Coman*, ECLI:EU:C:2018:385.

[20] Case T-340/14, *Andriy Klyuyev*, ECLI:EU:T:2016:496, para. 87; Case T-288/15, *Ahmed Abdelaziz Ezz*, ECLI:EU:T:2018:619, paras. 57–59: '57. First of all, it should be recalled that Article 2 TEU and Article 3(5) TEU require the institutions of the European Union to promote, in particular in international relations, the values and principles on which the European Union is founded, namely, in particular, respect for human dignity, the rule of law and fundamental rights. 58. Secondly, as the Court of Justice has pointed out, respect for those values and for the principles on which the European Union is founded is required of all actions of the European Union, including those in the area of the Common Foreign and Security Policy (CFSP), as is apparent from the provisions, read together, set out in the first subparagraph of Article 21(1), Article 21(2)(b) and (3) TEU, and Article 23 TEU (see, to that effect, judgement of 14 June 2016, *Parliament v Council*, C-263/14, EU:C:2016:435, paragraph 47). 59. In particular, Article 21(1) TEU provides that the European Union's action on the international scene is to seek to advance in the wider world, inter alia, the rule of law, the universality and indivisibility of human rights and respect for international law'.

[21] Charter of Fundamental Rights of the European Union [2016] OJ C202/389. Joined Cases C-404/15 and C-659/15 PPU, *Aranyosi*, ECLI:EU:C:2016:198, para. 87.

are protected under the framework decision establishing the European arrest warrant mechanism by virtue of its application.[22]

Although in these cases values were not explicitly appropriated by the citizen-litigants, the Court of Justice would go further, transcending the logic of protecting fundamental rights to explicitly place itself on the objective terrain of protecting values.[23] Fundamental rights protection is considered essential for the EU's existence, especially for safeguarding the Union's foundations and for forging membership in the European society being built. This logic has been used by the ECJ in politically sensitive disputes.

This was the case following the economic, financial and budgetary crisis that began in 2008, in the dispute over the austerity policies developed in the states that had recourse to financial support mechanisms. It was on this occasion that the rhetoric of values overtook that of fundamental rights for the first time, in the case that led to the judgment of the *Associação Sindical dos Juízes Portugueses (ASJP)*.[24] In this case, the Union of Judges of the Tribunal de Contas (Court of Auditors) brought an action before the Portuguese court against an administrative law providing for budgetary measures to reduce the remuneration of a number of civil servants and persons exercising functions in the public sector, including judges. This law implemented a 2014 law providing for a temporary reduction in the remuneration of persons working in Portugal's public administration. This austerity measure was adopted as part of an economic adjustment programme in return for financial assistance granted by the European Financial Stabilisation Mechanism (EFSM), the European Financial Stability Facility (EFSF) and the International Monetary Fund (IMF). Portugal's Constitutional Court declared the salary reduction measures unconstitutional for 2012 and 2013 (although no repayment or reimbursement was made for the two disputed years), while confirming their constitutionality for 2014 and 2015. The Union of Judges therefore appealed to the ECJ, arguing that the measures violated the principle of the independence of the judiciary, as enshrined in both Article 19(1) of the TEU and Article 47 of the CFR.

---

22 M. Fortunova, 'La fonction juridictionnelle et le mandat d'arrêt européen: la contribution des juges à la construction d'une Union de droit?' (2020) 635 *Revue de l'Union européenne* 95. *Minister for Justice and Equality*, above n. 21, para. 75. The mere finding of a violation of human dignity is not sufficient to suspend the execution of a European arrest warrant. The applicant and his or her lawyer have to provide evidence in support of their 'specific concerns' about the risk that these systemic or general failings will have an impact on his or her particular case, taking into account his or her personal situation, the nature of the offence for which he or she is being prosecuted and the factual context on which the arrest warrant is based.

23 The ECJ drew in part on the Opinions of its Advocates General: for example, see the Opinion of AG Jacobs, Case C-168/91, *Konstantinidis*, ECLI:EU:C:1992:504, para. 46; and Opinion of AG Tesauro, Case C-13/94, *P v. S*, ECLI:EU:C:1995:444, para. 9.

24 Case C-64/16, *Associação Sindical dos Juízes Portugueses (ASJP)*, ECLI:EU:C:2018:117.

This was not the first time that the legality of austerity measures had been in question. The decision to resort to financial aid and austerity measures had been at the centre of a major political crisis in Portugal, leading to an alliance of opposition parties and the resignation of Socialist Party Prime Minister José Sócrates in 2011, followed by ongoing tensions within Portuguese institutions. Every announcement of the introduction of austerity measures had led to a massive mobilisation of Portuguese society to reject this economic policy, as seen in successive general strikes and the significant social consequences of these austerity plans.[25] The courts, highlighting the violation of fundamental rights that these measures entailed, very quickly became the preferred means of challenging them. On several occasions, the Portuguese courts, and in particular the Constitutional Court, ruled that some of these measures were unconstitutional. One measure cut the salaries of civil servants.[26]

The ECJ was asked to rule on actions for annulment or preliminary rulings on the interpretation and assessment of the validity either of the national acts adopting the contested measures or directly against the protocols to the agreements and the economic adjustment programmes. However, it never ruled on the legality of these programmes.[27] In the *ASJP* case, it was not only

---

25 Le Monde, 'Grève générale massive contre l'austérité au Portugal', *LeMonde.fr* (24 November 2010) <https://www.lemonde.fr/economie/article/2010/11/24/les-portugais-en-greve-generale-contre-l-austerite_1444170_3234.html>; Le Monde, 'Grève générale au Portugal contre l'austérité', *LeMonde.fr* (24 November 2011) <https://www.lemonde.fr/europe/article/2011/11/24/greve-generale-au-portugal-contre-l-austerite_1608356_3214.html>; Le Monde, 'Grève générale et manifestations contre l'austérité au Portugal', *LeMonde.fr* (22 March 2012) <https://www.lemonde.fr/economie/article/2012/03/22/portugal-greve-generale-et-manifestations-contre-l-austerite_1674057_3234.html>; Le Monde, 'Au Portugal, nouvelle journée de protestation contre l'austérité', *LeMonde.fr* (30 May 2013) <https://www.lemonde.fr/economie/article/2013/05/30/le-portugal-proteste-contre-l-austerite_3421291_3234.html>. Historically, this rejection of calls for international financial assistance can be partly explained by the two previous interventions of the IMF in 1975 and 1983, which 'had resulted in an extremely severe austerity policy, breaking with the revolutionary hope linked to the fall of the dictatorship', see J.-F. Humbert, 'Austerity in Portugal', *Le Monde* (30 May 2013). J.-F. Humbert, 'La crise économique et financière au Portugal' (2011) Rapport d'information 249, *Senat*, p. 24 <https://www.senat.fr/notice-rapport/2010/r10-249-notice.html>.

26 M. Canotilho, T. Violante and R. Lanceiro, 'Austerity measures under judicial scrutiny: the Portuguese constitutional case law' (2015) 11(1) *European Constitutional Law Review* 155, 172; A.M. Guerra Martins, 'Constitutional Judge, Social Rights and Public Debt Crisis: The Portuguese Constitutional Case Law' (2015) 22(5) *Maastricht Journal of European and Comparative Law* 678; F. Pereira Coutinho, 'Austerity on the loose in Portugal: European judicial restraint in times of crisis' (2016) 8(3) *Perspectives on Federalism* 105.

27 In reference to Portugal: Case C-128/12, *Sindicato dos Bancários do Norte and Others v. BPN – Banco Português de Negócios SA*, ECLI:EU:C:2013:149; Case C-264/12, *Sindicato Nacional dos Profissionais de Seguros e Afins v. Fidelidade Mundial – Companhia de Seguros SA*, ECLI:EU:C:2014:2036; Case C-665/13, *Sindicato Nacional dos Profissionais de Seguros e Afins v. Via Directa – Companhia de Seguros SA*, ECLI:EU:C:2014:2327. In reference to Romania: Case C-434/11, *Corpul Naţional al Poliţiştilor v. Ministerul Administraţiei şi Internelor (MAI) and Others*, ECLI:EU:C:2011:830; Case C-134/12, *Corpul Naţional al Poliţiştilor*

the national measures that were at issue, but also, indirectly, the austerity programme that was the subject of negotiations with EU institutions, or at least its consequences.

Previously, the ECJ, refusing to position itself as an 'economic judge',[28] had refused or limited its review of these measures. However, the difference between this case and its predecessors is that it was presented not as an 'austerity case' but as a 'rule of law case', which, in the ECJ's words, concerns the very foundations of the EU. The reasoning was as follows: rule of law is one of the values protected by Article 2 of the TEU, which is concretised by Article 19(1) of the TEU on the organisation of the EU's judicial system, obliging each Member State to guarantee effective judicial protection in accordance with Article 47 of the CFR, and thus the independence and impartiality of courts.[29] Consequently, a breach of the principle of effective judicial protection would undermine the proper functioning of the EU's judicial system. This would call Article 2 of the TEU into question and, by the same token, the very foundation of the EU, since, as the ECJ pointed out, in accordance with Article 2 of the TEU, the 'Union is founded on values, such as the rule of law, which are common to the Member States in a society in which, inter alia, justice prevails'. Mutual trust between the Member States, and particularly between their courts, relies on the fact that these states share the common values on which the Union is based.[30]

The ECJ did not assess the legality of a particular policy, but rather its consequences – in particular, whether it undermined respect for the values on which the state's membership of the EU is based and on which the Union's very existence is founded. In the *ASJP* case, the ECJ concluded that the national measures in question were not such as to undermine the independence of the judiciary. But by relying on the rhetoric of values and by bringing within the scope of its review all national measures that may affect the organisation or functioning of national courts when the latter are called upon to rule on EU law, the Court of Justice considerably strengthened its power and reinforced its role as a constitutional court.

This reasoning has subsequently been taken up on a number of occasions, and even been developed further, as in the *Repubblika* judgment,[31] in which the ECJ developed the principle of non-regression of the rule of law under

Ministerul Administrației și Internelor and Others, ECLI:EU:C:2012:288; Case C-369/12, *Corpul Național al Polițiștilor – Biroul Executiv Central, reprezentant al reclamanților Chițea Constantin și al ții v. Ministerul Administrației și Internelor and Others*, ECLI:EU:C:2012:725.

28 P. Corre and N. Forster, 'Mesures d'austérité et droits fondamentaux devant la Cour de justice de l'Union européenne et la Cour européenne des droits de l'Homme: exception ou inadaptation?' (2018) 2 *Revue des affaires européennes* 289.

29 *ASJP*, above n. 24, paras. 31–32.

30 Ibid., para. 30.

31 Case C-896/19, *Repubblika v. Il-Prim Ministru*, ECLI:EU:C:2021:311, para. 63.

Article 2 of the TEU. In that case, the Maltese court asked a number of questions concerning the procedure for the appointment of judges, which had remained unchanged in the Maltese Constitution since 1964; the case was brought by a Maltese non-profit organisation for the protection of justice and the rule of law. It asked whether this procedure for appointing judges was compatible with Article 19(2) of the TEU and Article 2 of the TEU. The ECJ replied that, under Article 49 of the TEU, accession to the Union is conditional on respect for the values set out in Article 2 of the TEU. That continuing obligation, accepted by the Member State, gives rise to a principle of non-regression that prevents the state from amending its legislation in such a way as to undermine the protection of the value of the rule of law guaranteed by Article 2 of the TEU.

In disputes involving a confrontation between citizens or their representatives and a government that denies the basis of its adherence to, or even its participation in, the political project of European integration, the Court used this line of reasoning. This was the case in the *Wightman* judgment concerning the United Kingdom's withdrawal from the EU and interpreting Article 50 of the TEU. This case was the result of a referral by British Members of Parliament to their national court on the possibility of a vote by Parliament on a unilateral suspension of the procedure for withdrawal from the EU. Although the question of respect for values was not formulated in the question referred by the national court, the ECJ interpreted Article 50 of the TEU in light of those values, stating that:

> the importance of the values of liberty and democracy, referred to in the second and fourth recitals of the preamble to the TEU, which are among the common values referred to in Article 2 of that Treaty and in the preamble to the Charter of Fundamental Rights of the European Union, and which thus form part of the very foundations of the European Union legal order,[32]

means that a state 'cannot be forced to accede to the European Union against its will, neither can it be forced to withdraw from the European Union against its will'.[33]

These judgments are fundamental because with them the Court of Justice has developed a new line of reasoning that places the values enshrined in Article 2 of the TEU at the centre of the interpretation of the other provisions of the Treaty and the CFR. Although values were not directly invoked by the litigant or the referring court in these cases, this line of reasoning would subsequently be used on many occasions. Indeed, values are increasingly invoked to support actions brought before national and European courts.

---

32 Case C-621/18, *Wightman*, ECLI:EU:C:2018:999, para. 62.
33 Ibid., para. 65.

§ 2. CITIZENS' STRATEGIC USE OF THE RHETORIC OF VALUES

The reasoning developed in the *ASJP* and *Repubblika* cases would go on to be directly applied by litigants themselves. This can be seen in disputes concerning the Polish government's non-respect for the independence of the judiciary. To challenge the rules governing the organisation of the courts in Poland, the applicants appealed directly to values.

The reform of the Polish judicial system begun by the government of the Law and Justice Party (PiS) in 2015 has been the subject of numerous cases brought to the Supreme Court of Poland,[34] the Supreme Administrative Court,[35] and the lower courts.[36] These cases, giving rise to preliminary rulings, were brought by members of the public wishing to use the value of the rule of law to challenge all aspects of the judicial reform: the procedures for the recruitment and appointment of judges, the measures relating to the lowering of the retirement age for judges, the disciplinary procedures applicable to judges, and the independence of the disciplinary chamber of the Supreme Court. In these cases, judges and other litigants, in particular in criminal proceedings, brought actions challenging the measures taken against them as a result of this judicial reform, on the basis of Article 19(1) of the TEU and Article 47 of the CFR, read in light of Article 2 of the TEU.[37] Moreover, the national courts hearing these cases have, themselves, interpreted their role as national courts of EU law by submitting questions to the ECJ for preliminary rulings, the wording of which is more indicative of a request 'for the Court of Justice's approval than of a request for clarification of the meaning to be given to the provisions of European Union law'.[38] As Julie Teyssedre notes:

> the questions are targeted and sometimes particularly detailed [...] the national courts are clearly asking the Court of Justice to go beyond the limits of its preliminary ruling jurisdiction in order to rule not only on the interpretation of

---

34 For example, see Joined Cases C-585/18, C-624/18 and C-625/18, *A.K. and Others*, ECLI:EU:C:2019:982; Case C-522/18, *Zakład Ubezpieczeń Społecznych*, ECLI:EU:C:2020:42; Case C-537/18, *Krajowa Rada Sądownictwa*, ECLI:EU:C:2020:136; Case C-487/19, *W.Ż.*, ECLI:EU:C:2021:798; Case C-508/19, *Prokurator Generalny*, ECLI:EU:C:2022:201.

35 Case C-824/18, *A.B. and Others*, ECLI:EU:C:2021:153.

36 Joined Cases C-748/19 to C-754/19, *W.B. and Others*, ECLI:EU:C:2021:931; Joined Cases C-558/18 and C-563/18, *Miasto Łowicz*, ECLI:EU:C:2020:234.

37 *A.K. and Others*, above n. 34, paras. 51 and 52; *A.B. and Others*, above n. 35, para. 45; *W.B. and Others*, above n. 36, para. 62.

38 J. Teyssedre, 'La judiciarisation du contrôle du respect de l'État de droit: la Cour de justice au chevet des juges nationaux' (2020) 1 *Revue trimestrielle de droit européen* 23, 31.

national law but also on its compatibility with Union law and even to draw the consequences for the resolution of the dispute.[39]

The opposition to judicial reform in Poland is not the only instance of citizens appropriating values. Other examples include litigants invoking values in support of their interpretation of the conditions for admissibility of a case before the General Court and the Court of Justice. The case that led to the 2020 *Lukáš Wagenknecht* ruling is representative of this form of appropriation. In that case, a Czech senator brought an action before the General Court against the European Council's failure to act when it refused to exclude the Prime Minister of the Czech Republic from a Council meeting on the grounds of a potential conflict of interest due to his personal and family interests in companies belonging to the Agrofert Group, which is active in the agri-food sector and receives subsidies from the EU. The General Court dismissed the action as inadmissible, holding that, if the measure had been adopted, he would not have been directly and individually concerned by it, as if it had been addressed to him. In his appeal, the appellant invoked the 'fundamental value of justice as enshrined in Article 2 TEU'[40] and argued that the ECJ should interpret the conditions for the admissibility of a case for failure to act more flexibly, taking into account his status as a representative of Czech citizens. This approach highlights the fact that, in his view, the protection of the values of the EU, and in particular the need to combat conflicts of interest, should justify the granting of access to the EU Court of Justice to him as a representative of Czech citizens in order to uphold the ideal of justice, which is a value protected by the EU. Although the ECJ did not discuss or interpret the provisions in the sense sought by the applicant, the values were invoked before the Court in support of a vision of European society and the way in which political institutions should ensure they are respected.

The litigious appropriation of values has not only served to oppose certain choices made by political powers; it has also allowed citizens to participate in defining their meaning. The courtroom is a place of debate,[41] and democracy thrives on contradiction. In the context of a dispute or a reference to the Court of Justice for a preliminary ruling, the citizen contributes to defining

---

39 Ibid. In parallel, it should be noted that EU institutions have also used the rhetoric of values to support their actions against Poland for its failure to fulfil obligations in the dispute relating to the reform of the judicial system: see Case C-619/18, *Commission v. Poland*, ECLI:EU:C:2019:531; Case C-192/18, *Commission v. Poland*, ECLI:EU:C:2019:924. In the context of actions against Hungary for failure to fulfil obligations, the Commission even takes this rhetoric to the point of basing its action solely on Article 2 of the TEU, irrespective of any standard of implementation.

40 Case C-504/20 P, *Lukáš Wagenknecht*, ECLI:EU:T:2021:305, para. 38.

41 P. Noreau, above n. 1, p. 329.

the meaning of values, even if the ruling falls ultimately to the Court. The litigation concerning the European Citizens' Initiative (ECI), a 'fundamental instrument for European participatory democracy',[42] is an example of the way in which European citizens can rely on values in the exercise of their rights as citizens, as protected in Chapter V of the CFR, which is devoted to citizenship. Employing the obligation to state reasons stemming from the right to good administration, citizens have brought actions for annulment before the ECJ against Commission decisions that challenge the Commission's failure to adopt a position on the definition of the meaning to be given to certain values protected by Article 2 of the TEU. In doing so, citizens have proposed their own interpretation of what these values mean.

One example is the case of the 'One of Us' ECI initiative, which led to the *One of Us*[43] and *Puppinck*[44] rulings. The ECI, which was at the centre of the case, sought to get the EU to ban and stop funding activities involving the destruction of human embryos, in particular in the fields of research, development aid and public health, to respect human dignity and integrity. The Commission decided not to take any action, as it stated in a communication, i.e. not to exercise its legislative power, despite the fact that the ECI had collected the required number of signatures.[45] In support of its refusal to act, the Commission argued that EU law already provided the necessary legal framework to protect human dignity and public health. The Commission's reasoning is interesting in that it takes care not to comment on the fundamental thesis underlying the 'One of Us' initiative, according to which 'the human embryo is a human being [...] who therefore has human dignity'.[46] Yet the Commission's comments on the fundamental thesis was precisely the wish of the organisers of the initiative, based on Article 2 of the TEU. This desire, expressed in an action for annulment in the form of a complaint that the European Commission had failed to comply with its obligation to state reasons, illustrates the way in which European citizens turn to the courts to obtain, on the one hand, the definition of the EU values that they wish to assert, but also the importance of democratic mechanisms such as the ECI in contributing to the definition of these values. Here, by interpreting the European Commission's obligations in the ECI procedure, the court becomes the arbiter of the proper functioning of democratic mechanisms.

---

42 Opinion of AG Mengozzi, Case C-589/15 P, *Alexios Anagnostakis*, ECLI:EU:C:2017:175, para. 2.

43 Case T-561/14, *European Citizens' Initiative One of Us*, ECLI:EU:T:2018:210, para. 134.

44 Case C-418/18 P, *Puppinck and Others*, ECLI:EU:C:2019:1113.

45 'Communication from the Commission on the European Citizens' Initiative "One of us"', COM(2014) 355 final (28 May 2014).

46 *European Citizens' Initiative One of Us*, above n. 43, para. 134.

However, a word of caution: values can also be invoked in conflicts that are essentially political and do not seek to protect a model of society. For example, in the *Ingrid Alice Mayer* case,[47] the plaintiff invoked the value of the rule of law in a more pragmatic way, in support of her right to appeal in order to assert a subjective right to the renewal of her contract with the European Food Safety Authority. While the rhetoric of values has become an important dimension in highly political disputes, this represents a strategy, first employed by the Court and now by the citizen, to use increasingly higher legal standards in the hierarchy of European norms in order to circumvent certain obstacles that stand in the way of judicial review, by objectifying the protection of rights. Sometimes this is in favour of the protection of a model of society, but it is also used for more pragmatic purposes. The increasing use of values should not be misleading about their limited legal scope, even though they are invoked in support of all kinds of arguments.

SECTION III
THE LEGAL LIMITS OF THE APPROPRIATION OF VALUES

The purpose of each legal remedy, but also the role of European courts, imposes certain limits on the appropriation of values by citizens. On the one hand, it is not up to citizens to go beyond the limited legal scope of these norms on the basis of values. Nor is it up to them to use legal remedies beyond their purpose by widening access to the ECJ, a court with the exclusive jurisdiction to interpret values.

§ 1. THE LIMITED LEGAL SCOPE OF VALUES

The recognition of values as a legal norm does not allow their scope to be determined in the EU legal order, in particular their justiciability. In the first place, the justiciability of values derives from the specific nature of this category of norms. Values have a degree of generality and abstraction linked to the fact that they refer to an extra-legal and moral substratum, which has raised doubts as to whether citizens can rely on them before a court. Although case law shows that they have 'sufficient authority to lead to a positive concretisation of their content',[48] their scope is nevertheless limited. It follows from the case

47 Case T-493/14, *Ingrid Alice Mayer*, ECLI:EU:T:2017:100, para. 38.

48 J.H.H. Weiler, *The Constitution of Europe: 'Do the New Clothes Have an Emperor?' and Other Essays on European Integration*, Cambridge, Cambridge University Press, 1999, pp. 102–04, quoted from P. Zinonos, above n. 12, p. 121.

law that citizens cannot expect courts to exercise the full range of powers conferred on them by their office. The theory of 'invocability' helps to explain this observation.[49]

'Invocability' refers to the possibility for an individual to refer a matter to a court in order to ask it, on the basis of values, to: interpret national or European law in accordance with these values (invocability of interpretation); substitute the invoked rule for the national or European law that is contrary to EU law (invocability of substitution); annul the national or European law that is contrary to these values (invocability of exclusion); or hold the state or the Union liable for breaches of EU law (invocability of liability). Each of these, however, depends on certain conditions inherent to the norm, which values do not fulfil. Firstly, the grounds of exclusion and substitution must be ruled out insofar as they imply the direct effect of values. This has never been recognised by the ECJ in the current state of positive law. Without having to rule on the possibility of values by their very nature producing this type of effect, it appears that they are not unconditional, which is a central criterion for producing direct effect.[50]

Part of this limitation to the autonomous legal scope of values is the logic of concretisation developed by the Court of Justice. The EU's values have always been invoked in connection with principles or rights that have a direct effect, so that they result in excluding or precluding conflicting national rules. This is the case with the value of the rule of law, which is enshrined in Article 19(2) of the TEU and Article 47 of the CFR. The same applies to the value of democracy, enshrined in Article 11 of the Treaty on the Functioning of the European Union (TFEU),[51] which is linked to Article 8 of the Protocol on the Privileges and Immunities of the European Union,[52] and Article 10(1) of

---

[49] D. Simon, *Le système juridique communautaire*, 3rd ed., Paris, Presses Universitaires de France, 2001, p. 342. For an explicit reference to the modulation of the forms of invocability, see the Opinion of AG Léger, Case C-287/98, *Linster*, ECLI:EU:C:2000:3, para. 65.

[50] Opinion of AG Pikamäe, Case C-457/18, *Slovenia v. Croatia*, ECLI:EU:C:2019:1067, para. 132. In contrast, see, e.g. O. Kadlec and D. Kosar, 'Romanian Version of the Rule of Law Crisis Comes to the ECJ: The AFJR case is not just about the Cooperation and Verification Mechanism' (2022) 59(6) *Common Market Law Review* 1823; L.S. Rossi, 'Legal Value of Values: Article 2 TEU: Interplay with Other EU Primary Law Provisions and Judicial Remedies' (2020) 3 *Revue Trimestrielle de droit européen* 639, 657; M. Safjan, 'On Symmetry: In Search of an Appropriate Response to the Crisis of the Democratic State' (2020) *Il diritto dell'Unione* 673. The action for failure to fulfil obligations brought by the European Commission before the Court of Justice against Hungarian provisions violating the rights of LGBTQ+ persons, based solely on Article 2 of the TEU, should clarify this issue: see Pending Case C-769/22, *Commission v. Hungary*.

[51] Consolidated Version of the Treaty on the Functioning of the European Union [2016] OJ C202/47.

[52] Case C-163/10, *Patriciello*, ECLI:EU:C:2011:543, para. 31.

the TEU.[53] More generally, in its judgments on rule of law conditionality, the Court of Justice has established a link with the values and rights enshrined in the CFR. The Court has also identified other possible links between Article 2 of the TEU and other Treaty provisions. While Articles 6, 10 to 13, 15, 16, 20, 21 and 23 of the CFR 'define the scope' of the values of human dignity, freedom, equality and respect for human rights, Articles 8, 10, 19(1), 153(1) and 157(1) of the TFEU give substance to the values of equality, non-discrimination and equality between women and men.[54]

While this logic makes it possible to extend the legal scope of values, it does not lead to the recognition of their autonomous direct effect. Similarly, although the issue has never been before the Court of Justice, it is unlikely that in the current state of the law there will be recognition of the enforceability of reparation. The latter requires proof that the violation of the rule of law that has caused harm to an individual confers rights on that individual. Since values do not recognise subjective rights, it is again the rules that give effect to them that can be the basis of a claim for reparation before the national court or the General Court of the European Union.

Nevertheless, this logic of concretisation also allows citizens to appropriate values by reconciling them with principles or rights that concretise these values and to benefit from greater invocability. The use of values is not merely symbolic; the national or European court must interpret the rules of concretisation in light of these values. The invocability of interpretation does not impose any particular conditions on the rules interpreted. The only condition is that it should not lead to a *contra legem* interpretation.[55] The ECJ has made it clear in its case law that a provision that does not have direct effect may oblige the national authorities to interpret the law in accordance with the law of the EU,[56] and thus in accordance with the values set out in Article 2 of

[53] Case C-502/19 *Junqueras Vies*, ECLI:EU:C:2019:1115, para. 63; Case C-629/21 P, *Puigdemont i Casamajó and Others v. Parliament and Spain*, ECLI:EU:C:2022:413, para. 250; Case C-207/21 P, *Commission v. Poland (Protocol no. 36)*, ECLI:EU:C:2022:560, para. 81; *Puppinck and Others*, above n. 44, para. 64. For similar connections between Article 2 of the TEU and Article 10(1)/(2) of the TEU, see, e.g. Case T-624/16, *Gollnisch v. Parliament*, ECLI:EU:T:2018:121, para. 44; Case T-86/17, *Le Pen v. Parliament*, ECLI:EU:T:2018:357, para. 175; Case T-626/16, *Troszczynski v. Parliament*, ECLI:EU:T:2018:270, para. 163.

[54] Case C-156/21, *Hungary v. European Parliament and Council*, ECLI:EU:C:2022:97, paras. 157–58.

[55] Case C-14/83, *Von Colson*, ECLI:EU:C:1984:153, para. 26; D. Simon, 'La panacée de l'interprétation conforme: injonction homéopathique ou thérapie palliative?' in V. Kronenberger, M.T. D'Alessio and V. Placco (eds.), *De Rome à Lisbonne, les juridictions de l'Union européenne à la croisée des chemins: Mélanges en l'honneur de Paolo Mengozzi*, Bruylant, Brussels 2013, pp. 282–83.

[56] Case C-573/17, *Popławski*, ECLI:EU:C:2019:530, para. 72; Case C-308/19, *Whiteland Import*, ECLI:EU:C:2021:47, para. 30. The same applies, according to well-established jurisprudence, to directives lacking direct effect, Joined Cases C-397/01 to C-403/01, *Pfeiffer*, ECLI:EU:C:2004:584, para. 113.

the TEU.[57] Similarly, the interpretation of EU law by the Court of Justice has to be in accordance with the values of Article 2 of the TEU. In this respect, citizens are able to rely fully on them.

It should also be noted that the standard of application is important, as this determines the scope of the value. The scope will be limited to the field of application of EU law if the standard of application is a fundamental principle. Conversely, if the standard of application is a structural principle, such as in Article 19(1) or Article 10 of the TEU, the scope will be broader in that it refers to 'the field of implementation of Union law'. 'Implementing' is a generic term used to designate all the mechanisms used in the application of EU law.[58] This reasoning is different from the former; it provides better judicial protection of the values on which citizens can rely, and it does not do so in a way that is incompatible with the principle of subsidiarity.

Yet the scope of values is not the only obstacle to their appropriation for litigation. The conditional access to EU courts resulting from the operation of the remedies of the EU judicial system can also be cited.

§ 2. CITIZENS' CONDITIONAL ACCESS TO THE ECJ

In order to make European values their own, citizens must have access to the courts, and in particular to the Court of Justice, which has exclusive jurisdiction to interpret the values of the EU. However, this is not always the case. The conditions of access are often limited by the very purpose of the legal remedies.[59] Without going into detail, suffice it to say that the admissibility of actions for direct review of legality is limited to demonstrating conditions that are difficult to prove and that relate to standing. The infringement or the risk of infringement of Article 2 of the TEU does not justify a wider interpretation of the conditions for admissibility of actions for annulment.[60]

The protection of EU values by means of a reference for a preliminary ruling is also subject to certain restrictions. These restrictions derive from the conditions for admissibility of a reference for a preliminary ruling and prevent an abstract review of the conformity of a national or European rule with the values of the EU, or at least with the rules that give them concrete form.

57 C. Rizcallah, *Le principe de confiance mutuelle en droit de l'Union européenne*, Brussels, Bruylant, 2020, p. 353; M. Dougan, 'When worlds collide! Competing visions of the relationship between direct effect and supremacy' (2007) 44(4) *Common Market Law Review* 931, 946.

58 P. Auriel, *L'équivalence des protections des droits fondamentaux dans l'Union européenne*, Brussels, Bruylant, 2020, p. 135.

59 J. Wildemeersch, 'La jurisprudence récente relative aux conditions de recevabilité du recours en annulation devant la C.J.U.E.' (2021) 3 *Journal de droit européen* 102.

60 Case C-130/21 P, *Lukáš Wagenknecht v. Commission*, ECLI:EU:C:2022:226, para. 52.

A reference for a preliminary ruling may not be used to bring an action for failure to fulfil obligations – which allows the direct review of the legality of national measures – or to bring an action for annulment, failure to act or illegality. The admissibility of a reference for a preliminary ruling presupposes a link between the subject matter of the dispute and the provision whose interpretation is sought, in accordance with Article 267 of the TFEU. In addition, the admissibility of a reference for a preliminary ruling presupposes the existence of a dispute as to the substance of the case and proof that a reference to the Court of Justice is appropriate for the resolution of the dispute.[61] It is not for the Court to give advisory opinions on general or hypothetical questions, as the ECJ has repeatedly stated.[62]

This rule has led the Court of Justice to reject references for preliminary rulings in which the conformity of national law with EU values was raised without the national provisions in question having any direct connection with the provisions to be interpreted, or where the interpretation could not serve to resolve the dispute on the merits. For example, in the *Miasto Łowicz* judgment,[63] the ECJ rejected the preliminary questions referred by the Polish courts of Lodz and Warsaw on the grounds that the reference was irrelevant.[64] The main case concerned the payment of costs incurred by a Polish city in the performance of certain tasks entrusted to it in the field of public administration. The second case concerned criminal proceedings brought against certain individuals for involvement in kidnapping, in the context of which an exceptional sentence reduction was envisaged. The national courts, concerned about the disciplinary proceedings to which they might be subject as a result of the reference for a preliminary ruling or of any subsequent decision, asked the ECJ to rule on the compatibility of the provisions of the disciplinary system resulting from the reform of the judicial system in Poland with Article 19(1) of the TEU, read in conjunction with Article 47 of the CFR, which gives practical effect to Article 2 of the TEU. The ECJ, although traditionally more open to the admissibility of references for a preliminary ruling in the context of such disputes, found that the disputes in the main proceedings had no connection with Article 19(1) of the TEU, since the national measures interpreted had no connection with that Article, and its interpretation was not necessary in order to clarify the interpretation of those provisions of the Treaty.[65]

---

61 Joined Cases C-297/88 and C-197/89, *Dzodzi*, ECLI:EU:C:1990:360, para. 33; *Miasto Łowicz*, above n. 36, para. 44; Case C-223/23, *L.D.*, ECLI:EU:C:2023:1033, para. 51.

62 See cases in above n. 61; see also *Wightman*, above n. 32, para. 28.

63 *Miasto Łowicz*, above n. 36.

64 M. Jałoszewski, 'The "Disciplinary Chamber" has suspended Judge Tuleya and allowed criminal charges to be brought against him', *Rule of Law in Poland* (23 November 2020) <https://ruleoflaw.pl/the-disciplinary-chamber-has-suspended-judge-tuleya-and-allowed-criminal-charges-to-be-brought-against-him/>.

65 *Miasto Łowicz*, above n. 36, para. 49; see also *L.D.*, above n. 61.

Lastly, it should be borne in mind that individuals cannot bring actions directly before the ECJ, since the procedure can only be initiated by a court of a Member State. Consequently, the applicant can only raise the issue of the incompatibility of a national provision with EU values in the context of a preliminary question on interpretation, or the incompatibility of an EU provision with European values in the context of a preliminary ruling on validity, since only the national court is in a position to assess whether it is entitled or obliged to stay the proceedings.

SECTION IV
CONCLUSION

To conclude, the appropriation of values is one of the vectors of a still idealised collective identity. Values appear as 'the main pillar of the legitimacy of the European whole'[66] on which citizens base themselves. This approach is encouraged by the Court of Justice, which states that '[t]he values contained in Article 2 TEU [...] define the very identity of the European Union as a common legal order'.[67] The EU must, therefore, be able to defend these values within the limits of the powers conferred on it by the Treaties. This appropriation of values shows that they have, for citizens, the same function as European citizenship. So much so that one wonders whether the discourse on values is not destined to take precedence over that of European citizenship, which is more limited due to the limits of the status of EU citizen. In fact, values make it possible to construct 'a dynamic shared identity that transcends the plural nationalities of its components by establishing a status of belonging common to the members of the various state collectivities'.[68] Nevertheless, this appropriation is limited by the very conditions of litigation, which prevents considering that this appropriation will lead to developing an *actio popularis*. There is no doubt, however, that this appropriation of values is a powerful instrument to strengthen the identity of the EU in the eyes of its citizens, particularly in relation to the states, but also in relation to EU institutions, which are responsible for ensuring its future.

---

66 J. Lacroix, 'Une démocratie sans libertés? Réflexions sur la notion de démocratie illibérale' in J. Lacroix, *Les valeurs de l'Europe et l'indétermination démocratique*, Collège de France conference (15 November 2023).

67 Case C-157/21, *Poland v. Parliament and Council*, ECLI:EU:C:2022:98, para. 145; see also *Wightman*, above n. 32, paras. 62–63.

68 E. Dubout, 'L'échec de la citoyenneté européenne? Les mutations d'une citoyenneté complexe en période de crise identitaire' (July 2017) *JusPoliticum*, no. 18 <https://www.juspoliticum.com/articles/L-echec-de-la-citoyennete-europeenne-Les-mutations-d-une-citoyennete-complexe-en-periode-de-crise-identitaire>.

CHAPTER 8
THE PROTECTION OF PRIVACY AND PERSONAL DATA AS THE CORNERSTONE OF EUROPEAN DIGITAL CITIZENSHIP

Anastasia ILIOPOULOU-PENOT*

SECTION I
INTRODUCTION

The European Declaration on Digital Rights and Principles for the Digital Decade,[1] adopted on 15 December 2022 by the European Parliament, the Commission and the Council, announces the Union's 'aim to promote a European way for the digital transformation, putting people at the centre, built on European values and EU fundamental rights'. Using the term 'citizens' instead of 'people', the French version of the text further underlines the need to establish a mutually empowering and fulfilling relationship between values, fundamental rights and citizenship in an increasingly digitised society. Both the EU legislature and judiciary have been receptive to such a need and willing to participate in the ongoing construction of the 'right to have rights' in the algorithmic ecosystem.

Indeed, the case law of the Court of Justice on the protection of personal data has progressively developed a number of substantial rights and procedural guarantees for internet users and, more generally, for users of digital

* Professor of European Law, Paris-Panthéon-Assas University, Centre for European Law.

1 European Declaration on Digital Rights and Principles for the Digital Decade [2023] OJ C23/1 <https://digital-strategy.ec.europa.eu/en/library/european-declaration-digital-rights-and-principles>. This declaration can be seen as part of a broader phenomenon of the emergence of non-binding declarations of digital rights and principles, supported by civil society. On this phenomenon and the changes it leads to for the constitutional ecosystem, see E. CELESTE, *Digital Constitutionalism: The Role of Internet Bills of Rights*, Abingdon, Routledge, 2023.

technologies. These new entitlements are essentially the result of a creative reading of secondary law in the light of two provisions of the Charter of Fundamental Rights (CFR):[2] Article 7, which enshrines respect for private life, and Article 8, which constitutionalises protection of personal data. Asserting itself as both a human rights adjudicator[3] and a judge-regulator, the Court of Justice is patiently building a particular status[4] protecting both the individual and collective European values, especially privacy. This dynamic, initiated by the Court, has been further reinforced by the EU legislature. The adoption of the General Data Protection Regulation (GDPR)[5] defines a coherent set of rights of the 'data subject', giving flesh to a European vision of data privacy capable of producing a 'Brussels effect'.[6] The success story of the GDPR has paved the way for the adoption of the Digital Services Act (DSA)[7], the Digital Markets Act (DMA)[8] and the Artificial Intelligence Act (AI Act).[9] These instruments are emblematic expressions of the EU's 'digital Constitution'[10] and regulatory leadership in the sphere of new technologies.

This chapter begins by examining three central components of the status of the user of digital technologies. It then argues that it is possible to qualify this status as a 'European digital citizenship',[11] the essence of which is the

---

2 Charter of Fundamental Rights of the European Union [2016] OJ C202/389.

3 F. Fabbrini, 'The EU Charter of Fundamental Rights and the Rights to Data Privacy: The EU Court of Justice as a Human Rights Court' in S. de Vries, U. Bernitz and S. Weatherill (eds.), *The EU Charter of Fundamental Rights as a Binding Instrument: Five Years Old and Growing*, Oxford, Hart Publishing, 2015, pp. 261–86.

4 See J.-C. Bonichot, 'Données personnelles: l'invention européenne d'un monde nouveau' (2023) 185 *Pouvoirs* 97.

5 Council Regulation (EU) 2016/679 of 27 April 2016 on the protection of natural persons with regard to the processing of personal data and on the free movement of such data (General Data Protection Regulation/GDPR) [2016] OJ L119/1.

6 See A. Bradford, 'Digital Economy' in A. Bradford, *The Brussels Effect: How the European Union Rules the World*, Oxford, Oxford University Press, 2020, pp. 131–69. See also E. Fahey, *The EU as a Global Digital Actor: Institutionalising Global Data Protection, Trade, and Cybersecurity*, Oxford, Hart Publishing, 2022.

7 Council Regulation (EU) 2022/2065 of 19 October 2022 on a Single Market for Digital Services (Digital Services Act) [2022] OJ L277/1.

8 Council Regulation (EU) 2022/1925 of 14 September 2022 on contestable and fair markets in the digital sector (Digital Markets Act) [2022] OJ L265/1.

9 Council Regulation (EU) 2024/1689 of 13 June 2024 laying down harmonised rules on artificial intelligence and amending Regulations (EC) No 300/2008, (EU) No 167/2013, (EU) No 168/2013, (EU) 2018/858, (EU) 2018/1139 and (EU) 2019/2144 and Directives 2014/90/EU, (EU) 2016/797 and (EU) 2020/1828 (Artificial Intelligence Act), *OJ L, 2024/1689, 12.7.2024, ELI: http://data.europa.eu/eli/reg/2024/1689/oj.*

10 See A. Iliopoulou-Penot, 'La Constitution numérique européenne' (2023) 5 *Revue Française de Droit Administratif* 945.

11 See further A. Iliopoulou-Penot, 'The Construction of a European Digital Citizenship in the Case law of the Court of Justice of the European Union' (2022) 59(4) *Common Market Law Review* 969. Referring for the first time to a 'cybercitizenship', emerging from the Court's case law on the protection of personal data, see D. Simon, 'La révolution numérique du juge de l'Union: les premiers pas de la cybercitoyenneté' (2014) 7 *Europe* 4.

protection of privacy and personal data.[12] It contends that EU law and its actors have made a significant contribution to how citizenship can be understood and developed in the data era, in which peoples' lives and interactions increasingly unfold online.

SECTION II
THREE EMBLEMATIC RIGHTS OF THE INDIVIDUAL IN THE DATA ERA

Three rights of the individual consecrated by EU law are characteristic of the way in which the Court of Justice and the EU legislature strive to ensure that the autonomy, self-ownership and integrity of the individual in the digital ecosystem are reinforced rather than weakened. These rights, expressive and aspirational, are: (a) the right to be forgotten; (b) the right to defend oneself against electronic surveillance; and (c) the right to oppose certain profiling practices.

§ 1. THE RIGHT TO BE FORGOTTEN

The right to be delisted, also known as the right to be forgotten, is the prerogative of data subjects to have information about them removed from the list of results provided by online search engines following a search made on the basis of their name, if the lawfully displayed information has become 'inadequate, irrelevant [...] or excessive'.[13] The right was recognised in the seminal judgment in *Google Spain.*[14] It was derived from Directive 95/46, on the processing of personal data,[15] read in the light of the Charter of Fundamental Rights. Such a reading entailed, in practice, an application of fundamental rights in a *horizontal* relationship and imposed obligations on private intermediaries relating to the protection of privacy and personal data.[16] The right to be forgotten was then explicitly recognised in the GDPR, whose

---

12 On the added value of considering the two rights as distinct, see O. Lynskey, 'Deconstructing Data Protection: the "Added Value" of a Right to Data Protection in the EU Legal Order' (2014) 63(3) *International and Comparative Law Quarterly* 569.

13 Case C-131/12, *Google Spain v. Agencia Española de Protección de Datos (AEPD) and Mario Costeja González*, ECLI:EU:C:2014:317, para. 93.

14 Ibid.

15 Council Directive 95/46/EC of 24 October 1995 on the protection of individuals with regard to the processing of personal data and on the free movement of such data [1995] OJ L281/31.

16 House of Lords European Union Committee's Second Report of Session 2014–15, 'EU Data Protection Law: A "Right to be Forgotten"?', HL Paper 40 (30 July 2014).

Article 17 enshrines a broad right to erasure ('right to be forgotten'). The interpretation of Article 17 of the GDPR in several cases involving Google[17] has further shaped the right to be forgotten, which enables individuals to intervene in the active memory of the internet, embodied by search engines, in order to counteract the disruptive effects likely to be produced on the relationship between one's past and present.

In its case law, the Court of Justice charges search engines with the delicate task of balancing the 'right to oblivion' of some internet users and the 'right to know' of others, which is involved in assessing a request for dereferencing. The GDPR continues along the path opened up by the judgment in *Google Spain.* The data controller must weigh up antagonistic interests, thus becoming the arbiter in a conflict of fundamental rights in which that entity is also a party. This is no small development. It delegates fundamental rights adjudication to Google,[18] a powerful private firm, giving it responsibility to decide what is visible and what becomes invisible online. This invests the operator of a search engine with a decision-making power that closely resembles that of independent administrative authorities or courts, i.e. public bodies. The result is that Google is no longer just a company whose business model is based on data processing[19] and profit maximisation (therefore constituting a source of threat to online privacy);[20] the operator is turned into a decision-making body with the duty to contribute to the protection of personal data and e-privacy.

Google took the judgment of the Court seriously and swiftly put into place a mechanism to treat requests to remove online content. The operator has been proactive in setting up a procedure to facilitate the balancing, on a case-by-case basis, of internet users' right to privacy and the public's freedom of information. The criteria used for this weighing-up exercise were established by the Advisory Council,[21] a body set up for this purpose and composed,

---

17 Case C-507/17, *Google LLC v. Commission nationale de l'informatique et des libertés (CNIL)*, ECLI:EU:C:2019:772; Case C-136/17, *G.C. and Others v. Commission nationale de l'informatique et des libertés (CNIL)*, ECLI:EU:C:2019:773; Case C-460/20, *TU & RE/Google*, ECLI:EU:C:2022:962.

18 M. Tzanou, 'The Unexpected Consequences of the EU Right to Be Forgotten: Internet Search Engines as Fundamental Rights Adjudicators' in M. Tzanou (ed.), *Personal Data Protection and Legal Developments in the European Union*, Hershey, IGI Global, 2020, pp. 279–301.

19 Google has been described as 'the producer, extractor, refiner, distributor, and marketer of valuable data': S.M. Powers and M. Jablonski (eds.), *The Real Cyber War: The Political Economy of Internet Freedom*, Illinois, University of Illinois Press, 2015, p. 75.

20 S. Zuboff, *The Age of Surveillance Capitalism: The Fight for a Human Future at the New Frontier of Power*, London, Profile Books, 2019.

21 'The Advisory Council to Google on the Right to be Forgotten', *Google* <archive.google.com/advisorycouncil/>. The following statement is particularly telling: 'For each of these requests, we're required to weigh, on a case-by-case basis, an individual's right to be forgotten with the public's right to information. We want to strike this balance right. This obligation has been a new and difficult challenge for us […] We all have a shared interest in giving proper effect to the Court's decision and finding the best possible balance on this issue'.

for the most part, of members independent of the company. In this way, Google has taken on a new role in the algorithmic society, with the Court of Justice, followed by the EU legislature, enacting a certain privatisation of the enforcement of fundamental rights in the virtual ecosystem.[22] The judgment in *Google Spain* can thus rightly be seen as reflecting a more general trend consisting of 'the transformation of private actors such as transnational firms from profit-seeking entities to cocreators of standards and norms and subcontractors involved in their enforcement'.[23]

§2. THE RIGHT TO DEFEND ONESELF AGAINST ELECTRONIC SURVEILLANCE

The right to defend oneself against electronic surveillance has emerged in the strand of case law beginning with the groundbreaking judgment in the *Digital Rights Ireland* case.[24] This case law concerns traffic and location data, also called metadata, i.e. all data connected to telecommunications, including internet communications: date and duration of the call/connection, numbers called/websites visited, location of caller, subject matter heading of emails etc. Although metadata do not concern the actual content of communications, they may, taken as a whole, reveal habits, lifestyles, movements and places of residence, social relationships and environments frequented. As the Court underlines,[25] they may allow very precise conclusions to be drawn concerning the private lives of the persons concerned, including sensitive information such

[22] M. Bassini, 'Fundamental rights and private enforcement in the digital age' (2019) 25(2) *European Law Journal* 182. The privatisation of fundamental rights enforcement is a central feature of the EU governance of the internet. With the adoption of the Digital Services Act, the EU legislature also acknowledges the power of platforms to regulate freedom of expression online and tries to place some checks and balances on the exercise of this power, by introducing essentially procedural requirements.

[23] J.-M. Chenou and R. Radu, 'The "Right to be Forgotten": negotiating public and private ordering in the European Union' (2019) 58(1) *Business & Society* 74, 79.

[24] Joined Cases C-293/12 and C-594/12, *Digital Rights Ireland and Seitlinger and Others*, ECLI:EU:C:2014:238; Joined Cases C-203/15 and C-698/15, *Tele2 Sverige AB v. Post- ochtelestyrelsen and Secretary of State for the Home Department v. Tom Watson, Peter Brice and Geoffrey Lewis*, ECLI:EU:C:2016:970; Joined Cases C-511/18, C-512/18 and C-520/18, *La Quadrature du Net v. Premier ministre and Others*, ECLI:EU:C:2020:791; Case C-623/17, *Privacy International v. Secretary of State for Foreign and Commonwealth Affairs*, ECLI:EU:C:2020:790; Case C-140/20, *G.D. v. The Commissioner of the Garda Síochána and Others*, ECLI:EU:C:2022:258; Joined Cases C-793/19 and C-794/19, *SpaceNet AG and Telekom Deutschland GmbH*, ECLI:EU:C:2022:702; and Joined Cases C-339/20 and C-397/20, *VD and SR*, ECLI:EU:C:2022:703; Case C-470/21, *La Quadrature du Net and Others v Premier ministre and Ministère de la Culture*, ECLI:EU:C:2024:370.

[25] See in particular the judgment in *Digital Rights Ireland*, above n. 24, para. 27; the judgment in *Tele2*, above n. 24, para. 99; and the judgment in *Quadrature du Net*, above n. 24, para. 117.

as sexual orientation, political opinions, religious, philosophical, societal or other beliefs or state of health. Therefore, the collection and processing of metadata has the potential to become a powerful surveillance instrument.

The Court has firmly established the principle of prohibition of general preventive retention of metadata. More precisely, telecom operators cannot be obliged to systematically retain metadata in order to make them available to public authorities for law enforcement purposes. The Court admits an exception to this principle for the *sole* purpose of safeguarding *national security*[26] against a serious, genuine and present (or foreseeable) threat. In contrast, the purposes of combatting serious crime and safeguarding *public security* can only justify *targeted* metadata retention; in other words, retention has to concern certain categories of persons and/or certain geographical areas.

In its opposition to generalised and systematic metadata retention and by further requiring that access to such data must be framed by robust procedural safeguards, the Court implicitly recognises the right of individuals to defend themselves against practices of mass electronic surveillance. The case law echoes concerns shared by a wide number of Europeans. The Court refers to the way generalised data retention may affect the private life of a large part of the population, evoke a *feeling* of constant surveillance and have chilling effects on the exercise of other freedoms, especially freedom of assembly. The Orwellian language[27] of the Court has been taken up by the EU legislature in the recently adopted AI Act.[28] It is used in recital 18 in order to justify the prohibition of certain uses of biometric identification systems, which was one of the most hotly debated issues in the negotiations. The interpretation and application of the AI Act will hopefully further flesh out the right not to be the object of (mass) surveillance.

The right not to be subjected to surveillance was also at the heart of the two *Schrems* cases,[29] in which the activist Max Schrems successfully challenged – twice – the transfer of data of Facebook users towards the United States, and, at the same time, the world's largest data flow regime. The Court of Justice

---

[26] The safeguarding of national security 'encompasses the prevention and punishment of activities capable of seriously destabilising the fundamental constitutional, political, economic or social structures of a country and, in particular, of directly threatening society, the population or the State itself, such as terrorist activities': judgment in *La Quadrature du Net*, above n. 24, para. 135.

[27] Although it is worth mentioning that Daniel Solove considers that the right metaphor to capture the issues posed by data retention is not Orwell's *1984* but Kafka's *The Trial*: D. Solove, '"I've Got Nothing to Hide" and Other Misunderstandings of Privacy' (2007) 44 *San Diego Law Review* 745.

[28] Regulation (EU) 2024/1689.

[29] Case C-362/14, *Maximillian Schrems v. Data Protection Commissioner*, ECLI:EU:C:2015:650 (*Schrems I*); Case C-311/18, *Data Protection Commissioner v. Facebook Ireland Ltd and Maximillian Schrems*, ECLI:EU:C:2020:559 (*Schrems II*).

struck down the Commission's adequacy decision on the EU-US 'Safe Harbour' Framework[30] in *Schrems I*, and the 'Privacy Shield' Framework[31] in *Schrems II*, both of which authorised data transfers to servers located in the US. According to the Court, these decisions did not comply with the requirements of Directive 95/46 (in *Schrems I*) and the GDPR (in *Schrems II*), read in the light of Articles 7 and 8 of the Charter,[32] due to the excessively intrusive surveillance programmes in place in the United States.[33] The Court strategically chose to interpret 'adequate' data protection required for outward transfers as 'essentially equivalent' to that afforded by EU law, thereby considerably elevating the standard of protection of privacy and personal data.

§3. THE RIGHT TO OPPOSE CERTAIN PROFILING PRACTICES

The case law on the right to be forgotten and on the retention of metadata contains elements likely to contribute to the formulation of a right to defend oneself against certain uses of personal data that enable or are based on profiling. Both cases refer to *profiling* as being at the heart of the detrimental effects on privacy and respect of personal data. More precisely, in paras. 37 and 38 of the judgment in *Google Spain*, the Court explains that 'the activity of a search engine is [...] liable to affect significantly [...] the fundamental rights to privacy and to the protection of personal data', precisely because the list of results it provides, when a search is made on the basis of an individual's name, offers 'a structured overview of the information relating to that individual [...] enabling them to establish a more or less detailed profile of the data subject'. In the *La Quadrature du Net* case, the Court builds on its findings in *Digital Rights Ireland* to insist on the fact that metadata, which offer a window into peoples' personalities and lives, including sensitive information, provide 'the means of establishing a profile of the individuals concerned, information that is

30 Commission Decision 2000/520/EC of 26 July 2000 pursuant to Directive 95/46/EC of the European Parliament and of the Council on the adequacy of the protection provided by the safe harbour privacy principles and related frequently asked questions issued by the US Department of Commerce [2000] OJ L215/7.

31 Commission Implementing Decision (EU) 2016/1250 of 12 July 2016 pursuant to Directive 95/46/EC of the European Parliament and of the Council on the adequacy of the protection provided by the EU-U.S. Privacy Shield [2016] OJ L207/1.

32 The Court of Justice also found a breach of the right to an effective remedy, enshrined in Article 47 of the Charter, because data subjects do not have actionable judicial redress under the US regime.

33 The surveillance programmes of the National Security Agency (NSA), in cooperation with Silicon Valley operators, were revealed by Edward Snowden in 2013.

no less sensitive, having regard to the right to privacy, than the actual content of communications'.[34]

The EU legislature has also taken into account the dangers of profiling for individuals. The GDPR defines profiling[35] and provides for two rights in this respect: under Article 22(1), the right of the data subject 'not to be subject to a decision based *solely* on automated processing, including profiling, which produces legal effects concerning him or her or similarly significantly affects him or her';[36] and, under Article 15(1), the right to obtain information on:

> the existence of automated decision-making, including profiling [...] and, at least in those cases, meaningful information about the logic involved, as well as the significance and the envisaged consequences of such processing for the data subject.[37]

An important doctrinal debate exists as to whether the GDPR enshrines a 'right to explanation', going beyond mere information,[38] as recital 71 of the GDPR might suggest.[39]

The Court of Justice recently had the first occasion to interpret Article 22(1) of the GDPR in the *SCHUFA* case,[40] which illustrates the consequences that the utilisation of profiling techniques can have for individuals. In this case, a bank used the score provided by SCHUFA, a private company establishing

---

34 *La Quadrature du Net*, above n. 24, para. 117, referring to *Digital Rights Ireland*, above n. 24, para. 27 and *Tele2*, above n. 24, para. 99.

35 Under Article 4(4) of the GDPR, '"profiling" means any form of automated processing of personal data consisting of the use of personal data to evaluate certain personal aspects relating to a natural person, in particular to analyse or predict aspects concerning that natural person's performance at work, economic situation, health, personal preferences, interests, reliability, behaviour, location or movements'. A similar definition is provided by Article 3(4) of Council Directive (EU) 2016/680 of 27 April 2016 on the protection of natural persons with regard to the processing of personal data by competent authorities for the purposes of the prevention, investigation, detection or prosecution of criminal offences or the execution of criminal penalties, and on the free movement of such data [2016] OJ L119/89.

36 Article 22(1) of the GDPR (emphasis added). Exceptions are allowed in three limited cases, under Article 22(2) of the GDPR: if automated decision-making is strictly necessary for contractual purposes, if it is authorised by EU or national law, or if it is based on the data subject's explicit consent. In these cases, specific safeguards apply under Article 22(3) of the GDPR, such as the rights of the data subject to obtain human intervention, to express their own point of view and to contest the decision.

37 Article 15(1)(h) of the GDPR.

38 S. Wachter, B. Mittelstadt and L. Floridi, 'Why a right to explanation of automated decision-making does not exist in the General Data Protection Regulation' (2017) 7 *International Data Privacy Law* 76; C. Castets-Renard, 'Accountability of algorithms in the GDPR and beyond: A European legal framework on automated decision-making' (2019) 30(1) *Fordham Intellectual Property, Media & Entertainment Law Journal* 91.

39 Recital 71 refers to 'suitable safeguards, which should include specific information to the data subject and the right to obtain human intervention, to express his or her point of view, to *obtain an explanation* of the decision reached after such assessment and to challenge the decision' (emphasis added).

40 Case C-634/21, *OQ v. Land Hessen en presence de SCHUFA Holding AG*, ECLI:EU:C:2023:957.

consumer credit ratings, to refuse a loan applied for by a customer. The latter required SCHUFA to send her information on the personal data registered and to erase some (allegedly) incorrect data. In response, SCHUFA informed her of her score and outlined, in broad terms, the methods for calculating the scores. However, referring to trade secrecy, the company refused to disclose the various elements taken into account for the purposes of that calculation.

Following the Opinion of Advocate General Pikamäe, the Court of Justice considers that the score constitutes automated decision-making since it de facto predetermines the bank's decision. Indeed, according to established practice, evidenced by the referring court, an insufficient score leads in almost all cases to the refusal of the bank to grant the loan applied for. If the score were not considered as a decision within the meaning of Article 22(1) of the GDPR, individuals would not be able to ask the credit agencies to explain the underlying logic (since Article 22(1) of the GDPR would not apply). The bank would not be able to give this explanation either, as it does not establish the score. Therefore, in order to avoid a 'lacuna in legal protection',[41] the Court found that the credit agency score has to be included in the scope of Article 22 of the GDPR. In this way, the person concerned is able to contest the score, the use of which by several financial establishments could exclude him/her from access to loans, thus considerably limiting his/her capacity for action. In other words, the solution of the applicability of Article 22 is explained by the need to effectively guarantee individuals' rights. The broad scope of the concept of 'automated decision' reinforces the 'effective protection intended by' this provision.[42]

The right to be defended against practices based on profiling is further fleshed out in the AI Act, which follows the path opened by the GDPR, while further extending the protection it offers. For example, under the new Act, predictive policing based solely on profiling of natural persons is prohibited, while high-risk AI systems (listed in Annex III) involving profiling should be considered to pose significant risks of harm to the health, safety or fundamental rights of natural persons. The Act also introduces an individual right inspired by the GDPR and complementing it: the right to obtain clear and meaningful explanation from the deployer on the role of a high-risk AI system in the adoption of a decision that affects a natural person. The EU legislation further takes into account the risks created by profiling in the context of algorithmic recommendation systems used by social media and marketplaces, as well as online search engines. In consequence, Article 38 of the DSA requires very large online digital operators (platforms and search engines) to offer users a recommendation option that is not based on profiling.

---

41 Ibid., para. 61.
42 Ibid., para. 60.

SECTION III CAN THE NEW SET OF DIGITAL RIGHTS BE QUALIFIED AS DIGITAL CITIZENSHIP?

While the Court of Justice, supported by the EU legislature, is building a protective status for data subjects, neither the judiciary nor the lawmakers have so far used the term 'digital citizenship'. Nevertheless, it can be argued that the emerging set of digital rights can be described as such as it displays (even if it is not yet in a fully-fledged manner) a number of features which are commonly found in citizenship accounts. These include the protection of the individual against the exercise of power, an identity formed by certain values and, finally, the link with a territory.

First, the rights of the data subject are constructed as a status aiming at the protection of the individual both against the exercise of power by public authorities, now equipped with new technological means, and against unprecedented forms of power of private corporations.[43] While the case law on metadata retention concerns the need to defend individuals against the potential of data abuse by public authorities, in cooperation with private operators, the right to oppose automated decisions may concern both public and private entities using profiling techniques. Individuals need protection regarding knowledge constructed about them through profiling.[44] Such protection is a tool that aims to tackle power (and information) asymmetry between individuals and entities processing their data. This need to readjust the power balance[45] also underpins the right to be forgotten, invoked against private entities, whose economic dominance in the digital realm has transformed into considerable social and political influence. The high number of delisting requests received by Google[46] attests to the fact that this right meets a genuine

[43] Advocate General Jääskinen (who delivered the Opinion in *Google Spain*, above n. 13), describes this foundational judgment as 'a turning point in the evolution of EU Internet law and governance' as 'it opened a path for the subjection of the economic, social and political powers of Internet giants to judicial scrutiny from the perspective of an individual's fundamental rights, something that is indispensable in a society based on the principles of the Rule of Law'. N. Jääskinen, 'Google Spain and Google: Not to be forgotten!' in G. Barrett, J.-P. Rageade, D. Wallis and H. Weil (eds.), *The Future of Legal Europe: Will We Trust in It? Liber Amicorum in Honour of Wolfang Heusel*, Cham, Springer, 2021, p. 393.

[44] M. Hildebrandt, 'Profiling and the Identity of the European Citizen' in M. Hildebrandt and S. Gutwirth (eds.), *Profiling the European Citizen: Cross-Disciplinary Perspectives*, Dordrecht, Springer, 2008, pp. 303–26, especially p. 320.

[45] Remedying the power (and information) asymmetry between digital giants and individuals is also an essential aim of the EU's regulation on digital services and markets, namely the DSA and the DMA. See M. Eifert, A. Metzger, H. schweitzer and G. Wagner, 'Taming the giants: The DMA/DSA Package' (2021) 58(4) *Common Market Law Review* 987.

[46] See the information provided by Google at 'Requests to delist content under European privacy law', *Google* <https://transparencyreport.google.com/eu-privacy/overview?hl=en>. Google has accepted to delist about half of the links requested.

societal need and responds to a legitimate will of individuals to retrieve some form of control over their data. The right to be forgotten, just like the rights to oppose surveillance and certain uses of profiling, equip the individual in order for him/her to cope with the 'sense of powerlessness and helplessness'[47] felt in the face of personal data processing, which 'exposes individuals to the scrutiny of others in unprecedented ways'.[48] The new status of the data subject, in continual development by the Court and the EU legislature, aims to guarantee individual autonomy, empowerment and control over one's data.[49]

Second, the emerging status is built upon a distinctive equilibrium of values that forms a specific European identity. The case law on digital rights contributes to determining the collective values of the community of Europeans. The Court decides on inescapable conflicts between individual and collective values, and between collective values *inter se*. The Court has clearly prioritised e-privacy over conflicting fundamental rights and over weighty public interests. In the landmark judgment in *Google Spain*, delisting requested by an individual is presented as obligatory for the operator of a search engine as *a matter of principle* whereas its refusal is seen as an exception. The Court considers that the right to be forgotten must 'in principle' prevail over the public's right to information; it can only be sidestepped if there is a '*preponderant* interest' of the general public to have access to the disputed information.[50] In other words, there is a strong presumption in favour of e-privacy, which is difficult to rebut.

While celebrated in Europe as a victory for online privacy, the right to be forgotten has been described in the United States as an enemy of the First Amendment, threatening the free flow of information within a globalised society.[51] Its detractors raise the spectre of private censorship and the distortion

47 D. Solove, above n. 27, 757.

48 H. Nissenbaum, 'Towards an Approach to Privacy in Public: Challenges of Information Technology' (1997) 7(3) *Ethics and Behavior* 207, 218. Also H. Nissenbaum, 'Protecting Privacy in the Information Age: the Problem of Privacy in Public' (1998) 17 *Law and Philosophy* 559.

49 This is also the philosophy of the 'right to informational self-determination', which originated in the population census decision of the German Constitutional Court (BVerfG, Judgment of 15 December 1983, 1 BvR 209/83) and was later taken up by the ECtHR (*Satakunnan Markkinapörssi Oy and Satamedia Oy v. Finland*, no. 931/13, ECtHR, 27 June 2017 and *Benedik v. Slovenia*, no. 62357/14, ECtHR, 24 April 2018).

50 Judgment in *Google Spain*, above n. 13, para. 97 (emphasis added). Such 'preponderant interest' has to be justified by 'particular reasons, such as the role played by the data subject in public life' (para. 97).

51 K. Byrum, *The European Right to Be Forgotten: The First Amendment Enemy*, Lexington Books, Lanham (MD) 2018. However, in defence of the solution of the Court of Justice since it reflects the European value of online privacy, see '*Google Spain SL v. Agencia Española de Protección de Datos*: Court of Justice of the European Union Creates Presumption that Google Must Remove Links to Personal Data upon Request' (2014) 128(2) *Harvard Law Review* 735 <https://harvardlawreview.org/archives/vol-128/google-spain-sl-v-agencia-espanola-de-proteccion-de-datos/>.

of history and government intervention.[52] Other critics from across the Atlantic argue that the Court of Justice fails to understand the contribution of search engines to the emergence of a 'public' capable of forming public opinion, a *sine qua non* condition for the existence of a democratic public sphere.[53] These criticisms are based on the fact that while, in its groundbreaking 2014 ruling, the Court refers to the interest of the public to have access to information, it does not frame this as the fundamental freedom of expression and of information.[54]

Indeed, initially, the Court of Justice did not seem to take sufficient account of the consequences for the freedom of expression and information[55] as well as for the freedom to conduct business, which are also guaranteed by the Charter (respectively by Articles 11 and 16). In the follow-up case *TU & RE/Google*,[56] the German Federal Court rightly drew attention to the issue of the balancing exercise involving rights that are *equally* fundamental. The Court of Justice was convinced by this and moved in the direction suggested by the German court. Its judgment expressly refers to the weighing up of several fundamental

---

52 K. Byrum, above n. 51.

53 R.C. Post, 'Data Privacy and Dignitary Privacy: Google Spain, the Right To Be Forgotten, and the Construction of the Public Sphere' (2018) 67(5) *Duke Law Journal* 981: 'the CJEU misunderstands the relationship between Google and the construction of the contemporary public sphere. *Google Spain* dismisses Google as a mere profit-making, data-processing corporation. But that interpretation of Google fails to appreciate how Internet search engines underwrite the virtual communicative space in which democratic public opinion is now partially formed. Google should have been accorded the same legal status as print media'. The author supports this assertion by showing how newspapers created the modern democratic public sphere in an analogous way in the US in the 19th and 20th centuries.

54 E. Frantziou, 'Further Developments in the Right to be Forgotten: The European Court of Justice's Judgment in Case C-131/12, *Google Spain, SL, Google Inc v Agencia Espanola de Proteccion de Datos*' (2014) 14(4) *Human Rights Law Review* 761, 769: 'The judgment mislabels a widely protected fundamental right as an "interest", subjects it to a presumption of non-applicability and hence fails to take account of its equal weight in the "fair balance" discussion'.

55 See also C. Kuner, 'The Court of Justice of EU's Judgment on the "Right to be Forgotten": An International Perspective', *EJIL: Talk!* (20 May 2024) <https://www.ejiltalk.org/the-court-of-justice-of-eus-judgment-on-the-right-to-be-forgotten-an-international-perspective/>: 'The judgment has the potential to create a kind of "EU Internet" separate from the global Internet, with search results and other web content displayed differently in the EU from how they are in the rest of the world. This could adversely affect the right of EU individuals to receive information "regardless of frontiers" under Article 19 UDHR and Article 19 ICCPR. In sum, while the Court's determination to grant individuals greater control over the processing of their personal data is to be welcomed, it has insufficiently considered the global nature of the Internet, and failed to take into account the fundamental rights of Europeans to communicate across borders'.

56 *TU & RE/Google*, above n. 17.

rights that needs to be undertaken when a request for dereferencing is made. It also underlines that:

> Where the information in question is likely to contribute to a debate of public interest, it is appropriate, in the light of all the circumstances of the case, to place particular importance on the right to freedom of expression and of information.[57]

Despite this welcome recalibration, the presumption in favour of privacy remains.

The Court's case law on metadata retention can also be seen as a victory of privacy over security concerns. The prohibition of generalised data retention is formulated as *a rule* and its authorisation as *an exception*, within a democratic society.[58] Several national courts have raised eyebrows concerning the Court's choice to give priority to e-privacy over security.[59] Led by the French Conseil d'État, which has strongly expressed its discontent and disagreement,[60] the Belgian Constitutional Court,[61] the Federal Administrative Court of Germany,[62] the Irish Supreme Court,[63] the French Cour de Cassation[64] and the Italian Corte di Cassazione[65] have all formulated reservations about the Court's findings. Their counter-arguments are not to be taken lightly. After all, as Article 4(2) of the Treaty on European Union (TEU) recognises, ensuring security is an essential function of the State: indeed, it is one of its *raisons d'être*.[66] Why should a state, whose cardinal mission is to protect its citizens, be deprived of an efficient instrument in the fight against serious criminality? Several referring courts have pointed out the complexity of putting into place targeted data retention, and its lesser effectiveness compared to generalised data retention. They have further underlined that, in certain cases, generalised data retention is the *only* effective means for investigating or for proving or

---

57 Ibid., para. 73.

58 *La Quadrature du Net*, above n. 24, para. 142; *G.D. v. The Commissioner of the Garda Síochána*, above n. 24, para. 84.

59 For an overview of national reactions, see F.-X. Millet, 'Le glissement jurisprudentiel en matière de données de connexion: l'expansion des compétences de l'Union et sa réception dans les États membres' (2023) 4 *Revue Française de Droit Administratif* 606. This author is also critical of the position of the Court of Justice.

60 This disagreement is expressed in the judgment applying the Court's answer in *La Quadrature du Net*: Conseil d'État, Assemblée, 21 April 2021, *French Data Network e.a.*, nos. 393099, 394922, 397844, 397851, 424717, 424718.

61 See the preliminary decision of the Belgian Constitutional Court in the case *La Quadrature du Net*, 19 July 2018, no. 96/2018.

62 *SpaceNet AG and Telekom Deutschland GmbH*, above n. 24.

63 *G.D. v. The Commissioner of the Garda Síochána*, above n. 24.

64 *VD and SR*, above n. 24.

65 S. Bellè, 'La réception italienne de la jurisprudence européenne sur les données de connexion' (2023) 1 *Revue des affaires européennes* 203.

66 Consolidated Version of the Treaty on European Union [2016] OJ C202/13.

prosecuting criminal offences. Examples concern financial market abuse and online criminal offences, such as large-scale copyright infringements. Last but not least, there is the issue of guaranteeing victims' rights and avoiding impunity, which has been raised by victims' associations, inter alia on the occasion of the *G.D. v. The Commissioner of the Garda Síochána* case, a high-profile murder case in Ireland in which evidence had been obtained from illegally retained data.

Despite this, the Court of Justice takes a strong position in favour of privacy. This is likely because, in the eyes of the Court, respect for e-privacy is not only a private interest linked to the realisation of individual freedom but 'a public good that concerns a citizen's freedom from unreasonable constraints on the construction of her identity'.[67] It has an impact on public life and, therefore, *a collective value*. Three elements support this explanation. First, the Court underlines the wide-ranging interference of generalised data retention 'with the fundamental rights *of practically the entire European population*'.[68] Second, it places increased emphasis on the 'feeling', likely to be generated in the minds of those concerned, 'that their private lives are the subject of constant surveillance'.[69] Third, the Court refers to the 'deterrent effect' of generalised data retention on the 'exercise of the freedom of expression' and information,[70] which is a cornerstone of democratic society. Deprived of guarantees of e-privacy (in other words, without freedom from the feeling that somebody is watching them online), citizens would no longer be able to participate freely and meaningfully in a space of social interaction and democratic practice.[71] The Court thus defends a specific democratic vision that is firmly opposed to the logic of mass surveillance. It implicitly invites one to move beyond an individualistic prism and adopt a social understanding of respect for e-privacy as a collective good, as a *sine qua non* prerequisite for the development of meaningful interpersonal relationships and the sustainable functioning of democracy.[72]

---

67 M. Hildebrandt, 'Profiling and the rule of law' (2008) 1 *Identity in the Information Society* 55 <https://doi.org/10.1007/s12394-008-0003-1>.

68 *Digital Rights Ireland*, above n. 24, para. 56 (emphasis added).

69 Ibid., para. 37.

70 Ibid., para. 28.

71 See N.M. Richards, 'The dangers of surveillance' (2013) 126(7) *Harvard Law Review* 1934.

72 See S. Seubert and C. Becker, 'The Democratic Impact of Strengthening European Fundamental Rights in the Digital Age: The Example of Privacy Protection' (2021) 22(1) *German Law Journal* 31, 32: 'by strengthening people's personal freedom, European privacy protection is, at the same time, proving to be essential for the development and flourishing of democratic practices conceptualized as collective acts of free communication'.

Protection of privacy and personal data has, therefore, rightly been seen as a tenet of European constitutional identity.[73] Such an evolution can be linked to another development that has taken place in the Court's case law in a different (but related) context. In the twin Assembly judgments of 16 February 2022 in the budget conditionality cases,[74] the Court of Justice explicitly refers to the identity of the Union as a common legal order, which is based on the values of Article 2 of the TEU and which the Union must be able to defend. The values of Article 2 of the TEU include respect for human rights, which itself includes protection of privacy and personal data. Such protection has thus become a stepping stone for expressing, fostering and asserting a collective European identity, embedded in the Charter of Fundamental Rights. This evolution confirms the capacity of the Union's Bill of Rights to contribute to the progressive building of a European identity,[75] that is promoted within the Union and outwardly projected.[76]

Third, the emerging status is linked to the territory of the Union, as the personal data of the individuals present in the EU can only be transferred to third countries offering data protection standards that are not simply 'adequate' (the term used in Directive 95/46 and the GDPR) but 'essentially equivalent' to those afforded by EU law. This finding, based on a teleological interpretation, has provoked strong reactions. On the one hand, some have decried the EU's 'judicial imperialism' and 'peculiar arrogance about imposing its personal data law on the rest of the world' and leading a 'campaign of harassment' against the United States.[77] In a more moderate vein, others have criticised the praetorian brandishing of constitutional values as 'weapons',[78] and the attempt to build 'a

---

73 B. Petkova, 'Privacy as Europe's First Amendment' (2019) 25(2) *European Law Journal* 140. According to this author, the Court's case law places emphasis on Europe's 'otherness' in relation to third countries, especially the United States.

74 Case C-156/21, *Hungary v. European Parliament and Council*, ECLI:EU:C:2022:97; Case C-157/21, *Poland v. European Parliament and Council*, ECLI:EU:C:2022:98.

75 See A. Iliopoulou-Penot and L. Xenou, 'Propos introductifs. De la capacité de la Charte de façonner une identité de l'Union dans un contexte pluraliste' in A. Iliopoulou-Penot and L. Xenou (eds.), *La Charte des droits fondamentaux, source de renouveau constitutionnel européen?*, Brussels, Bruylant, 2020, p. 17.

76 It is important to note that the right to be forgotten, consecrated in *Google Spain*, above n. 13, has influenced the global debate over 'privacy versus free expression', as it emerges through decisions of national and international courts. This is shown by K.H. Youm and A. Park, 'The Right to Be Forgotten: *Google Spain* as a Benchmark for Free Speech versus Privacy?' (2023) 24(1) *Chicago Journal of International Law* 167. The authors conclude that the groundbreaking approach of the Court of Justice will undoubtedly remain an important part of the global debate, with the balance shifting away from free speech and free press and toward the right to privacy.

77 S. Baker, 'How Can the U.S. Respond to Schrems II?', *Lawfare* (21 July 2020) <https://www.lawfaremedia.org/article/how-can-us-respond-schrems-ii>.

78 J. Atik and X. Groussot, 'A Weaponized Court of Justice in *Schrems II*' (2021) 4(2) *Nordic Journal of European Law* 1, 18: 'Constitutional values of one party are ill-suited to satisfactorily resolve a legal conflict between two parties. A constitutional court, such as

European fortress of personal data'.[79] On the other hand, the Court has been praised for pioneering high privacy standards in data flows and for sending a vibrant message: the Union stands up for the protection of its citizens and their personal data. It is a virtuous global actor seeking to promote a demanding conception of online privacy that must be preserved, if necessary, by opposing the laws and practices of external authorities.

It seems then that, in *Schrems I* and *Schrems II*, the Court further develops the narrative of the territory of the Union, which is found in EU citizenship law.[80] This narrative appeared in the *Ruiz Zambrano*[81] line of case law, on the right to family reunification of static EU citizens in the state of origin. It developed further in the *Petruhhin*[82] strand of case law placing limits on the extradition of Union citizens to third countries. In this case law, as Niamh Nic Shuibhne explains, the territory of the Union is conceived of as a special legal place underpinned by common distinctive values and as a place where the EU legal order is engaged to protect Union citizens.[83]

European digital citizenship is intimately linked to this 'territory of the Union' and sets red lines for cooperation with third countries, including long-standing allies such as the US, if their conception of privacy is substantially different from that prevailing in Europe. These red lines are effective. For example, the US authorities had to make serious efforts[84] to address the difficulties identified in *Schrems II* in the context of the negotiations with the EU on the new Transatlantic Data Privacy Framework. This framework was announced in March 2022 and led, in July 2023, to the adoption by

---

the CJEU – that sees its own law and not that of the counterparty to the conflict – makes reconciliation and resolution far less likely. Europe may "win" this contest with the United States – and the CJEU's judgment in *Schrems II* may contribute to its policy success. But such a "win" reflects the exercise of power more than law'.

79 O. Pollicino, *Judicial Protection of Fundamental Rights on the Internet: A Road Towards Digital Constitutionalism?*, Oxford, Hart Publishing, 2021, especially Chapter 3, 'Judges, Privacy and Data Protection: From Atoms to Bits Across the Atlantic', p. 99.

80 N.N. Shuibhne, 'The "Territory of the Union" in EU Citizenship Law: Charting a Route from Parallel to Integrated Narratives' (2019) 38(1) *Yearbook of European Law* 267, building on the work of L. Azoulai, 'Transfiguring European Citizenship: From Member State Territory to Union Territory' in D. Kochenov (ed.), *EU Citizenship and Federalism: The Role of Rights*, Cambridge, Cambridge University Press, 2017, p. 178.

81 Case C-34/09, *Gerardo Ruiz Zambrano v. Office national de l'emploi (ONEm)*, ECLI:EU:C:2011:124.

82 Case C-182/15, *Aleksei Petruhhin v. Latvijas Republikas Ģenerālprokuratūra*, ECLI:EU:C:2016:630.

83 N.N. Shuibhne, above n. 80.

84 The Executive Order on Enhancing Safeguards for United States Signals Intelligence Activities, signed by President Biden on 7 October 2022, implements the commitments taken by the US towards the EU.

the European Commission of a new adequacy Decision.[85] While the latter has already been challenged[86] and is not entirely immune to a *Schrems III* ruling,[87] its negotiation already proves that governments of third countries cannot treat European data requirements as a paper tiger. This also applies to digital operators, as illustrated by the record fine (1.2 billion euros) imposed by the Irish Data Protection Authority on Meta (the owner of Facebook) in May 2023,[88] for the transfer of personal data on the basis of standard contractual clauses that do not offer guarantees equivalent to those of EU law.

SECTION IV CONCLUSION

Both the Court of Justice and the EU legislature are patiently building a status for users of digital technologies that aims to defend both the individual and society in the face of (public and private) power in the data era. The status gives expression to a European vision of respect for privacy and personal data, which is an integral part of the Union's identity, to which the Court now explicitly refers. As such, this status is attached to the territory of the Union, conceived as a special legal place underpinned by common values. All these elements (protection, identity and the link to a territory) indicate the citizenship quality of the new status. It can be argued that an incipient form of digital citizenship, sustained by fundamental rights, has come into life. Such citizenship is a building block of the European digital constitutionalism,[89]

85 Commission Implementing Decision EU 2023/1795 of 10 July 2023 pursuant to Regulation (EU) 2016/679 of the European Parliament and of the Council on the adequate level of protection of personal data under the EU-US Data Privacy Framework [2023] OJ L231/118.

86 Philippe Latombe, a deputy in the French National Assembly and member of the French authority for the protection of personal data, the National Commission on Technology and Liberty (CNIL), has brought annulment proceedings against the Decision before the General Court: Case T-553/23, *Latombe v. Commission.*

87 NYOB, 'European Commission gives EU-US data transfers third round at CJEU', *noyb.eu* (10 July 2023) <https://noyb.eu/en/european-commission-gives-eu-us-data-transfers-third-round-cjeu>. The European Parliament has pointed out the weaknesses of the new mechanism in the light of the *Schrems*' criteria in its Resolution of 11 May 2023 on the adequacy of the protection afforded by the EU-US Data Privacy Framework (2023/2501 (RSP)). For a detailed evaluation of the validity of the decision see M. Barczentewicz, 'Schrems III: Gauging the Validity of the GDPR Adequacy Decision for the United States', *International Center for Law & Economics* (25 September 2023) <https://laweconcenter.org/resources/schrems-iii-gauging-the-validity-of-the-gdpr-adequacy-decision-for-the-united-states/>.

88 '1.2 billion euro fine for Facebook as a result of EDPB binding decision', *European Data Protection Board* (22 May 2023) <https://www.edpb.europa.eu/news/news/2023/12-billion-euro-fine-facebook-result-edpb-binding-decision_en>.

89 G. De Gregorio, *Digital Constitutionalism in Europe: Reframing Rights and Powers in the Algorithmic Society*, Cambridge, Cambridge University Press, 2021; G. De Gregorio, 'The Rise of Digital Constitutionalism in the European Union' (2020) 19(1) *International*

which is shaped by a new generation of EU legislative instruments (such as the GDPR, the DSA, the DMA and the AI Act) that have federal characteristics. Combining the logic of the (internal) market and of (fundamental) rights, these instruments aim to guarantee certain European values, such as respect for privacy and other fundamental rights, the integrity of public discourse and deliberative process, and fairness of and within markets. The adoption of the new legislation is a result of Europe's geopolitical awakening;[90] it gives body to the narrative of Europe protecting its citizens, its interests and its values or, in other words, the Union's claim to sovereignty.[91] The link between sovereignty, constitutionalism and citizenship in the new environment created by digital technologies bears further exploration. In the years to come, EU law will hopefully continue to contribute to the elaboration of a triangular social contract for online society: a contract among citizens, public authorities and private corporations.

Journal of Constitutional Law 41; O. Pollicino, 'The quadrangular shape of the geometry of digital power(s) and the move towards a procedural digital constitutionalism' (2023) 29(1–2) *European Law Journal* 10.

90 L. van Middelaar, *Le réveil géopolitique de l'Europe*, Paris, Éditions du Collège de France, 2022.

91 The most eloquent expression of this narrative is found in the Sorbonne speech on the new initiative for Europe pronounced by French President Emmanuel Macron on 26 September 2017: 'President Macron gives speech on new initiative for Europe', *Élysée* (26 September 2017) <https://www.elysee.fr/en/emmanuel-macron/2017/09/26/president-macron-gives-speech-on-new-initiative-for-europe>.

CHAPTER 9
HUMAN RIGHTS AND THE PRECARIAT

Dr Andrew FAGAN*

SECTION I INTRODUCTION

This chapter addresses the European human rights community of scholars, jurists, policymakers, opinion-formers, and practitioners. It aims to attract this community's attention with an urgent and heartfelt plea on behalf of another, much larger, constituency of people. Specifically, I shall argue that we must urgently and robustly recognise and engage with social class as a recurring and highly significant element of ongoing and pervasive human rights violations and injustice within Europe. While the human rights project has made massive strides in recognising a wide range of many peoples' identities, this recognition rarely extends to include social class, despite the extent to which class identity is demonstrably implicated with human rights violations and wider forms of social injustice. I hope to raise a far greater awareness of the importance of class within the human rights community and that this may, in turn, lead to more effective and concerted scholarly and practical efforts to address class-based human rights violations and injustice. Following the innovative and highly influential scholarship of Guy Standing, I shall specifically focus upon a

---

* Andrew Fagan was born and raised in poverty. He left formal schooling aged 14 without any qualifications. He was the Director of the Human Rights Centre at the University of Essex from 2020–24, where he remains a Senior Lecturer in the Law School. He has taught human rights at Essex for over 20 years. His interdisciplinary research focuses upon a range of core challenges to human rights theory and practice, including poverty and inequality, populism and illiberalism, and religious and cultural diversity. His articles have been published in several leading journals, including *Human Rights Quarterly*, the *Critical Review of Social and Political Philosophy*, and the *Journal of Applied Philosophy*. He is also the author of several books, including *Human Rights and Cultural Diversity* (Edinburgh, Edinburgh University Press, 2017) and *The Atlas of Human Rights* (California, University of California Press, 2010).

diverse and growing class of people who he terms the 'precariat'.[1] I will argue that the human rights of many people amongst the European precariat are being violated and that our failure to recognise them as a distinct constituency of systemically vulnerable people compounds the injustices they suffer. One must first name a problem in order to begin developing responses to it and, when applied to class, this truism requires the human rights community to unequivocally name and identify those who are most affected by class injustice itself.

My argument, then, will add to the growing body of scholarly critiques of human rights.[2] It is important, however, to understand that what I offer here (as I have offered elsewhere) is a *critique* of human rights.[3] I aim not to deny or refute the wider normative claims or purpose of human rights. Rather, I will draw attention to an area which human rights must urgently recognise and effectively engage with. I thus seek not to further diminish the standing or normative aspirations of the European human rights project, but to add to our work and our understanding of the transformative potential of human rights. While many significant challenges confront any scholarly attempt to recognise social class as a human rights category, engaging effectively with social class has the potential of popularising and perhaps thereby strengthening the European human rights project. As human rights appear to have become increasingly unpopular within many European societies, effectively engaging with social class provides the basis for effectively confronting and perhaps even reversing this trend in ways which can make human rights 'real' and relevant for the many in desperate need of a far better protection of their human rights amidst what could be a more socially just European order.

SECTION II
HUMAN RIGHTS AND THE RECOGNITION OF IDENTITY

Generations of philosophers have debated the question of whether and, if so, how human rights should engage with specific forms of identity. Against the background of the moral individualist foundations and tenor of the liberal

---

1 G. Standing, *The Precariat: The new dangerous class*, London, Bloomsbury, 2014.

2 See S. Moyn, *Not Enough: Human Rights in an Unequal World*, Cambridge (MA), Belknap Press, 2018; S. Hopgood, *The Endtimes of Human Rights*, New York, Cornell University Press, 2013; D. Kennedy, 'The International Human Rights Movement: Part of the Problem?' (2002) 15 *Harvard Human Rights Journal* 101, 109. For a response to these criticisms, see K. Sikkink, *Evidence for Hope: Making Human Rights Work in the 21st Century*, Princeton (NJ), Princeton University Press, 2017.

3 A. Fagan, 'The Gentrification of Human Rights' (2019) 41(2) *Human Rights Quarterly* 283; A. Fagan, 'Taking Social Class Seriously' (2023) 45(2) *Human Rights Quarterly* 260.

rights project, disagreements have raged over whether and to what extent peoples' identities should figure within normative and legal human rights frameworks. While some continue to defend approaches which seek to exclude any significant consideration of identities from the grounding and application of human rights instruments, the dominant perspective within Europe in particular, has recognised the undeniable truth that some peoples' identities are targeted in ways which manifestly violate their human rights and that effectively responding to this state of affairs requires the legal recognition of such identities and the granting of various negative and positive rights' entitlements to the individual members of many such communities.[4] The so-called 'colour-blind' approach of certain forms of liberal moral individualism has shifted substantially and significantly towards the legal establishment of rights protections which are reserved for specific communities of people whose visible and sometimes not so visible identities expose them to forms of harmful prejudice, discrimination, and inequality.

Based upon the fundamental ideals of non-discrimination and equality, human rights law comprises a robust collection of identity-focused protections for specific constituencies of people, which extend to include protections against discrimination on the grounds of race, colour, sex, gender identity, language, religion, disability, indigeneity, political or other opinion, national or social origin, property, birth or other status. These protections are a crucial component of a far wider political and social effort that concertedly seeks to eradicate discrimination and inequality from our societies. Indeed, some prominent human rights scholars have gone so far as to claim that some of the greatest successes of the human rights project, particularly within liberal democracies, are best seen in the advances made in the promotion of an assortment of recognition rights, which offer legal protection against racism, sexism, religious intolerance, homophobia, ableism and the like.[5] Recognition rights provide a powerful symbol for the commitment to defending some of the most vulnerable in our societies and a much-needed good news story for a human rights project which is facing a barrage of criticisms from many different quarters.[6] These achievements are profoundly important and should, of course, be celebrated and rigorously defended. Seeking to exclude recognition of the existence of vulnerable minority communities compounds

4 See B. Barry, *Culture and Equality: An Egalitarian Critique of Multiculturalism*, Cambridge, Polity Press, 2001; T.M. Franck, *The Empowered Self: Law and Society in the Age of Individualism*, Oxford, Oxford University Press, 2000; M. Fineman, 'The Vulnerable Subject: Anchoring Equality in the Human Condition' (2008) 20(1) *Yale Journal of Law and Feminism* 1.

5 K. Sikkink, above n. 2.

6 See the Office of the UN High Commissioner for Human Rights, 'The global backlash against human rights', *United Nations* (12 March 2018) <https://www.ohchr.org/en/statements/2018/06/global-backlash-against-human-rights>.

the injustices which many members of such communities suffer. While the legal recognition of such identities raises a vast panoply of questions and issues which are far beyond the scope of this chapter to engage with, it should be clear that so-called 'colour-blind' approaches have no place within an effective human rights framework.

The human rights project must and does take identity seriously on the grounds and to the extent that peoples' identities play a significant role in the human rights violations and injustices they suffer. These extend to include visible and less visible forms of identity through which peoples' human rights are violated.[7] Recognition rights are particularly predicated upon and are a response to the vulnerabilities and harms which specific communities of people are exposed to. The legitimate possession of such rights is therefore necessarily limited to communities whose existence is constituted and shaped by the harms they suffer. There are many communities of such people in our societies who are afforded such protections to varying degrees. However, and as I shall now argue in detail, a distinct (though highly diverse and intersectional) constituency of vulnerable people exist who are largely ignored within the global human rights project generally and the European human rights framework, in particular: those who suffer human rights violations and systemic forms of inequality as a direct consequence of their social class identity. We largely fail to even acknowledge the existence of social class, let alone take it seriously as a ground of, or key factor in, systemic human rights violations and wider forms of injustice. This failure serves to compound the fate which so many suffer and warrants our urgent attention.

[7] For an illustrative, though non-exhaustive, list of relevant international standards, see Articles 1 and 55 of the Charter of the United Nations (1955); Articles 22 and 25 of the Universal Declaration of Human Rights (1948); Articles 9, 11, 12 and 13 of the International Covenant on Economic, Social and Cultural Rights (1966); Article 6(1) of the International Covenant on Civil and Political Rights (1966); Article 5 of the International Convention on the Elimination of All Forms of Racial Discrimination (1965); Articles 11, 12, 13 and 14 of the Convention on the Elimination of All Forms of Discrimination against Women (1979); Articles 24 and 27 of the Convention on the Rights of the Child (1989); Articles 24 to 30 and 43 of the International Convention on the Protection of the Rights of all Migrants Workers and Their Families (1990); Article 28 of the Convention on the Rights of Persons with Disabilities (2002); Articles 4, 11 to 17, and 19, 23, 30 and 31 of the European Social Charter (revised) (1961); and Article 4 of the Additional Protocol to the European Social Charter (1988). See also Sustainable Development Goal 10 (of the United Nations' (UN's) 17 Sustainable Development Goals).

SECTION III
THE EXISTENCE OF SOCIAL CLASS

Social class is a notoriously complex and (for some) controversial category of identity. Whether social class exists in any objectively verifiable way and, if so, what it consists of and what implications it may hold for law and politics have all been, and continue to be, topics of intense scholarly debate. While I cannot begin to engage with, let alone resolve, such concerns here, my argument does require a coherent account of social class. It is necessary to show that social class exists for the purposes of analysing and developing responses to human rights violations and wider forms of injustice which, I have asserted, should be an urgent cause of concern for defenders of human rights within the European framework.[8]

I have a deep personal relationship with social class. For me, social class was and remains very real. I was born and raised within a deprived working-class neighbourhood in inner London. My mother was German and had been abandoned by her husband, my father, to raise three children on her own and in poverty. My recollection of the social housing estates I lived on is of high levels of unemployment, poverty, violence, and criminality. Overcrowding was widespread and it was relatively rare to see anyone live much beyond their late 60s or 70s. I remember many people suffering from various forms of chronic physical and mental illnesses, which often went undiagnosed and untreated. My schooling was similarly poor, with no one ever mentioning the possibility of any of us going to university. Social mobility was largely non-existent and very few people (myself excluded) successfully 'escaped' from these materially deprived surroundings. The neighbourhoods I grew up in were also multiracial and were blighted by habitual forms of racism and prejudice. Occasionally this racial tension escalated into forms of violence. Similarly deprived neighbourhoods can still be found across Europe. My experiences, while unusual for someone who became a university professor, are certainly not that unusual for a great many people. Countless millions of people have been shaped by similarly difficult and deprived working-class environments.[9] While I came to learn about academic debates concerning the existence of class,

---

[8] My own scholarly approach to class is heavily influenced by the highly sophisticated framework developed by Pierre Bourdieu. Bourdieu's notion of capital comprising four distinct forms (economic, social, symbolic, and cultural) deeply informs my own approach. See P. Bourdieu, 'The Forms of Capital' in J. Richardson (ed.), *Handbook of Theory and Research for the Sociology of Education*, New York, Greenwood Press, 1986, pp. 241–58. See also P. Bourdieu, *The Weight of the World: Social Suffering in Contemporary Society* (trans. P. Parkhurst Ferguson), Stanford (CA), Stanford University Press, 1999.

[9] For an intimate study of the realities of social class in the UK and the US, see A.R. Hochschild, *Strangers in Their Own Land: Anger and Mourning on the American Right*, New York, The New Press, 2016; D. McGarvey, *Poverty Safari: Understanding the*

I knew and know that class exists and is undeniably real for vast populations of people whose human rights are increasingly vulnerable and precarious. I also know, as an academic, that defining class or identifying any specific class category is challenging.

Despite ongoing scholarly debates concerning the existence of class, many European states formally recognise the existence of different socio-economic classes or categories in their official recordings and surveys of the social demographics of their populations.[10] State recognition of social class hierarchies often influences important government decisions over public expenditure and programmes for action covering a wide array of different state services and provisions. The criteria that states deploy for distinguishing between different socio-economic categories typically include such indicators as median family income, occupational status, or educational attainment, all of which are designed to afford a sufficiently objective standing for the categories which states recognise. As I shall consider shortly, such forms of class categorisation enable states and others to identify who is most exposed to a variety of forms of harm and human rights violation. One does not have to be from a working-class background, or to be a Marxist to see and to accept that social class continues to exist, and that class continues to fundamentally affect the lives and opportunities of many of those people who occupy the lower rungs of the social class ladder. While one may legitimately debate the causes and consequences of social class, no one should dispute its existence any longer.

I argued above that the granting of recognition rights is dependent upon the existence of diverse and distinct forms of vulnerability and harm which, in various ways, serve to shape, if not constitute, a distinct community of people. This requirement grounds and justifies the rights' protections afforded to a diverse constellation of minority communities within a great many European societies. It must also be satisfied if we are to begin to seriously countenance human rights' recognition of social class, alongside those other categories which have been legally recognised across much of Europe. How then does social class adversely affect some peoples' enjoyment of their human rights?

Efforts to address this crucial question must proceed very carefully. There is a constant danger of inadvertently contributing to pervasive forms of social prejudice and stigmatisation when claiming that those who occupy the 'lower' rungs of the social ladder necessarily lead diminished or deprived lives.

Anger of Britain's Underclass, Edinburgh, Luath Press, 2017; J.C. Williams, *White Working Class: Overcoming Class Cluelessness in America*, Boston (MA), Harvard Business Review Press, 2017.

10 For example, five separate social classes are officially recognised in the UK. See Office for National Statistics, 'The National Statistics Socio-Economic Classification (NS-SEC)', *ONS.gov.uk* <https://www.ons.gov.uk/methodology/classificationsandstandards/otherclassifications/thenationalstatisticssocioeconomicclassificationnssecrebasedonsoc2010>.

That being working class, for example, is a condition reasonable people have good reason to avoid. Notwithstanding my appeal to states' nominal acknowledgment of social class and the limited criteria this is based upon, one must acknowledge that class identities are extremely complex social phenomena, through which many other forms of identity also intersect. Alongside the more material attributes of class that I have referenced above, one must also acknowledge the more distinctly socio-cultural attributes of class, which play crucial roles in reproducing differing forms of class identity across time and space. One might, as advertisers and marketers routinely do, distinguish between different lifestyle manifestations of class identity, which will extend to include personal preferences and behaviour across and within different socio-cultural spaces and domains.[11] Against those who advertently or inadvertently distinguish between the alleged intrinsic advantages of more stereotypically middle- or upper-class tastes, modes of dress, patterns of speech and the like, one must vigilantly avoid implying or asserting that working-class lifestyles are necessarily grounded in and are evidence of diminished forms of existence, or that the working classes can be defined and identified by their alleged preferences for so-called 'lower tastes'. The unstated norm of middle-classness (so to speak) should be rejected as robustly as any of those other hegemonic, discriminatory, unstated norms, which the human rights community (amongst others) has done much to expose and challenge. Whilst I am not denying that lifestyle preferences are deeply connected to the distribution of more overtly material capital within European societies, I believe that the less demanding normative aspirations of a human rights-based approach to injustice demands a more rigorous focus upon more overtly material forms of harm. Whether or not one prefers football to rugby, beer over wine, or musicals over the opera are not legitimate human rights issues, but systemic material deprivation and disrespectful social stereotyping are.[12]

It is important to be clear that I am not arguing for the need to recognise the European working classes as in need of specific human rights' recognition and protection *tout court*. Rather, I am arguing that a subdivision of the more traditional working classes has emerged over the past half century or so and that their lives are increasingly beset by systemic and pervasive forms of injustice which, in many cases, amount to human rights violations. Following the scholarship of Guy Standing, I shall henceforth refer to this constituency of people as the precariat.[13] A human rights-based engagement with social class

11 For an analysis of this, see E. Paulson and T. O'Guinn, 'Working-Class Cast: Images of the Working Class in Advertising, 1950–2010' (2012) 644 *The Annals of the American Academy of Political and Social Science* 50.

12 For a highly astute and influential analysis of this, see P. Bourdieu, *Distinction: A Social Critique of the Judgement of Taste*, Abingdon, Routledge, 2010.

13 G. Standing, above n. 1.

must focus resolutely upon the extensive forms of harm and injustice many amongst the precariat are exposed to.

In a much cited and highly influential publication, Standing developed the term the 'precariat' to designate a rapidly expanding social constituency whose members' lives are principally characterised by precarity and chronic insecurity, despite their residing in many of the wealthiest societies on earth. Standing seeks to identify the distinct socio-economic suffering of this expanding constituency of people. The precariat is a large and growing constituency, including the young, the old, the frail, the chronically ill and disabled, migrant workers, refugees and asylum seekers, the unemployed, the many in employment but on zero-hours contracts, and many others who may not yet be considered bona fide members of this unenviable constituency but for whom the loss of an increasingly insecure livelihood might result in them becoming 'precariatised'. The precariat inhabit deprived social housing estates across Europe, including the fateful Grenfell Tower in London in which 71 residents died from a massive and preventable fire which engulfed the tower block in June 2017.[14] The precariat can routinely expect to lead shorter and more unhealthy lives than their middle- and upper-class counterparts. Many of the precariat quite literally risked their lives during the Covid-19 pandemic as they continued to venture out during successive lockdowns to precarious but socially and economically essential employment. A disproportionate number of the precariat across Europe succumbed and died from Covid-19, a statistic which rarely attracts any concerted attention any longer.

The lives of the precariat are increasingly beset by poverty and widening socio-economic inequality. As a result of decades of stagnating wages and benefits, the profound shock of the global financial crisis of 2008–09, the resulting austerity programmes which many governments introduced, the ongoing consequences of Covid-19, and most recently the so-called cost of living crisis, many millions of people living within some of the world's richest economies have descended into poverty and destitution. Increasing numbers of some of the most vulnerable sections of our societies have become largely dependent upon diminishing state welfare support and employment within a growing low-wage sector of the economy in which profits are accrued, in part, as a direct result of low wages and 'flexible' working conditions. Over the past couple of decades, this grim state of affairs has been compounded by the increasingly precarious condition of other previously more secure sections of the population as the automatisation of many industries threatens to render even some middle-class professionals and skilled workers effectively redundant, pensioners face ever-diminishing state pensions, the rising cost of

[14] For an analysis of Grenfell and a criticism of the human rights community's response, see A. Fagan, 'The Gentrification of Human Rights', above n. 3.

housing and diminishing provision of affordable public housing leaves many people unable to afford a home of their own and vulnerable to poorly-regulated private landlords, and rising interest rates threaten to seriously impact those large sections of many societies who are carrying historically high levels of personal debt.

The data and statistics which support this characterisation of the precariat make for grim reading. I will begin with the United Kingdom.[15]

The UK is the seventh most unequal society within the Organization for Economic Cooperation and Development (OECD). In the UK, the richest 10% of the population owns 45% of the nation's wealth, while the poorest 50% owns 8.7% of the wealth. Around one in five of the UK population (20%) were in poverty in 2020/21. This amounts to some 13.4 million people. Of these, 7.9 million are working-age adults; 3.9 million are children, and 1.7 million are pensioners. Across the poorest fifth of families, around six in ten low-income households are not able to afford an unexpected expense, over half are in arrears on their housing rent, around a quarter use credit to pay for essential bills, and over seven in ten families are going without essentials every week. This abysmal state of affairs was also highlighted by the UN Special Rapporteur for extreme poverty in his 2018 UK country report. Philip Alston was scathing in his condemnation of the failures of successive UK governments to uphold many of the core human rights of many of its most vulnerable citizens and he attracted sustained criticism from the UK government as a consequence.[16] It should also be noted that there remain huge variations in poverty rates by ethnicity. Around half of all people in households headed by someone of Bangladeshi ethnicity were in poverty in 2020/21. This figure was over four in ten for people in households headed by someone of Pakistani or Black ethnicity. This is over twice the rate of people in households headed by someone of white ethnicity, although, of course, the precariat also contains a great many vulnerable white people.

The Member States of the European Union also contain large precariat populations.[17] Thus, the number of people at risk of poverty or social exclusion in the EU in 2022 was 95.3 million. 72.7 million people were at risk

---

15 The following UK figures are taken from The Joseph Rowntree Foundation, 'UK Poverty 2023', *JRF.org.uk* (26 January 2023) <https://www.jrf.org.uk/work/uk-poverty-2023-the-essential-guide-to-understanding-poverty-in-the-uk>.

16 See P. Alston, 'Statement on Visit to the United Kingdom' (16 November 2018) <https://www.ohchr.org/sites/default/files/Documents/Issues/Poverty/EOM_GB_16Nov2018.pdf>; P. Alston, 'Visit to the United Kingdom of Great Britain and Northern Ireland: Report of the Special Rapporteur on extreme poverty and human rights', UN Doc A/HRC/41/39/Add.1 (23 April 2019), pp. 3–7.

17 The following figures are taken from the European Commission, 'Key Figures on European Living Conditions 2023 edition' (2023) <https://ec.europa.eu/eurostat/documents/15216629/17704280/KS-HC-23-001-EN-N.pdf>.

of poverty. In relative terms, 21.6% of the population in the EU was at risk of poverty or social exclusion in 2022. This proportion was slightly higher for females (22.7%) than for males (20.4%). In 2022, the severe material and social deprivation rate in the EU was 6.7%, up from 6.3% in 2021. This rate was also higher for females (7.0%) than for males (6.4%).

Despite the important differences amongst the precariat in respect of other forms of identity, the precariat share a common exposure to poverty, low wages, and the resulting insecurity this material deprivation entails. The effects of this extend across areas of life which include a wide range of human rights. The precariat suffer civil and political and social and economic rights violations Some of the most visible and harmful instances consist of discriminatory and stigmatising attitudes and beliefs exhibited by public officials and other members of the same society towards those considered to be poor. These stigmatising attitudes are widespread and have been shown to significantly affect, for example, peoples' access to public spaces and amenities,[18] affordable housing,[19] access to healthcare,[20] exposure to and treatment by the criminal justice system,[21] peoples' access to and willingness to take up available welfare benefits,[22] and even parents' custody over their own children, solely on the grounds of their precarious economic circumstances.[23] In many countries, distinctive terms of abuse have arisen, which intentionally denigrate and demean the poor, reflecting widespread and documented prejudice towards them.

The final feature of the precariat condition which I wish to highlight concerns social mobility, or rather, the lack of social mobility, which increasing numbers of people are subjected to.

---

18 C. Rollot, 'Une famille pauvre exclue du musée d'Orsay', *Le temps* (31 January 2013) <https://www.letemps.ch/culture/une-famille-pauvre-exclue-musee-dorsay>.

19 L. Jamet and C. Thouilleux, 'Davantage de victimes de vol ou d'agression parmi les sans-domicile', *Institut national de la statistique et des études économiques (Insee)* (18 November 2012) <https://www.insee.fr/fr/statistiques/1304053>.

20 G. Moscelli, L. Siciliani, N. Gutacker and R. Cookson, 'Socioeconomic inequality of access to healthcare: Does choice explain the gradient?' (2018) 57 *Journal of Health Economics* 290.

21 Human Rights Watch, 'US: Criminal Justice System Fuels Poverty Cycle: UN Official Speaks Out for Reform', *hrw.org* (21 June 2018) <https://www.hrw.org/news/2018/06/21/us-criminal-justice-system-fuels-poverty-cycle>.

22 H. Dubois and H. Ludwinek, Eurofound, 'Access to social benefits: Reducing non-take-up', Publications Office of the European Union, Luxembourg, 2015 <https://www.eurofound.europa.eu/publications/report/2015/social-policies/access-to-social-benefits-reducing-non-take-up>.

23 *Soares de Melo v. Portugal*, no. 72850/14, ECtHR, 16 February 2016; *Wallova and Walla v. Czech Republic*, no. 23848/04, ECtHR, 26 October 2006. For an analysis, see A.-D. Mornington and A. Guyard-Nedelec, 'Is Poverty Eroding Parental Rights in Britain? The Case of Child Protection in the Early Twenty-First Century' in N. Brando and G. Schweiger (eds.), *Philosophy and Child Poverty: Reflections on the Ethics and Politics of Poor Children and their Families*, Dordrecht, Springer, 2019.

Defenders of the neoliberal economic and political order argue that class is an entirely contingent and provisional identity, which largely results from the economic decisions individuals make. It is frequently asserted that no one is condemned to lifelong membership of a deprived social class, and that talented, hard-working individuals can ascend the social ladder through their own efforts.[24] Some do 'escape' a precariat fate. I did. But such rare exceptions do not prove the rule. The vast majority of people born and raised within some of the poorest and most precarious communities never manage to 'ascend' the social ladder. This is borne out by a huge and growing body of statistical data and evidence.

The World Economic Forum (WEF), which few would describe as a particularly radical champion of the 'have-nots', is just one body which has provided compelling evidence that the vast majority of people do not change their socio-economic status and conditions across their lifetimes. Few people born to middle- and upper-class parents descend into the 'lower' classes and even fewer people born into the 'lower' classes successfully ascend the social class ladder over the course of their lives. This lack of social mobility has been worsening over the past two to three decades. Having developed a Global Social Mobility Index, the WEF has painted a gloomy picture of the prospects for social advancement within most societies. In their 2020 report, they assert that:

> there are only a handful of states with the right conditions to foster social mobility. Furthermore, most countries underperform in four areas: fair wages, social protection, working conditions and lifelong learning.[25]

More specific evidence of the lack of social mobility in the UK has also recently been provided by the previous Conservative Government's own Social Mobility Commission, who, in their 2021 report proclaim that:

> Every critical measure of low social mobility – child poverty, income inequality, access to stable housing, unemployment for young people and gaps in school attainment – was poor in 2019. The impact of COVID-19 is threatening to make each of these factors worse.[26]

---

24 See M. Friedman, *Capitalism and Freedom*, Chicago (IL), University of Chicago Press, 1962 and 2002.

25 World Economic Forum, 'The Global Social Mobility Report 2020: Equality, Opportunity and a New Economic Imperative', Geneva 2020 <https://www3.weforum.org/docs/Global_Social_Mobility_Report.pdf>.

26 Social Mobility Commission, 'State of the nation 2021: Social mobility and the pandemic', HMSO, 2021, p. xv <https://assets.publishing.service.gov.uk/government/uploads/system/uploads/attachment_data/file/1003977/State_of_the_nation_2021_-_Social_mobility_and_the_pandemic.pdf>.

The overwhelming majority of children raised in poor families and neighbourhoods are faced with systemic barriers to their sharing in the privileges of their counterparts in more affluent and secure settings. Poverty, and many of the economic, political, and socio-cultural effects of that, has become an inescapable fate for a great many people amongst us. As one academic has recently written:

> in the UK today the most determinative fact in relation to most people's life chances is their socio-economic origin and status. This is particularly the case relative to the impact of the other protected characteristics.[27]

Leaving the precariat is a privilege which very few are able to enjoy.

To conclude this section, while social class is an intellectually challenging construct, the existence of class is unquestionably confirmed and demonstrated by the conditions of the lives many endure within increasingly unequal European societies. The lifestyle differences which provide markers of different class identities are not, in and by themselves, causes of concern for a human rights-based approach to class. However, material deprivation and social stigmatisation of some of the most vulnerable members of our societies undoubtedly raise profoundly important and urgent human rights concerns. Poverty and marginalisation have been described by some as posing an existential threat to liberal democracy.[28] As such, they clearly demand a robust and effective response from a doctrine and project which claims to be fundamentally concerned with promoting social justice. I am arguing that a fundamental obstacle to our ability to address this existential threat remains our failure to concertedly and unequivocally name those who are most directly affected by these systemic human rights violations. While the human rights community has largely embraced a wide array of different identities, it has routinely failed to extend this recognition to social class and the precariat, in particular. Before I proceed to set out an outline of what any such effort will need to include, I want to strengthen my central claim further by acknowledging those, albeit ineffectual and unrepresentative, human rights-based attempts to engage with social class.

---

27 K. Malleson, 'Equality Law and the Protected Characteristics' (2018) 81(4) *Modern Law Review* 598, 612.

28 See W.A. Galston, 'The Enduring Vulnerability of Liberal Democracy' (2020) 31(3) *Journal of Democracy* 8.

SECTION IV
DESPERATELY SEEKING SOCIAL CLASS

It would be unfair to some sections of the human rights community to claim that social class has been entirely ignored by human rights scholars and practitioners. I want to briefly discuss examples of some such engagement. However, I begin by addressing what might be misconstrued as an acknowledgment of social class within international human rights law.

The particularly observant reader might recall that my earlier list of identity-based characteristics which are afforded protections within, for example the two core UN human rights covenants – the International Covenant of Civil and Political Rights (ICCPR) and the International Covenant of Economic, Social and Cultural Rights (ICESCR) – include social origin as a protected characteristic. One might be forgiven for assuming that this addresses and refutes my criticism of human rights' neglect of social class. It is also worth noting, given the specific European focus of this chapter, that social origin is included as a protected characteristic in the anti-discrimination provision of Article 14 of the European Convention on Human Rights (ECHR) and Article 1 of Protocol No. 12 of the ECHR. The European Social Charter, Article E also prohibits discrimination on grounds of social origin or other status. Finally, Article 21 of the Charter of Fundamental Rights of the European Union[29] forbids discrimination on grounds of 'social origin'. However, none of these instruments provide protection for people on the basis of their social class or socio-economic standing.

Thus, the treaty monitoring body for the ICESCR, the Committee on Economic, Social and Cultural Rights, has clarified in its General Comment 20, that social origin is an inherited social status, based upon descent and does not extend to include social class. A similar interpretation has been delivered by the European Committee for Social Rights, and rulings of the European Court for Human Rights.[30] Thus, despite initial appearances to the contrary, social origin has been explicitly distinguished from social class in both UN and European human rights law. The problem remains.

Greater progress has been made towards affording legal recognition to social class within several European nation-states. Thus, domestic legal protections specifically against the stigmatisation of the poor exist in Belgium, Bulgaria,

[29] Charter of Fundamental Rights of the European Union [2016] OJ C202/389.

[30] For a detailed analysis of this, see J. Gerards, 'Chapter One: Discrimination Grounds' in D. Schiek, L. Waddington and M. Bell (eds.), *Cases, Materials and Text on National, Supranational and International Non-Discrimination Law*, Oxford, Hart Publishing, 2007.

Croatia, Czechia, Hungary, Latvia, Lithuania, Romania and Slovakia.[31] Article 14 of the ECHR also affords applicants the opportunity to claim protections against discrimination on grounds of their social condition.[32] While entirely welcome, it is important to note that these protections are rarely claimed and even more rarely granted. As an academic scholar with expertise in this area has written:

> Many national, European, and international anti-discrimination provisions prohibit discrimination based on a person's socioeconomic situation. It is striking, however, that this is barely applied in practice. There is little case law related to this at national, international and European levels.[33]

At the level of international human rights law, the previously mentioned General Comment No. 20 of the UN Committee on Economic, Social, and Cultural Rights explicitly acknowledges that:

> A person's social and economic situation when living in poverty or being homeless may result in pervasive discrimination, stigmatization and negative stereotyping which can lead to the refusal of, or unequal access to, the same quality of education and health care as others, as well as the denial of or unequal access to public places.[34]

Similarly, the UN Guiding Principles on Extreme Poverty and Human Rights expressly state that individuals have the right to be protected from the negative stigma attached to the conditions of poverty, without going so far as to identify the poor as a distinct category or class of people. One might conclude that while the problem has been recognised, the identities of those who are most affected by it have not.

Beyond human rights law and its institutions, a small number of academic scholars have sought to draw attention to social class as a ground for discrimination and stigmatisation. These include, Shreya Atrey, Sandra Fredman, Sarah Ganty, Kate Malleson, Wayne MacKay and Natasha Kim, Juan Carlos Benito Sánchez, and Geraldine Van Bueren, all of whom have presented critical analyses of the general exclusion of social class from international, regional and domestic discrimination law, whilst simultaneously arguing, in

---

31 S. Ganty, 'Poverty as Misrecognition: What Role for Anti-discrimination Law in Europe?' (2020) *European University Institute Department of Law Research Paper* 2020/12, p. 28 <https://ssrn.com/abstract=3715003>. Republished at (2021) 21(4) *Human Rights Law Review* 962 <https://doi.org/10.1093/hrlr/ngab016>.

32 S. Ganty, *European University Institute Department of Law Research Paper* 2020/12, above n. 31.

33 Ibid., p. 2.

34 Committee on Economic, Social and Cultural Rights, 'General Comment No. 20: Non-discrimination in economic, social and cultural rights', E/C.12/GC/20 (2 July 2009), clause 35.

most cases, for inclusion of social class as a protected characteristic.[35] Thus, Ganty has written:

> Poor people themselves are subjected to stereotyping, prejudice, stigma and discrimination because of their precarious situations. In this regard, poverty is not only a consequence but also a cause of discrimination, creating a vicious cycle. In other words, misdistribution raises important issues of recognition resulting from a person's socioeconomic status.[36]

Van Bueren has been even more explicit in her call for the recognition of social class within the UK's domestic anti-discrimination mechanisms when she states, 'It is an extraordinary lacuna, that to discriminate on the basis of someone's class is lawful in the UK and in the domestic legislation of many countries of the world'.[37] She then states unequivocally:

> I argue that the time is now overdue for the inclusion of an express prohibition against class discrimination in law—national, regional and international—because the reliance upon existing standards has proven grossly inadequate.[38]

There are many terms of abuse reserved for particularly stereotyped poor working-class people in the English language. These include such terms as 'white trash', 'redneck', 'chav', 'hosers' and 'wiggers'.[39] They constitute particularly visible elements of a wider political and socio-cultural environment which discriminates against people on their grounds of their (apparent) class identity. Van Bueren (herself from a working-class background) is surely correct to draw our attention to this and to insist that such forms of discrimination should cause as much concern and outright condemnation as the many other terms of abuse directed towards other communities of discriminated against people. The recognition of social class as a protected characteristic is certainly a measure worthy of support, as is a concerted zero-tolerance attitude towards class-based forms of discrimination. However, combatting class-based discrimination is a necessary, but not a sufficient, component of the far more robust (and

---

35 S. Atrey, 'The Intersectional Case of Poverty in Discrimination Law' (2018) 18(3) *Human Rights Law Review* 411; S. Fredman, 'Redistribution and Recognition: Reconciling Inequalities' (2007) 23(2) *South African Journal on Human Rights* 214; W. MacKay and N. Kim, 'Adding Social Condition to the Canadian Human Rights Act' (2009) *Final report for the Canadian Human Rights Commission*; J.C. Benito Sánchez, 'Towering Grenfell: Reflections around Socioeconomic Disadvantage in Antidiscrimination Law' (2019) 5(2) *Queen Mary Human Rights Law Review* 1; G. Van Bueren, 'Inclusivity and the law: do we need to prohibit class discrimination?' (2021) 3 *European Human Rights Law Review* 274.

36 S. Ganty, *European University Institute Department of Law Research Paper* 2020/12, above n. 31, p. 2.

37 G. Van Bueren, above n. 35, 274.

38 Ibid., 275.

39 See O. Jones, *Chavs: The Demonization of the Working Class*, London, Verso, 2016.

demanding) response that I shall proceed to outline shortly. One must also acknowledge that there are significant weaknesses to the anti-discrimination approach, which engaging with class serves to clearly highlight.

Recognition rights are typically granted on the basis that members of particular communities suffer distinct forms of disadvantage as a consequence of their identities. The negative and positive rights which comprise recognition rights seek to provide various forms of redress to members of communities who have been or are being harmed in significant ways as a consequence of how others perceive and treat them.[40] The human rights-based instruments which seek to combat racism, sexism, anti-Semitism, Islamophobia, transphobia, and the like include an acknowledgment that members of these communities deserve and are entitled to specific protections because the wider prejudices they are exposed to are both real and entirely unreasonable. Recognition rights are constituted from a complex set of dynamics which both include an acknowledgment that certain groups of people suffer harm because of how others perceive them, and that justice requires enabling people to be who they are without having to endure pervasive harm as a consequence. Recognition rights should enable people to celebrate who they are and take pride in the traditions, beliefs, practices, and characteristics which they consider to be essential to their identity and sense of belonging. Not everyone accepts that granting rights to such identities is a legitimate response to such forms of harm and injustice.[41] However, and for the sake of argument, let us allow that this approach is conceptually coherent and has resulted in affording legal protections to a great many vulnerable peoples. This does not mean that the conventional legal instruments extended to, say, women, African Americans, Muslims, Jews, or the disabled are appropriate for responding to the harms suffered by the precariat, a class which, of course, includes many such people.

The limitations of this conventional, recognition rights-based response are well illustrated by considering the existing phenomenon of 'pride days', or annual events, which enable vulnerable and marginalised peoples to celebrate their identities and which call upon the wider society to affirm the rights of, for example, the LGBTQI+ community, or the historical and current contributions of people of African descent to European society and culture. In these ways, peoples' identities and their commitments are upheld as worthy of esteem and

40 See L. Alcoff, *Visible Identities: Race, Gender and the Self*, Oxford, Oxford University Press, 2007; A. Honneth, *The Struggle for Recognition: the Moral Grammar of Social Conflicts* (trans. J. Andersom), Cambridge, Polity Press, 1996; A. Honneth, *Disrespect: The Normative Foundations of Critical Theory*, Cambridge, Polity Press, 2007; A. Shachar, *Multicultural Jurisdictions: Cultural Differences and Women's Rights*, Cambridge, Cambridge University Press, 2001; C. Taylor, 'The Politics of Recognition' in A. Gutmann (ed.), *Multiculturalism: Examining the Politics of Recognition*, Princeton (NJ), Princeton University Press, 1994, pp. 25–73.

41 B. Barry, above n. 4.

respect. Would the establishment of Pride Days for the Precariat perform a similar function and have similar value? Think about it.

Being poor and destitute is a condition which should not be celebrated or esteemed. Working in poorly paid and insecure employment, living sicker and shorter lives, having higher rates of functional illiteracy, being overly dependent upon inadequate state welfare and charity both constitute and simultaneously severely harm members of the precariat. These are conditions which are part of the injustices the precariat suffer and should not form any part of any proposed remedy or solution to their plight. Yes, we must adopt a zero-tolerance attitude towards derogatory terms of abuse directed towards the precariat, but we must also go much further and seek to develop policies and radical programmes which address the underlying causes of their plight, beyond the surface symptoms of injustice.

This reference to addressing causes and not merely symptoms also raises another important issue and highlights another limitation to the conventional over-reliance upon combatting discrimination in so much human rights thinking and action. As others have argued in respect of the defence offered for many more recognised recipients of recognition rights, too much emphasis has been placed upon changing the discriminatory attitudes directed towards many vulnerable minorities.[42] We have already seen evidence that discriminatory attitudes can have very tangible consequences for peoples' access to public goods and spaces, as well as for many peoples' own sense of self-worth and self-respect. They are not an irrelevance. However, one may successfully eradicate or significantly diminish racist or sexist attitudes without this having any significant impact upon the more overtly material deprivation and harm people continue to suffer from as a result of systemic, structural injustices in the distribution of wealth, capital and opportunity.[43] We may (rightly) take pride in having contributed to rights-based campaigns to efforts to eradicate commonplace racism from high-profile public spaces for example, whilst simultaneously ignoring the less visible poverty and destitution which many ethnic minorities continue to suffer from within Europe and beyond. Combatting discriminatory attitudes is necessary and valuable, but its benefits are limited and can address only part of the wider injustice the precariat are exposed to. Campaigns which focus overwhelmingly on protecting civil and political rights will have little effect if they do not also extend to include robust social rights protections. This is obviously particularly important in efforts to combat the material injustices suffered by the precariat.

---

42 For an analysis of this, see W. Benn Michaels, *The Trouble with Diversity: How We Learned to Love Identity and to Ignore Inequality*, 10th Anniversary ed., New York, Henry Holt & Company, 2016; O.O. Táíwò, *Elite Capture: How the Powerful Took Over Identity Politics (and everything else)*, London, Pluto Press, 2022.

43 See W. Benn Michaels, above n. 42 and O.O. Táíwò, above n. 42.

The precariat clearly and undeniably suffer systemic and egregious human rights violations. The question this raises for the human rights community is: what are we going to do about it?

SECTION V
WHAT IS TO BE DONE?

In earlier publications I have analysed what I consider to be some of the core factors in human rights' continuing class blindness.[44] Suffice it to say that there are many likely causes to this blindness, including ideological sensitivities surrounding the very category of class, genuine difficulties in delineating who should be considered to belong to the social classes human rights should pay due attention to, the overwhelming dominance of professional, well-educated, middle-class people within the European human rights community, and more broadly, what I have referred to as the 'gentrification of human rights'. I shall not return to those arguments here and encourage interested readers to engage with these earlier publications for a far more substantial explanation of why the human rights community largely fails to take class seriously. I shall use the remainder of this chapter to focus upon what we might constructively do to begin the process of overcoming our neglect of such a large constituency of people in need of support.

Developing a robust and effective human rights-based response to the plight of the precariat as a social class will require sustained and arduous scholarly and practical work from many different quarters. My own contribution will be modest at best. However, for the remainder of this chapter it will consist of asserting three clear demands. In order to take class seriously and to add the significant weight of human rights to the struggle against injustices which afflict the lives of over 100 million people across the EU and the UK, the European human rights community must urgently and robustly do the following: add social class to our understanding of who should enjoy recognition rights; significantly transform our understanding of the harms such people suffer in ways which accord far greater significance to social rights; and finally, seek to engage more concertedly and effectively with the precariat as a potential ally in the European human rights cause. I shall briefly discuss each of these in turn.

---

44 See above n. 3.

§ 1. RECOGNISE THE PRECARIAT

As I have argued above, the human rights community has made lasting and highly valuable contributions to combatting the wider legal, political, and social injustices which marginalised communities of people are unfairly exposed to. Racism and sexism, for example, could only be addressed by first identifying the victims of these injustices. Flesh must be put, so to speak, on the otherwise identity-less members of our societies in order to begin to fashion remedies and protections. I am arguing that the same act of recognition must be extended to the precariat as a social class.[45]

I have shown above that the precariat suffer harms and injustices as a consequence of their confinement within a social class which is routinely discriminated against and whose defining attributes include a material deprivation and vulnerability which very few are able to 'escape' from on their own efforts.

The precariat are, of course, a highly diverse and heterogeneous constituency of people. These internal differences extend to include many of the personal characteristics which are legally recognised as deserving of specific protection. The problem here is that the exclusion of poverty as a distinct and shared condition which all of the precariat suffer fails to address some of the most tangible and harmful injustices which women, people of colour, religious minorities, and the disabled, for example, suffer. While even wealthy members of legally recognised minorities are still exposed to prejudice and stigma, their lives and their conditions are not additionally afflicted by a poverty and precarity which affect many other members of many such communities. The complex bundle of injustices suffered by *poor* people of African descent, or women, or Muslims or the disabled are not adequately recognised or engaged with by remedial instruments which ignore the distinctly material, socio-economic components of their lives. Justice is not fully served by simply promoting the interests of minority communities if the compounding effects of poverty and precarity are absent from the remedies provided.[46]

Adding poverty and precarity to our efforts to combat identity-based human rights violations will necessarily require us to recognise that members of the

---

[45] While she does not concertedly appeal to human rights, the philosopher Iris Marion Young has engaged robustly with class and injustice. See I.M. Young, *Justice and the Politics of Difference*, Princeton (NJ), Princeton University Press, 2011. For a contemporary analysis of capitalism and inequality, see N. Fraser and R. Jaeggi, *Capitalism: A Conversation in Critical Theory*, Cambridge, Polity Press, 2018. See also T. Piketty, *Capital in the Twenty-First Century* (trans. A. Goldhammer), Cambridge (MA), Belknap Press, 2014; J. Whyte, *The Morals of the Market: Human Rights and the Rise of Neoliberalism*, London, Verso, 2019.

[46] This argument is also made by W. Benn Michaels, above n. 42 and O.O. Táíwò, above n. 42 and N. Fraser, *The Old is Dying and the New Cannot be Born: From Progressive Neoliberalism to Trump and Beyond*, London, Verso, 2019.

otherwise dominant ethnic white constituency in many, if not all European societies, deserve our attention and support. Not on the grounds of their 'being White', but of their belonging to the wider precariat class. After all, 'white' people are just as diverse and complex as any other recognised constituency of people. White people are not exposed to the racial prejudice and discrimination suffered by people of colour, for example. However, many are similarly afflicted by the poverty and precarity I summarised earlier in this chapter. Similarly, and within a conventionally designated constituency of 'white' people, many white men will not be exposed to the harmful conditions which many white women have to endure, but an approach which ignores poverty and precarity results in a false generalisation of those who enjoy various forms of unjustified privilege.[47] Simply pronouncing that all white people share a fundamental condition of economic, legal, political, and social privilege is a ludicrous generalisation which has counterproductive consequences for the European human rights project.

The precariat is a profoundly intersectional class of diverse people, which crosses and encompasses many, if not all, of the recognised forms of minority identity. As Dr Martin Luther King Junior himself recognised towards the end of his life, despite all the efforts to divide different ethnic communities of people from each other, many such communities share a common condition of being poor and this shared fate requires our urgent recognition and engagement.[48] We must urgently add the precariat to our recognition of those communities who are systemically afflicted by violations of their human rights.

§2. PROPERLY RECOGNISE SOCIAL RIGHTS

The status of and support for social rights has long been discussed within the global human rights community. Notwithstanding repeated UN announcements that all human rights are equally important and deserving of respect, there remains a long-standing view, espoused and celebrated by some and denounced by others, that social rights do not and should not be accorded as much importance and weight as their civil and political rights counterparts.[49] Irrespective of the scholarly debates, it seems undeniable that

---

47 See A.R. Hochschild, above n. 9 and R. DiAngelo, White Fragility: Why It's So Hard for White People to Talk About Racism, Boston (MA), Beacon Press, 2018.

48 See T. Shelby and B.M. Terry, *To Shape a New World: Essays on the Political Philosophy of Martin Luther King, Jr.*, Cambridge (MA), Belknap Press, 2020.

49 See A. Neier, 'Social and Economic Rights: A Critique' (2006) 13(2) *Human Rights Brief* 1. It was also repeated more recently in C. Tomuschat, *Human Rights: Beyond Idealism and Realism*, 3rd ed., Oxford, Oxford University Press, 2014; G. MacNaughton, D. Frey and C. Porter (eds.), *Human Rights and Economic Inequalities*, Cambridge, Cambridge University Press, 2021.

many in power do not consider poverty and destitution to be as egregiously intolerable and wrong as the suspension of peoples' right to vote, or the wholesale denial of a free press. Social rights are not, demonstrably, taken as seriously by those with the power and duty to defend human rights. However, it is important to acknowledge that the European human rights system takes a significantly different approach to social rights than, say, the United States does. Social rights enjoy legal standing in Europe where they have been consistently denied and rejected across the Atlantic. The European system, generally, does recognise social rights as human rights. It just does not do a very good job of implementing the legal standards it has ratified. The system also relies far too heavily on legal remedies for addressing social rights violations.

As readers are likely to be aware, the European Convention on Human Rights (ECHR) consists of civil and political rights. It does not extend to include social rights, which have been assembled in a separate European Social Charter (ESC), which all the EU Member States, and the UK are party to. While the ESC purports to guarantee citizens' enjoyment of their fundamental social and economic rights, its implementation and enforcement mechanisms are significantly weaker than those of the European Court of Human Rights (ECtHR), which oversees the ECHR. It should also be pointed out that all the EU Member States and the UK have also ratified the International Covenant on Economic, Social and Cultural Rights. Unlike in the US, social rights have been widely recognised within the European human rights framework. Despite the existence of these legal instruments, what I am referring to as the European precariat number over 100 million people and are the victims of systemic human rights violations. The European social rights regime is manifestly failing to effectively defend the social rights of a vast population of people.

As with other areas of the global human rights regime, the relative success in the setting of standards and the ratification of social rights protections has not extended to the effective implementation of the legal rights protections which citizens should be able to enjoy. The absence of any forms of robust institutional mechanisms for holding states to account in respect of their social rights obligations is obviously a crucial and much discussed factor.[50]

Other scholars have also gone further and have argued that even those social rights which do exist are far too modest in respect of the minimal conditions required for determining that the rights are being upheld.[51] Many have argued that social rights in their current configuration cannot provide an

---

50 See P. O'Connell, *Vindicating Socio-Economic Rights: International Standards and Comparative Experiences*, Abingdon, Routledge, 2012.

51 See S. Moyn, above n. 2; G. de Búrca, *Reframing Human Rights in a Turbulent Era*, Oxford, Oxford University Press, 2021; M. Goodale, *Reinventing Human Rights*, Stanford (CA), Stanford University Press, 2022; D. Harvey, *A Brief History of Neoliberalism*, Oxford, Oxford University Press, 2005.

effective instrument for overcoming the pervasive forms of inequality which neoliberalism is particularly characterised by because they typically aspire for little more than mere subsistence. Social rights surprisingly appear to be largely consistent with the simultaneous existence of gross forms of inequality. Clearly, a robust response to the human rights violations and inequalities suffered by the precariat will require a substantial transformation of social rights in ways which significantly raise the bar on the minimal conditions required for the enjoyment of rights to housing, healthcare, education, reproductive health and social security, amongst others.

Finally, the proper recognition of social rights will also entail our moving away from an undue reliance upon legal remedies and litigation as the principal instruments by which human rights may be upheld. As others have argued, social rights' protections are not best served by an over-reliance upon the decisions of judges alone but require concerted support and action at the level of policy-making and, prior to this, the robust support of elected political officials and governments.[52] Confronting and eradicating the injustices endured by the precariat obviously cannot be achieved on a case-by-case basis, but requires concerted, collective, political action. We should, I believe, be moving towards the creation of an environment in which the eradication of poverty is widely viewed as an essential requirement of any legitimate, human rights-respecting state. Indeed, lest this sound unduly utopian and against those who repeatedly argue that this politicisation of human rights does not have the public support it requires, there exists a sizeable body of evidence that voters in many European societies routinely rank social rights concerns as the most important and valuable for them.[53] Properly recognising social rights enjoys widespread and well-established public support.

§ 3. ENGAGE WITH THE PRECARIAT

Who (and on what terms) the human rights community recognises and engages with raises many complex issues and questions, generally. One must, for example, always be alert to and critically conscious of the complex relational dynamics entailed by any attempt to ally with the life experiences of others.[54] This is particularly pertinent in respect of our engagement with the precariat.

52 See P. O'Connell, above n. 50.

53 See the surveys assembled by YouGov, 'Welfare & Benefits', *yougov.co.uk* <https://yougov.co.uk/topics/politics/explore/academic_area/Welfare_Benefits>.

54 For a critical study of the relationship between human rights 'saviors' and 'victims', see M. wa Mutua, 'Savages, Victims, and Saviors: The Metaphor of Human Rights' (2001) 42 *Harvard International Law Journal* 201.

As I (and others) have written previously, the human rights community within most high-income, European societies is not socially representative in respect of social class.[55] The human rights community appears to be largely constituted by scholars, students, activists, and professionals who have, generally, had little direct experience of the lives of those endured by the precariat. To be blunt, most human rights 'people' appear to be largely middle-class, despite also being highly diverse in respect of race, gender, sexuality, religious affiliation and the like. The human rights community's lack of concerted engagement with the precariat and social class more generally itself appears to reflect the broad class composition of the community. While some others may disagree, I do not believe this to be inevitable or an insuperable obstacle to developing a far more effective engagement with the precariat, as I am calling for.

We obviously need to actively build a more socio-economically diverse and representative European human rights community to include far more people who have had or continue to have direct experience of precarity and poverty. To achieve this, we will need to accord far more importance to the kinds of issues and human rights violations which cause so much harm and suffering to so many people. Thus, whilst some of us must and will continue to focus upon more conventional human rights issues, such as asylum, migration, unfair trials, torture, the abuse of state power, and the like, others amongst the human rights community must also begin to engage far more concertedly with many of the issues which afflict the poor in our midst.[56] Taking the precariat seriously will also require a greater interest in such issues as unionisation and working conditions, housing, mortality, healthcare, state welfare, public transport, peoples' access to public libraries, the wider forms of social exclusion suffered by the poor, and the systemic indignities inflicted by the neoliberal state upon those who turn to it for essential support in times of need.

Engaging properly with the precariat will also inevitably involve far more difficult conversations surrounding politics and the perceived support for populist right-wing political candidates and policies amongst some of the poorer and particularly less educated sections of society.[57] While condemning discrimination must always remain a fundamental condition of anyone's

55 See F. Mégret, 'Human Rights Populism' (2022) 13(2) *Humanity: An International Journal of Human Rights, Humanitarianism, and Development* 240.

56 One excellent example of a community human rights organisation undertaking this kind of work is the human rights-based activities of the civil society organisation, Participation and the Practice of Rights (PPR), based in Belfast, which campaigns for rights to work, welfare and housing: <https://www.nlb.ie>. For other examples of similar community-based human rights work, see F. Hunt, 'Social Rights Are Human Rights: But the UK System is Rigged', Centre for Welfare Reform, 2017.

57 I intend to explore these challenges in a subsequent publication, provisionally entitled 'Human Rights and the Deplorable'.

support for human rights and a red line for the human rights community, we must strive to resist sweeping generalisations which portray entire communities as 'deplorable'.[58] We need to robustly demonstrate the relevance of human rights for so many people who might otherwise be persuaded by others that so-called 'ordinary people' have no interest in or need of human rights. This is clearly not true and particularly at a time when so many are suffering such egregious violations of their human rights.

We need to pay far greater attention to the human rights violations which are increasingly taking place so close to home and to those conditions which expose so many people to forms of despair and resentment which are almost always associated with political extremism.[59]

SECTION VI
HOPING FOR TOO MUCH?

Taking class seriously is going to require radical changes to how we engage with power and privilege. It will also require a level of critical self-reflection, which many will wish to avoid. Taking class seriously will require far-reaching and radical changes to how we operate and even who we collectively are. There will be those who will conclude that the vision I am seeking to develop is simply far too demanding and utopian. Radical change is not to everyone's liking, nor in many peoples' interests. However, while more conventionally recognised human rights challenges will continue to blight our world and will demand our engagement, poverty and inequality within high-income, European states also demand our recognition and engagement. The fact that so little attention has been paid to the victims of systemic injustice on our own doorsteps should be a cause of some collective shame. Knowing what we now know about the impact of poverty and inequality upon the poor as a class of people, our continuing failure to acknowledge and engage with this injustice will, for me, seriously call into question the moral authority of what remains the dominant platform for justice within so many societies and parts of the

---

58 For an example of what I understand to be a particularly one-dimensional depiction of this over-generalisation see Office of the High Commissioner for Human Rights, 'Zeid warns against populists and demagogues in Europe and U.S.', *United Nations* (5 September 2016) <https://www.ohchr.org/en/statements/2016/09/zeid-warns-against-populists-and-demagogues-europe-and-us?LangID=E&NewsID=20452>. See also Human Rights Watch's similar depiction of populism in their report, Human Rights Watch, 'The Pushback Against the Populist Challenge', *hrw.org* (2018) <https://www.hrw.org/world-report/2018/pushback-against-the-populist-challenge>.

59 Philip Alston makes a similar argument without discussing social class in any detail: P. Alston, 'The Populist Challenge to Human Rights' (2017) 9(1) *Journal of Human Rights Practice* 1.

world. Failing to take the precariat seriously runs the risk, I believe, of fatally undermining the entire standing of the global human rights project, the failure of which would be catastrophic. At the normative core of human rights is, I believe, a deep aversion to and rejection of systemic forms of inequality and injustice. The proper and necessary response to a worsening set of conditions is not to adjust our normative aspirations to better fit such a terrible set of conditions, but to double down on our principles and seek to strengthen the project by more effectively and robustly recognising and engaging with the most vulnerable amongst us. Settling for less is, I passionately believe, a betrayal of the human rights project.

www.ingramcontent.com/pod-product-compliance
Ingram Content Group UK Ltd.
Pitfield, Milton Keynes, MK11 3LW, UK
UKHW051905290926
8980IPUK00017B/1780

9 781839 704390